The Ages of Superma

The Ages of Superman

*Essays on the Man of Steel
in Changing Times*

Edited by JOSEPH J. DAROWSKI

McFarland & Company, Inc., Publishers
Jefferson, North Carolina, and London

LIBRARY OF CONGRESS CATALOGUING-IN-PUBLICATION DATA

The ages of Superman : essays on the Man of Steel in changing
times / edited by Joseph J. Darowski.
    p.   cm.
Includes bibliographical references and index.

ISBN 978-0-7864-6308-4
softcover : acid free paper ∞

1. Superman (Fictitious character)   2. Comic books, strips,
etc.— United States.   3. Literature and society — United States.
I. Darowski, Joseph J.
PN6728.S9A37 2012
741.5'973 — dc23   2011048458

BRITISH LIBRARY CATALOGUING DATA ARE AVAILABLE

Front cover design by Rob Russell

Cover photograph © 2012 iStockphoto

Manufactured in the United States of America

*McFarland & Company, Inc., Publishers
  Box 611, Jefferson, North Carolina 28640
  www.mcfarlandpub.com*

Table of Contents

Preface

JOSEPH J. DAROWSKI

Some may consider Superman quaint or outdated. There are certainly edgier and grimmer characters that have been created. But Superman has had one of the most profound impacts on American popular culture of any fictional character and to this day he remains a profit-generator. First published in the early days of the comic book industry, the Man of Steel gave birth to the superhero genre. This genre, though most closely linked to the comic book medium where it began, has influenced all aspects of the entire entertainment industry. And it all began in 1938 when Superman, created by Jerry Siegel and Joe Shuster, first appeared on the cover of *Action Comics #1* (Jun. 1938).

The elements of the superhero genre fully came together for the first time when Superman first appeared, and he was soon followed by Batman, Wonder Woman, and hundreds of others. Costumed superheroes are among of the defining figures of American entertainment, as iconically American as the Western cowboy. Superheroes, though always present in some form in our entertainment, have enjoyed a resurgence in popular culture in the last decade. At the same time that superheroes have been the stars of children's cartoons and live-action dramas on television, dominated the Hollywood box office, and taken another troubled step onto Broadway stages, the academy has given greater notice to comic book superheroes. Numerous books have been published looking at individual creators, the history of the industry, or topics such as superheroes and philosophy or superheroes and religion. This book will attempt to do something different. It will explore the evolution of a popular culture icon, Superman, and how he has remained relevant for more than seven decades of uninterrupted narratives.

One of the most intriguing aspects of Superman is that new stories have been told featuring the character continually since his creation. While many other franchises of the entertainment industry, such as James Bond or Star Trek, have had new chapters added across a long period of time, there are often years in between the new stories being produced. Superman comics

1

have been published continuously since 1938, with a new story, or even four or five or six new stories, appearing on a more-or-less monthly schedule. This long-running narrative allows for a fascinating look at the evolution of Superman.

While Superman from World War II era comic books is easily identified as the same character as the Superman of Cold War era comics, there are clear and obvious distinctions when they are looked at closely. By exploring how this popular culture icon has changed through the years we can track how our entertainment mirrors the changes in American society. Superman began as a crusading social avenger at the end of the Great Depression, became a patriotic hero during World War II, saw his powers increase in the early years of the Cold War, entered a period of flux during the Vietnam War, was killed and returned at the end of the Cold War, and has looked for his place in the superhero world since the turn of the century. Near the end of 2011 the character experienced yet another reimagining, this one a more serious break from his previous stories. This collection will analyze the character, primarily through his comic book adventures, in chronological order until this most recent reimagining of the Man of Steel. Stories from each decade of his existence will be analyzed in the context of society at that time. Our popular entertainment does not exist in a vacuum, and though it may serve as escapist fare it still reflects the real world.

The collection begins with Todd S. Munson examining the Superman comics from the World War II era in "'Superman Says You Can Slap a Jap!': The Man of Steel and Race Hatred in World War II." While the comic book stories themselves rarely touched on the war effort, Superman was an agent of American propaganda. Especially on comic book covers and adaptations into other media, Superman was frequently shown battling America's enemies.

Lori Maguire and Peter Lee each look at Superman stories from the 1950s during the Cold War era. In "Supervillains and Cold War Tensions in the 1950s," Maguire examines the villains Superman faced in relation to the fears that dominated American society at the time. Lee explores the relationship between Kryptonite and the nuclear age in "Kryptonite, Radiation and the Birth of the Atomic Age."

Louie Dean Valencia García provides a different view of this American icon, by analyzing Superman's influence in Spain during the 1950s and 1960s. "Truth, Justice, and the American Way in Franco's Spain" looks at translations of Superman comics at a period when Francisco Franco was attempting to control as much of Spain's popular culture as possible. While Superman may often be seen as an unproblematic symbol of virtue in America, in Spain at this time the American ideals embedded in Superman comic books were considered radical and often censored. This alternative view of Superman allows for an understanding of how the American values Superman embodied could be perceived from different perspectives.

Thomas C. Donaldson and Christopher B. Zeichmann each look at Superman's supporting cast in comic books published in the 1970s. The characters experienced significant changes and revisions in apparent reaction to social movements in America. Donaldson's "The Inflexible Girls of Steel: Lois Lane, Supergirl, and the Subversion of Second Wave Feminism" explores the expanded Superman family in the context of the feminist movement. While in "Black Like Lois: Confronting Racism, Configuring African American Presence" Zeichmann looks at a story in which Lois Lane becomes African American for a day in relationship with the Black Power movement.

Jason M. LaTouche and Paul R. Kohl examine a story published during a time when DC Comics attempted to make their characters more relevant in relation to real-world events. In "Red, White and Bruised: The Vietnam War and the Weakening of Superman" LaTouche examines a Superman story arc called "The Sandman Saga" and uses the United States' increasingly unpopular involvement in the Vietnam War as a means of interpreting the message. Kohl examines the same story in "The Struggle Within: Superman's Difficult Transition into the Age of Relevace," but with a different societal parallel. Kohl uses the changing role of the news media and the counterculture movement as societal touchstones that inform the story. Both analyses are equally thorough and insightful.

One of the most significant eras for Superman comic books is a reboot of the character following DC Comics universe-altering event *Crisis on Infinite Earths*. Following this event, the character's origins were reimagined in a miniseries by writer/artist John Byrne. Daniel J. O'Rourke and Morgan B. O'Rourke analyze that mini-series in light of the Reagan era in "'It's Morning Again in America': John Byrne's Re-Imaging of the Man of Steel." Jack Teiwes's essay, "The New 'Man of Steel' Is a Quiche-Eating Wimp! Media Reactions to the Reimagining of Superman in the Reagan Era," also looks at the mini-series, but more specifically the media's reaction to it in light of American attitudes towards masculinity in the 1980s. Michael Smith examines the stories that followed this reinterpretation of Superman, but still were firmly entrenched in the American culture of the 1980s in "More Human than (Super) Human: Clark Kent's Smallville and Reagan's America."

Entering the 1990s Superman comics became more closely connected and told larger, more inter-connected narratives. Matthew J. Smith discusses this era in general and why America was particularly well-positioned for this type of grander storytelling at that time in "The 'Triangle Era' of Superman Comic Books: Continuity, Marketing and Grand Narratives in the 1990s."

In "Searching for Meaning in 'The Death of Superman,' Joseph J. Darowski positions one of the most famous Superman stories of all time in light of America's identity crisis at the conclusion of the Cold War. José Alaniz writes about the funeral for Superman and the act of mourning in American culture in "Death, Bereavement, and the Superhero Funeral."

Stefan Buchenberger's "Superman and the Corruption of Power" evaluates a series of "Elseworlds" tales, or stories that are not part of the official Superman continuity. In each of these stories, Superman is corrupted or abuses his powers in some way. The manner in which these corruptions take place reveals fears about America's powers and influence if not used in a responsible manner.

Jeffrey K. Johnson considers another DC Comics event, *Infinite Crisis*, and the manner in which the narrative contrasts the present day Superman with the earliest Golden Age version of the character in "This Isn't Your Grandfather's Comic Book Universe: The Return of the Golden Age Superman."

In recent years there have been multiple storylines published by DC Comics which are driven by the absence of Superman rather than his presence. John Darowski's "In a World Without Superman, What Is the American Way?" discusses *52*, *Trinity*, and *The World of New Krypton* and what each one reveals about the Superman's symbolic meaning.

Randy Duncan's "Travelling Hopefully in Search of American National Identity: The 'Grounded' Superman as a 21st Century Picaro" looks at the final story to be published before the 2011 reboot of the Superman franchise. In a story called "Grounded" Superman decides to walk across America to reconnect with his adopted country. Duncan uses the tradition of the picaresque journey to analyze this story.

While the general public may have a broad, largely shared conception of who Superman is, the character has been far from static. Many different variations of the character have been published. If Superman had failed to adapt to changing times in America he would have become a relic of a bygone era. Instead, in looking at the many changes the character has undergone to remain relevant we can learn as much about America as about the Champion of Truth, Justice, and the American Way.

"Superman Says You Can Slap a Jap!"

The Man of Steel and Race Hatred in World War II

TODD S. MUNSON

But the unwritten success of the war was the smash comeback of the Oriental villain. He had faded badly for a few years, losing face to mad scientists—but now he was at the height of his glory. Until the war we always assumed he was Chinese. But now we knew what he was! A Jap; a Yellow-Belly Jap; a Japa-a-nazi Rat....

—Jules Feiffer, *The Great Comic Book Heroes*[1]

In *War Without Mercy: Race and Power in the Pacific War,* John Dower argues that World War II was in large part a race war, a conflict that "exposed raw prejudices and was fueled by racial pride, arrogance, and rage on many sides."[2] The primary target of this hatred was not the Germans—who in ethnic makeup were similar to most Americans—but rather the Japanese, who even in friendlier times were seen as a culture and ethnicity diametrically opposed to our own. However, in the same way that our visceral responses to the Japanese in the 1940s have largely faded from the collective American consciousness, so too have our memories of Superman reflecting and perpetuating such responses. In fact, due to the paucity of such stories in his comic books, Superman is seen as having played virtually no role in the war effort (save perhaps his frequent rejoinders to purchase war bonds).[3] Such was not the case. As we survey the various iterations of the character in comic books, newspaper comic strips, radio, and cartoons it will become evident that the "race war" against the Japanese was very much a part of Superman's adventures, and that the so-called Man of Tomorrow was very much a man of his time.

Superman Comic Books Cover the War

The Japanese began to appear on American comic book covers in early 1942, approximately the same time that the Imperial Army and Navy were enjoying a string of victories in Southeast Asia — and that Japanese Americans were being herded into interment camps on the West Coast. In contrast to the negligible role the character played in the interior pages of *Action Comics,* *Superman,* and *World's Finest,* "cover Superman" was fighting on the front lines of the war from the very beginning. In fact, between 1942 and 1945 approximately fifty percent of the covers of the Superman titles feature World War II in a prominent fashion, though the stories inside the covers rarely addressed the war. Before he was drafted in May 1942, artist Fred Ray drew a series of Japan-related Superman covers. The first of these, *Action Comics #48* (May 1942),[4] was obviously inspired by the events of December 7, 1941. Superman lands a dramatic mid-flight punch to the propeller of a Japanese biplane, while the aircraft carrier that launched the jet is seen below. The Japanese pilot, at far left, appears to have sustained the blow himself— his grimace reveals a set of sharpened buck-teeth, though his slanted eyes betray no outward emotion. In illustrations such as these Ray drew on the many stereotypic images of Japan popular at the time: Japanese as de-personalized, diminutive, sub-human creatures with fangs and yellow skin — without the airplane, a foe scarcely worth Superman's time.

A second Ray illustration, from the cover of *Superman #17* (July 1942),[5] shows Superman standing astride the earth, holding Hitler and Japanese Prime Minister Hideki Tojo by the scruffs of their necks, as though they were errant children. The image harks back to a short comic story that ran in *Look* magazine in 1940, in which Hitler and Stalin are roughly escorted by Superman to stand trial for war crimes at the League of Nations' World Court in Geneva.[6] Here, Tojo dresses the familiar part of the military officer, with knee-high leather boots and sword in scabbard, and bears the typical Japanese open-mouthed expression of anguish — revealing his buckteeth, slanted eyes, and signature round eyeglasses.

In *Superman #18* (Sep. 1942),[7] the title character rides a bomb plummeting through cloud and sky, accompanied by four dive-bombers streaking downward at a similar trajectory. The geographical setting is indeterminate, save for the caption at right: "WAR SAVINGS BONDS AND STAMPS DO THE JOB ON THE JAPANAZIS!" The caption — considered along with the early 1942 publication date — suggests that the Doolittle raid may have been an inspiration for Ray, as he imagined how the Man of Steel might have retaliated for the Pearl Harbor attacks of the previous year.

The other cover artist who set Superman against the Japanese enemy was

Jack Burnley. During World War II he drew over a dozen covers with war-related themes, among them several memorable images featuring the Japanese. For example, Burnley's cover for *World's Finest #8* (Winter 1942)[8] features Batman, Superman, and Robin selling war bonds to children under a sign that reads "SINK THE JAPANAZIS WITH BONDS & STAMPS," while *World's Finest #9* (Spring 1943),[9] boasts a fanciful cover reminiscent of a propaganda poster. Against a bright yellow background, Superman, Batman, and Robin hurl baseballs at the literal heads of the Axis powers, who poke out from behind a sheet reading "Knock Out the Axis With Bonds & Stamps." Tojo, at far right, is the ugliest of the bunch (Mussolini is a close second), with typically exaggerated features drawn from the stock images of the day — save the hue of his skin, which an unknown colorist mysteriously rendered a Caucasian pink, the same as the others in the scene.

The spring and summer of 1943 brought another cluster of war- (and Japan-) related covers to *Action Comics*, all drawn by Burnley. In *Action Comics #58* (March 1943), Superman uses his mighty arm muscles to turn a photo-realistically drawn printing press, which churns out a flier reading "Superman says: *YOU* can slap a Jap with WAR BONDS and STAMPS."[10] A familiar refrain, to be sure, but this particular iteration boasts a visual of a "Jap" — with banana-yellow skin, x-ed out eyes, and a tongue protruding from buckteeth — being slapped by a giant Caucasian hand. *Action Comics #62* (July 1943) boasts a dramatic rendering of Superman swooping downward to save a wounded G.I. from Japanese aircraft fire.[11] The bullets bounce off the Man of Steel, while the young soldier, wrapped in bloodied bandages, looks on. The setting of the cover — a tropical jungle in the foreground, and a purplish mountain range in the distance — evokes the island of Guadalcanal, where a bloody campaign between Japan and the Allies cost thousands of lives in 1942–1943. Superman, who obviously could not have been portrayed as playing an active role in the outcome of this conflict, nonetheless makes his own modest contribution by preventing the strafing of a soldier — and one can imagine him punching out the airplane "off camera" moments later.

Indeed, the following month's cover featured Superman performing just such a feat. On Burnley's cover to *Action Comics #63* (Aug. 1943), we see an enraged Superman straddling the airplane, raising his fist to pummel the pilot directly.[12] The Japanese pilot, whose skin color mirrors the bright yellow hue of the comic itself, puts up his hands in an obviously futile gesture to protect himself. In fact, he looks as though he has already been struck: his goggles have flown off behind him, and his head reels back in anguish.

Burnley's last Japan-themed cover, on *Action Comics #86* (July 1945), echoes his earlier printing press cover in its use of photo-realistic detail and emphasis on war bond sales.[13] A determined looking Superman buries Tojo alive in a tremendous heap of bond certificates for the seventh war loan, which was in itself the largest bond drive of the Second World War.

Finally, Wayne Boring, who would go on to become the definitive Superman illustrator of the 1950s, made one very memorable contribution to the canon of Japan-related Superman covers from World War II. The cover of *Action Comics #76* (Sep. 1944) nearly leaps off the page: Superman, at left, lands a mighty punch on a speeding Japanese motorcycle.[14] As a result, two Japanese soldiers — one who had been driving, another in the sidecar — are violently flung upwards into the title graphic itself. Though this scene presents a physical impossibility (surely the riders would have been thrown forward, rather than upward, if their motorcycle had stopped suddenly) it is nonetheless successful in its striking use of space.

In the comic books, Superman was rarely involved in the war outside of the cover images. However, shortly after the comic book adventures of Superman became popular, adaptations into other media followed. In newspaper comic strips, in cartoons, and on the radio Superman was depicted as much more involved in the war effort.

The Newspaper Comic Strips

From its humble beginning in three newspapers in January 1939 (and only six months after the character's comic book debut) the *Superman* daily comic strip eventually appeared in over three hundred daily newspapers across the country, and had an estimated audience of twenty to twenty-five million Americans — a figure that thoroughly dwarfed sales of the monthly comic books. Though a February 1942 strip saw Clark Kent flunk his Army physical (mistakenly reading the eye chart in the next room with his x-ray vision), "comic strip Superman" was ready and able for duty in the Pacific theater.

In a remarkable narrative written by Whitney Ellsworth and Al Schwartz[15] that ran from June 28 to August 21 1943, Clark Kent and Lois Lane are sent to investigate conditions at one of the Japanese internment camps established shortly after the Japanese attack on Pearl Harbor. "The public is interested in knowing the full details of what goes on inside a typical Jap relocation camp where alien Japs, as well as American citizens of Japanese ancestry, have been sent after being evacuated from the West coast and elsewhere," explains *Daily Planet* editor Perry White long-windedly. Upon arrival at the fictional "Camp Karok," Lois and Clark are reassured of the democratic freedoms enjoyed by the denizens of the camp. "While armed soldiers guard the camp, the relocation center's internal affairs are run by civilians and representatives of the interned Japanese themselves," assures a camp officer. "The Japanese here have their own schools ... their own newspapers. We provide them with worthwhile work projects, for, as you know, idle hands breed mischief." Clark concurs that it is a "more than reasonable set-up." The officer confides that the Army's primary source of concern is not "loyal Japs of American ancestry," but rather "enemy sympathizers who would be glad to sabotage our national welfare at the first opportunity."

Clark, correctly suspecting that there are indeed "enemy sympathizers" among the camp's residents, investigates further as Superman — and is buried alive by Japanese saboteurs, who gloat that the "the highly vaunted Superman falls victim to Japanese ingenuity ... added proof that America is destined to become a vassal state of Japan!" Needless to say, the Man of Steel soon escapes and sets after his pursuers. In a bizarre twist, however, he elects to go undercover as a Japanese by contorting his super-facial muscles: "it's easy — to make myself— look like a Jap," he says, over the course of the three-panel transformation. At the appropriate moment, Superman reveals his identity and proceeds to punch his way through a "horde of enraged enemy Japs." Their leader encourages them onward — "Don't give ground! You can't lose insomuch as you have the divine protection of Hirohito!" — but he is no match for Superman, who slams him into a large Japanese flag hanging on the wall. "Here's your place in the rising sun!"

The tale concludes with a half-hearted reminder from Superman that "most Japanese Americas are loyal citizens.... Not one act of sabotage was perpetrated in Hawaii or territorial U.S. by a Japanese-American." This message may have been a sop to the Office of War Information, which was horrified by the advance strips it had received, noting that the narrative "was about disloyal Japanese, with only a passing mention of loyal Japanese." The OWI had no censorship powers, however, and the McClure Syndicate — which distributed the strip to newspapers nationwide — declined their request to retract the entire episode. This narrative also drew some protests from the public, who criticized the strip for both "inciting race hatred" and implying that "the Army is lax enough to allow concealed weapons" to into the camps. Tellingly, none of the complaints were directed toward the practice of interning tens of thousands of Japanese and Japanese-American citizens.[16]

During the war, the full-color Sunday version of comic strip ran a feature called "Superman's Service for Servicemen," in which the title character offered aid and assistance to American soldiers overseas. In one long-running serial from April and May of 1944, Superman receives a highly unusual request from the *Japanese* army. Lois Lane is outraged — "of all the nervy, arrogant, cheeky things!" — but Superman flies off to the Pacific to meet "Major Sukiyaki" and his men. Sukiyaki explains that while the "more fortunate sons of Hirohito have pleasure defeating miserable enemies," his own troops are growing restless and bored, and would greatly appreciate some entertainment. The Man of Steel opens the show with an acrobatic exhibition, noting "you Japs used to be great jugglers and acrobats back in our vaudeville days." When Superman "accidentally" drops the two Japanese soldiers he was juggling, the officer is unconcerned: "one break arm, one break leg, no matter, simply shoot." Superman tells Sukiyaki that he needs to prepare a special entertainment, and flies to the nearest American base—where he promptly gives away the Japanese location and leads the Allies back for a bombing raid. As the Japanese soldiers run screaming for their lives, Superman says, "You asked for music, dancing, entertainment! Well, you look plenty excited, you're doing your own dancing, and if those guns aren't music I'll eat my hat!"

Though Superman rarely took enemy lives, another intriguing serial from late in the war (July 1945) featured multiple Japanese deaths for which the Man of Steel was at least indirectly responsible. The Japanese army orders a kamikaze attack on Superman—as one pilot says, "I now have honor to die for Emperor while destroy Superchap. Hope also ancestors have Breakfast ready!" Plane after plane explodes against Superman's chest, until the last pilot is allowed to escape unharmed to "dig up more opposition." Back at Imperial HQ, the army calls on the services of one Captain Slapahapa, the "bravest suicide pilot in all Japan." Slapahapa—a slight fellow with predictably buck teeth and slit eyes—proclaims that he "is looking forward with much enjoyment to joining honorable ancestors," and takes off in an airplane loaded to the gills with explosives. Upon impact Slapahapa and his craft are blown to smithereens, while an unscathed Superman flies to Japan to capture the army officers responsible for the attack.

Radio and Animation

In addition to print, Superman thrived in other media during the war years, most noticeably radio and animated cartoons. In February 1940, the *Adventures of Superman* radio program was first broadcast on WOR in New York City. The program, which was the origin of the Jimmy Olsen character, as well as the phrase "It's a bird! It's a plane! It's Superman!" was a smash hit, eventually reaching over eighty-five stations on the Mutual Network and producing over two thousand episodes before its cancellation in 1951. Although in the comics Clark Kent remained a civilian during World War II, in the radio serial he was commissioned as an undercover Secret Service agent, which opened the door to several adventures involving Superman and the Axis powers.

Of the extant audio recordings, there are two serials that feature the Japanese enemy. In the first (Jan.-Feb. 1945), Clark and Lois meet a runaway princess from Illyria, a hidden South American country recently fallen under the sway of the evil Grand Master Saki.[17] During the mission to restore the princess to the throne, Superman overhears two soldiers who have just parachuted into a nearby clearing. Speaking in heavy "Yellowface" accents, the pair leave no doubt as to their nationality and mission: "Oh, is great honor Emperor has bestowed upon us, the first Japanese to land in America as conquerors! There will be peace only when Japan rules the world! We will kill any living thing that interfere with great and glorious plan of the emperor!" Superman jumps out at the paratroopers — "I wouldn't miss this for all the rice they've stolen from China!" — but their rifle bullets bounce off his chest. In a nod to the perceived penchant among Japanese for self-extermination, one of the pair then exclaims "[he] is devil! He will not take me! I go to my ancestors! I die honorable death!" Rather than use his super-speed to prevent the solider from shooting himself, Superman waits for the deed to be completed — and then calmly says, "that's *one*."

Superman grabs the remaining paratrooper, and with a shout of "up, up, and away," proceeds to juggle the terrified, screaming man around in midair. The Man of Steel makes no attempt to extract any intelligence from the soldier by means of this technique (as he often did to petty criminals in the comic book), but rather his sole intent is to inflict panic and shock. All while he chants to himself a sort of revenge mantra: "That somersault is for the Chinese," he says, as he spins the paratrooper around in the air; "and this one is for our boys in Bataan, and here's a turn for Saipan, and another for Tarawa." Superman leaves the soldier tied up in the jungle, and heads off to confront the evil Saki, revealed to be a Japanese spy. After defeating — in the words of the narrator — "hordes of bloodthirsty Japanese" at the gates of Illyria, Superman returns the grateful princess to her people.

Another serial from 1945, now lost save for a single fifteen-minute episode originally broadcast on May 8th of that year, features an experimental Japanese super-weapon of such power that it could force an end to the war. It is not a nuclear bomb that promises to wreak such destruction — that would come soon enough in real life — but rather a hallucinogen that convinces its victims that they are under attack from their inanimate surroundings, such as flowers, trees, or patterned wallpaper. We hear the sad tale of "Sing Song," the only survivor of Japan's first test run of the weapon on a small island in the Pacific. The island was a paradise for three thousands souls, who lived in peace until a group of "yellow men with guns" disrupt their idyll: "We Japanese own whole world pretty soon.... We come do you great honor. We make experiment here with great new weapon. If work, all of you here die for Emperor, go to honorable Japanese heaven. Then we kill all Yankee dogs and own whole world." The island's headman (Sing Song's father) resists and is summarily shot. One hour later, the entire population is exterminated save Sing Song, who is spared for reasons unknown — sadly, no other episodes of this serial exist.

The *Superman* animated cartoon, produced by Fleischer Studios, appeared in movie theaters on a roughly monthly schedule from September 1941 until the summer of 1943. While the initial villains were robots, dinosaurs, and mad scientists, Japan found its way into storylines when Fleischer was bought out by Paramount Studios, whose animated features boasted an unusually high percentage of war-related content in the early 1940s.[18] "Japoteurs," written by Carl Meyer and William Turner, premiered on September 18, 1942. Given the long lead time required for the production of these elaborate animated features, it was likely conceived soon after the attack on Pearl Harbor some nine months previous. The cartoon opens with a Japanese man seated at a desk, reading about the "world's largest bombing plane" in the *Daily Planet*. He pushes a button on his desk, transforming a framed image of the Statue of Liberty into a Rising Sun flag, in front of which he stands and makes a deep bow. Along with two accomplices, the man hijacks the plane with the intention of diverting the craft to Tokyo. Here Superman steps in, easily dispatching the henchmen — but in so doing, allows the third man enough time to smash the controls and transform the bomber into the world's largest kamikaze mission, headed straight for Metropolis. Superman races ahead and catches the plane by the nose, landing it gently.

The second cartoon featuring Japanese was also written by Meyer and Turner, and reached theaters in November 1942. "Eleventh Hour" is one of the few examples in any media of Superman taking the fight to Japan, as it is set the port city of Yokohama. The narrative begins, unusually, *in medias res*: Clark and Lois have been kidnapped, and are interred under armed guard in separate (but adjoining) hotel rooms. We do not know how long they have been held in captivity, but we understand that Clark has been changing into Superman at precisely eleven o'clock every evening, breaking out of his room, and wreaking havoc on the nearby naval yards for which Yokohama was famous. In addition to damaging or destroying several ships, he also blows up bridges, tanks, and so forth, plainly killing several soldiers in the process. In response the Japanese post fliers threatening to execute Lois unless the attacks cease immediately. Superman apparently fails to see any of the fliers, and continues his attacks unabated. After destroying a large naval cruiser, the Man of Steel is temporarily trapped underneath a steel scaffolding — just as Lois is sent off to face the firing squad. Superman emerges from the rubble at the last moment, spots the message on a fallen girder, and rescues Lois as the executioners' bullets bounce off his chest. In an unusual twist, though, we learn at cartoon's close that Clark Kent remains a Japanese prisoner of war — but as the now-rescued Lois relays the situation, he will surely be safe because Superman is there to protect him. Perhaps needless to say, this plot point was dropped, and no mention of Japan was ever made in the cartoons again.

Fighting, but Not Winning, the War

William W. Savage, Jr., in his pioneering *Comics Books and America 1945–1954*, neatly summarized the dilemma comic book publishers faced during the war years: "were the United States to unleash [superheroes] upon the Axis, the war could reasonably be expected to end in an hour or less. Some explanation of why that would not happen had to be forthcoming if the credibility, and ultimately, the utility, for the heroes were to be maintained, even among unsophisticated juvenile audiences."[19] And yet, our survey of Superman across multiple media formats reveals the character to have been far more involved in the war effort that has hitherto been recognized. While he may not have challenged the Axis powers in the interior pages of *Action Comics, Superman,* or *World's Finest*, Superman was nonetheless an integral part of the war effort in all other manifestations of the character during the mid–1940s.

Moreover, as we noted at the beginning of this essay, the Allied conflict with Japan during World War II was — in John Dower's words — marked by "racial pride, arrogance, and rage."[20] This characterization resonates quite strongly with character of Superman in his earliest years: he was a quick-tempered vigilante, who showed little remorse for enemies injured or killed in the name of "justice." It is interesting to note in closing, however, that Superman's renegade nature began to transform in the mid–1940s. By the close of America's conflict against Japan, Superman had firmly moved to the side of law and order — and in so doing, had become a symbol of American values. I highlight this issue here because the Superman we have seen in these pages is far closer to that original intention than to the modern character: his anger, his violence, and his wit were all very much in evidence as he took on the Axis powers, among whom the Japanese surely engendered the most visceral responses. Superman's clash against the Axis powers on comic book covers, newspaper strips, radio, and cartoons was a part of the character's transformation from a social avenger to the patriotic defender of "truth, justice, and the American way"— a fact which has too often been obscured in the collective American memory.

CHAPTER NOTES

1. Feiffer, Jules, *The Great Comic Book Heroes* (New York: Dial Press, 1965; reprint, Fantagraphics Books, 2003), 59.

2. Dower, John, *War Without Mercy: Race and Power in the Pacific War* (New York: Pantheon, 1986), 4.

3. In the otherwise excellent *Men of Tomorrow: Geeks, Gangsters, and the Birth of the Comic Book* (New York: Basic Books, 2004), Gerard Jones notes that DC Comics publisher Jack Leibowitz forbad Superman from participating in the war since "too many isolationists out there had the power to keep their kids from buying comics" (p. 165). This thesis is problematic, as the comics market was bursting with stories of costumed heroes fighting the Japanese and Nazis — presumably because they had a positive, not negative, impact on comic book sales. Ian Gordon, meanwhile, suggests Superman was kept out of the war because of narrative difficulties due to the fact he could so easily have ended it; see *Comic Strips and Consumer Culture, 1890–1945* (Washington, D.C.: Smithsonian Institution Press, 1998), 146.

4. Ray, Fred (cover artist). *Action Comics #48* (May 1942). New York: DC Comics.

5. Ray, Fred (cover artist). *Superman #17* (July 1942). New York: DC Comics.

6. *Look*, February 27, 1940. Reprinted in *Superman Sunday Classics, 1939–1943*. New York: Sterling Publishing Co., Inc., 2006. 187–190.

7. Ray, Fred (cover artist). *Superman #17* (Sep. 1942). New York: DC Comics.

8. Burnley, Jack (cover artist). *World's Finest #8* (Winter 1942). New York: DC Comics.

9. Burnley, Jack (cover artist). *World's Finest #9* (Spring 1942). New York: DC Comics.

10. Burnley, Jack (cover artist). *Action Comics #58* (March 1943). New York: DC Comics.

11. Burnley, Jack (cover artist). *Action Comics #62* (July 1943). New York: DC Comics.

12. Burnley, Jack (cover artist). *Action Comics #63* (Aug. 1943). New York: DC Comics.

13. Burnely, Jack (cover artist). *Action Comics #86* (July 1945). New York: DC Comics.

14. Boring, Wayne (cover artist). *Action Comics #76* (Sep. 1944). New York: DC Comics.

15. Jerry Siegel, the co-creator of Superman and original artist for the newspaper comic strip had been drafted into the U.S. Army at the time of this story.

16. Gordon H. Chang, "'Superman is About to Visit the Relocation Centers' and the Limits of Wartime Liberalism," *Amerasia Journal* 19:1 (1993), pp. 37–60.

17. Of the eleven episodes that made up the story, only eight are still extant — but given the show's practice of recapping the previous episode's action, it is possible to recreate the narrative.

18. Shull, Michael S., and David E. Witt, *Doing Their Bit: Wartime American Animated Short Films, 1939–1945* (McFarland & Company, Inc., 2004 second edition), 46.

19. William W. Savage, Jr., *Comic Books and America 1945–1954* (Norman: University of Oklahoma Press, 1990), 10.

20. Dower, John, *War Without Mercy: Race and Power in the Pacific War* (New York: Pantheon, 1986), 4.

BIBLIOGRAPHY

Boring, Wayne (cover artist). *Action Comics #76* (Sep. 1944). New York: DC Comics.
Burnley, Jack (cover artist). *World's Finest #8* (Winter 1942). New York: DC Comics.
_____. *World's Finest #9* (Spring 1942). New York: DC Comics.
_____. *Action Comics #58* (March 1943). New York: DC Comics.
_____. *Action Comics #62* (July 1943). New York: DC Comics.
_____. *Action Comics #63* (Aug. 1943). New York: DC Comics.
_____. *Action Comics #86* (July 1945). New York: DC Comics.

Chang, Gordon H. "'Superman Is About to Visit the Relocation Centers' and the Limits of Wartime Liberalism." *Amerasia Journal* 19:1 (1993), pp. 37–60.

Dower, John. *War Without Mercy: Race and Power in the Pacific War.* New York: Pantheon, 1986.

Feiffer, Jules. *The Great Comic Book Heroes.* New York: Dial Press, 1965; reprint, Fantagraphics Books, 2003.

Gordon, Ian. *Comic Strips and Consumer Culture, 1890–1945.* Washington and London: Smithsonian Institution Press, 1998.

Jones, Gerard. *Men of Tomorrow: Geeks, Gangsters and the Birth of the Comic Book.* New York: Basic Books, 2004.

Ray, Fred (cover artist). *Action Comics #48* (May 1942). New York: DC Comics.

_____. *Superman #17* (July 1942). New York: DC Comics.

Savage, William W., Jr. *Comic Books and America 1945–1954.* Norman: University of Oklahoma Press, 1990.

Shull, Michael S., and David E. Witt. *Doing Their Bit: Wartime American Animated Short Films, 1939–1945,* 2d ed. Jefferson, NC: McFarland, 2004.

Siegel, Jerry (w), and Joe Schuster (a). *Look,* February 27, 1940. Reprinted in *Superman Sunday Classics, 1939–1943.* New York: Sterling Publishing, 2006.

Supervillains and Cold War Tensions in the 1950s

Lori Maguire

In the United States, the 1950s were a period of immense power and growth but also one of great fear, especially since the Soviet Union had exploded its first atomic bomb in 1949. America was no longer the only nuclear superpower and found itself threatened. The development of Soviet rocket technology, the descent of the "iron curtain" over various Eastern European countries after World War II, and the communist victory in China in 1949 reinforced American disquiet. Danger was also found to exist inside the country, whether from communists (the revelation of various Soviet spies which contributed to the panic of McCarthyism) or from the arms race (reports of nuclear contamination that occurred because of testing). Many of these anxieties found their expression in the popular culture of the time and comic books were one of the most significant places.[1]

Superman holds a special place in any analysis of this question for a number of reasons.[2] To begin with, scholars have observed that Superman represents human triumph over technology and in particular over "mechanized urban society."[3] Since so many anxieties of the time were linked to technology, it would seem obvious that they would find a reflection in his stories. Furthermore, to a large extent because of the *The Adventures of Superman* television series (1952–1958), alone among superheroes, Superman's popularity actually increased in the early 1950s. Finally, he is in many ways quintessentially American. Like his fellow citizens, he is an immigrant in a country where the immigrant experience is a defining one. Raised in Kansas, in the heartland of the nation, he has completely accepted the values of his adoptive, farmer parents. He is thus an immigrant who has embraced mainstream values and who has fully integrated into his new society. As Gary Engle notes in his essay, "What Makes Superman So Darned American?": "Superman's victories over criminals, foreign tyrants and extraterrestrial invaders are always testimony that the American way is the true way, the just way."[4] His resemblance to the heroes of Westerns has also been noted.[5] He is thus an obvious symbol of an idealized vision of America as superpower working, through its strength, for democracy and justice in the world.[6]

The famous opening of the television series illustrates this idea with Superman in front of a flag "fighting for truth, justice and the American way." However, the series itself, perhaps for budgetary reasons, mainly consisted of simple detective stories and rarely contained any Cold War propaganda. Since the comic book stories were usually linked to the series, Superman found himself limited to fighting crime in Metropolis or having rather silly adventures.[7] While World War II had figured largely in all superhero comics, the Korean War received barely a mention.[8] But after the cancellation of the show and with the start of the so-called "Silver Age" age of comics, Superman began to face more challenging adversaries, fighting often on a cosmic level against villains as strong as himself. In such cases, he can be viewed as showing human superiority to technology and a kind of soulless science but also as a reflection of America's foreign policy — at least in the idealistic way it was presented to the public at the time. America's role internationally then becomes that of a superpower who maintains order in the world through the use of force against bad guys, helps the worthy poor, and protects private property (after all, communism is opposed to such a notion). Champion of humanity and its greatest values, Superman fights against outrageous villains who seek to dominate the world for their own ends. And, of course, he always wins. But, interestingly enough, he rarely wins by using his strength and power.

This chapter aims to examine the major villains during this time frame and assess to what extent they reflect certain Cold War tensions.[9] Clearly the world seemed a more frightening place after Hiroshima and Nagasaki. Taking the lead from Susan Sontag's essay "The Imagination of Disaster," a great deal of work has already been done on the expression of anxieties related to nuclear power in the science fiction cinema of the time.[10] Most of these themes can also be found in the Superman comics of the period. While before the war Superman had promoted New Deal ideals and worked against corruption, and during the war he had supported the war effort (although leaving most of the fighting to the military), in the 1950s his universe became progressively more charged with the trappings of science fiction and as the villains he opposed grew in stature so did he. By the end of the decade, the villains were much too powerful for any human institutions to control and Superman had become a demi-god — but one whose physical strength was often surprisingly unimportant.

Among the major villains there is, first and foremost, Lex Luthor, most famous of all Superman's opponents.[11] Luthor first appeared in *Action Comics*

. *#23* (April 1940).[12] He has undergone a number of transformations since then but he began — with a full head of red hair — as a "power-mad, evil scientist."[13] By 1950, though, he had descended to a criminal bent on robbing banks and finding any way to annoy and humiliate Superman. For example, in "Superman's Super-Magic Show," *Action Comics #151* (Dec. 1950), he teamed up with the Prankster and Mr. Mxyztplk to make the Man of Steel "super-ridiculous."[14] The man who had, in the 1940s, provoked wars, threatened earthquakes, stopped the flow of oil, and turned American financiers into his tools now was happy with simply embarrassing Superman — such was the decline of villains in this period. Luthor, however, still remained a scientific genius and his often bizarre inventions reflected this fact. Luthor, of course, represents fear of scientific advance — especially of its misuse — particularly in relation to weapons technology. He also became more threatening as the decade advanced.

The late 1950s saw the arrival of a host of new villains, most of them showing the influence of science fiction. Brainiac, a threatening space alien, first appeared in 1958. The following year saw Metallo, a highly dangerous part-man, part-robot, and Bizarro, the flawed, accidental duplicate of Superman, introduced to readers. The year 1959 also saw the first appearance of the monkey who was transformed through voyaging in space into the giant ape, Titano. Furthermore, we can also note the preoccupation with Krypton at this time and the villains that Superman faced from there.

An analysis of these figures and their presentation can reveal a great deal about the anxieties of the time. In particular, three themes stand out (although there is some overlapping between them): fear of nuclear radiation, fear of invasion, and fears related to the space race. Underlying each, of course, is fear of technology being turned to the wrong ends and used to take away freedom and establish dictatorship or, quite simply, to destroy.

Fear of Nuclear Radiation

At this time the effect of nuclear testing was attracting a great deal of attention especially since there was evidence that it was affecting the food supply. In the 1950s, nuclear testing was done above ground and often within the U.S., in particular in the desert regions of Nevada and Utah. It became more and more clear that, in spite of government denials, the areas around these testing sites — and thus the people who inhabited them — were being contaminated by fallout. This occurred most dramatically in the 1954 tests by the U.S. which spread high levels of fallout over thousands of miles in the Pacific, causing acute radiation sickness and even death among Japanese fishermen. The following year radioactive rain fell on Chicago. Later still, radioactivity was found to affect the food supply, especially milk — which is closely linked to the nourishment of children. It seemed that future generations were being adversely affected.[15]

Three subsequent events dramatized the situation even more. In September 1957 the Kyshtym disaster occurred in Russia which would be the greatest nuclear accident of all time until Chernobyl. The USSR, however, tried to cover it up and it only reached the Western press the following year. Less than a month later, in November 1957, the Windscale disaster in Britain caused the release of radioactive material into the environment. A few months later, in March 1958, a B–47 bomber accidentally dropped an atom bomb in South Carolina. Although this injured a number of people, massive disaster was avoided because atomic fission failed to occur. The risk of being destroyed by your own side seemed very real. Although earlier in the decade, the government had tried to reassure people and minimize the results of a nuclear attack, by this time, the public had become aware of its devastating consequences.

In Superman, radiation is associated most frequently with kryptonite. Although appearing in the Superman radio series as early as 1943, its first use in the comic books, interestingly enough, occurs just a few months after the USSR exploded its first atomic bomb in August 1949.[16] The only thing capable of weakening and even killing Superman, it paradoxically comes from Superman's home planet — so the origin of his superpowers is also, potentially, the source of his destruction.[17] In a similar way the military and particularly the atomic power of the U.S. could also destabilize and even destroy the nation.[18] Kryptonite has been most closely associated with Lex Luthor. Indeed, Luthor managed to develop a synthetic version of it in *Action Comics #141* (Feb. 1950).[19] However, for much of the decade he was only the shadow of the villain he had been.

In *Action Comics #249* (Feb. 1959), though, he came back with a vengeance as the Kryptonite Man.[20] In this story, Luthor actually finds a way to make a serum of kryptonite and takes it himself. Through his various inventions, Luthor has already become too powerful for any regular human authority to defeat, but by taking kryptonite he becomes lethal to the only remaining authority that can contain him.[21]

Interestingly enough, many things about kryptonite have associations with nuclear power. For one thing, in *Superman #130* (July 1959), Superman nearly dies from kryptonite in Death Valley — not terribly far from nuclear test sites.[22] Furthermore, the term "radiations" is frequently used. In "The Kryptonite Man," Luthor glows and so we actually see the green radiations that would, in time, kill Superman.[23] Reflecting concerns after Sputnik, Luthor puts a satellite in orbit to further hurt Superman. The superhero finds himself with no protection at all and must abandon earth for the moon. He is saved, however, by his own ingenuity, scientific knowledge and technical prowess and so, in the end, manages once again to defeat Luthor who is imprisoned.

Another ray appears in the story of Bizarro, although this time it is a duplicator ray. First appearing as the imperfect replicate of Superboy, the technology is later stolen by Luthor who creates a Bizarro version of the adult Superman in the hope of using him against the Man of Steel.[24] A disguised Luthor lures Superman to his lab with the promise of an antidote to kryptonite. What emerges does not live up to Luthor's hopes but still represents a threat. Bizarro admires Superman and wishes to imitate him but with often disastrous results. He represents strength without a consciousness of the consequences of one's actions. He is not nasty or power hungry — he just is unable to foresee the damage he can do unintentionally to weaker creatures. This, in fact, represents Superman's fear of his own power.[25] In the same way, America, the superpower, could destroy itself and others at any time as a consequence of its very strength.

Metallo, who first appeared in 1959, is another villain associated with kryptonite.[26] Formerly the corrupt and murderous journalist John Corben, Metallo comes into being after Corbin is saved from a car accident by having his brain transferred into a robot. Since he is powered by a uranium heart, the link with nuclear power is clear. A robot body and a uranium heart make him a threat to American society but not to Superman — at least not until Metallo learns that kryptonite would be a superior power source. Indeed, Superman, and presumably the world, is only saved because Metallo steals fake kryptonite and so dies.

Fear of Invasion

Threats coming from outer space were a continual theme in science fiction from the very start of the 1950s and they occur in the Superman comics regularly. A few examples will suffice. In *Superman #65* (July-Aug. 1950), three survivors of Krypton arrive on earth, all possessing powers equal to Superman and all evil.[27] Indeed, the story begins with what appears to be an attack on Metropolis which leaves skyscrapers shaking throughout the city. Through his incredible strength and speed, Superman manages to save the city and then seeks the reason for the near disaster. He finds the three Kryptonians and discovers their history. Mad scientists, they had tried, through one of their inventions, to force the citizens of Krypton to accept them as dictators. In true Cold War spirit, the Kryptonians refused to give into their demands, saying that: "We cannot ... live under dictatorship! It is better ... to die." They were finally saved by the superior scientific genius of Superman's father, Jor-El but Superman does not have the same resources. He finally defeats them through tricking them into fighting each other.

Later, in *World's Finest Comics #68* (Jan.-Feb. 1954), earth was threatened by a meteor which human science could perceive but not destroy — making it an obvious job for Superman.[28] He forces the asteroid to orbit the earth, preventing a direct collision, but this wreaks havoc with the weather. Throughout the world there are massive tidal waves, cyclones and floods as the polar caps melt. The twist is that Superman must handle all this and destroy the asteroid while experiencing amnesia. He does so through a strong sense of duty.

In other cases Superman defeats spies who are analyzing the possibility of invasion. In *Superman #122* (July 1958), a freakish accident with lightning gives an ordinary American soldier the same powers as the Man of Steel.[29] The latter uses this incident to convince spies from an unidentified foreign power that he can transfer his powers at will to any number of persons. They report that: "Superman can create an army of super-soldiers overnight by transferring his powers.... That is America's new secret weapon.... Abandon all attack plans." So, in spite of all his powers, it is once again through a ruse that he saves the U.S.

He does this again in *Action Comics #244* (Sep. 1958) in which he meets a merman, Vul-Kor and his merdaughter, Lya-La, although this time he saves the entire planet from invasion.[30] In true Mata Hari fashion, Lya-La tries to seduce Superman into helping them in their nefarious plan and seems to have succeeded. Indeed, Vul-Kor explains:

> Will you be sorry to see the Earthlings wiped out? The human coil will hurl a super heat-ray at earth's poles! As the ice-caps melt, flood waters will deluge the continents, drowning the earth forever! Human civilization will sink without a trace! Then my sea-breathing people can colonize this new water-world! Thus we will conquer earth without having to use our space warships and drop super-bombs! It's a good thing my daughter's charms swayed you into throwing in with us. Now I'll start the infra-coil! Zero hour is here!

Of course, Superman has not thrown in his lot with someone bent on Earth's destruction and has actually sabotaged the machine. But once again he succeeds through subterfuge rather than fighting. He convinces Vul-Kor that earth's water is poisonous to him and so he leaves peacefully.

A different point of view on spying occurs in another story from that year.[31] Here Jimmy Olsen makes a wish on an ancient totem for Superman to meet his parents. He sees them when young, before their marriage and is horrified to discover that they are traitors, working with Kil-Lor, an evil, would-be dictator. However, when the Krypton Bureau of Investigation intervenes, Jor-El claims that he and Lara are actually undercover agents. Unfortunately, the only person aware of their identity has just died and so Superman's parents are sentenced to 100 years in a prison satellite. Once there, though, Superman helps his future parents to defeat Kil-Lor, and, at the end, they find the necessary evidence to clear themselves. In this story it is not spies who are the real threat but a too easy condemnation of innocent people. The KBI is well ahead of the conspiracy but its own secrecy jeopardizes its agents. Of course, this is well after McCarthyism but it does seem to be a warning against such excesses, especially in the aftermath of Sputnik.

Fears Related to the Space Race

The United States' Space Race with the Soviet Union began after World War II. Succeeding with the first supersonic flight in 1947, America seemed well in advance. This caused a certain complacency which received a sharp jolt in October 1957 when the USSR launched the world's first satellite, Sputnik. This provoked panic in the U.S. as the nation rushed to catch up and, feeling terribly vulnerable, to protect its citizens. A month later, the Gaither Report called for the construction of more missiles and an expansion in the numbers of fallout shelters.[32] In December the first American attempt at sending a satellite into space failed, increasing the feelings of vulnerability—although Explorer 1 was successfully launched a month and half after that. Suddenly satellites and space ships were everywhere in popular culture. The creation of NASA in 1958 attracted even more attention to the subject. This was an obvious theme to use in the Superman comics.

In *Action Comics #242* (July 1958), Clark Kent and Lois Lane take off on the Columbus, described as "the first experimental spaceship with humans aboard."[33] They enter space and break all records for the distance a rocket has traveled from earth. However, all is not perfect for they discover the arrival of Brainiac, probably the greatest threat from outer space that Superman faced in the period. In this initial manifestation Brainiac is a bald, green extraterrestrial and former dictator who lost his empire to a plague. He has since traveled the universe shrinking cities from various planets in order to reconstitute them later on his home world — and so recreate his lost dictatorship. Superman watches as he shrinks Earth's major cities and fails completely to stop him. In fact, Brainiac, through his science, possesses greater powers than Superman. In the end, the Man of Steel wins, of course, but only because Brainiac has gone into suspended animation for his return flight. Furthermore, while Superman manages to restore earth's cities, he can do nothing to help the others, including Kandor, a city taken from Krypton (although he does take the latter to his Fortress of Solitude in the hope of one day finding a way to restore it).

Even the act of exploring space can hold risks in the story of "Titano the Super-Ape," *Superman #127* (Feb. 1959).[34] This story is obviously inspired by the Russians sending a dog named Laika with Sputnik II in November 1957 and the Americans putting two monkeys into space a few months after this comic book appeared. In the story, an intelligent, gentle but mischievous chimp is launched into space aboard a satellite but, while in space, is affected by two meteors containing, significantly, uranium and Kryptonite. When he returns to earth, he becomes a giant ape whose eyes radiate Kryptonite. After a number of difficulties, Superman finally manages to send Titano into pre-history where he can no longer harm human civilization. The warning about potential dangers in rushing ahead into explorations of the unknown is clear.

In another story, "The Man No Prison Could Hold," *Action Comics #248* (Jan. 1959), we see a more insidious danger.[35] While flying around the earth, Superman notices an unknown satellite and seeks to discover what country has launched it. He finds an island containing a former Nazi scientist and people he has enslaved to work on his project. His goal is to launch a much larger satellite that will allow an "international crime syndicate" to spy on the police, banks and any other group of interest to them. The threat of surveillance from space comes from an old enemy, but the idea resonates with the period when the comic book was published. Superman here uses his strength and superpowers to defeat them.

In the Superman comics, as elsewhere in the popular culture of the time, we can find reflections of leading preoccupations in society. In particular, supervillains exemplify some of the dominant periods experienced by Americans in the 1950s. Significantly, all too frequently, the villains are more powerful than Superman — that all too obvious symbol of an idealized America. Time after time it is not Superman's superior strength that makes him win but his resourcefulness and even wiliness. He continually fools his opponents into giving up. His strength is important but it is generally used to prevent catastrophe and save innocent lives. It is not Superman's, or America's, strength that is key to success but the way in which that strength is cleverly employed. Superman's foes may possess equal or greater strength, but the values America holds dear allow Superman to persevere and triumph over the comic book enemies that represent the real-world threats America feared.

CHAPTER NOTES

1. William Savage in *Comic Books and America, 1945–1954* (Norman: University of Oklahoma, 1990) p. ix, asserts that: "Comic books in the postwar decade, through a unique

combination of text and pictures, offered a world view to a large segment of the American population (primarily children and adolescents, but, as we shall see, some adults as well) that did not yet have one; the world after 1945, as historians are wont to say, was a more confusing place that [sic] it had ever been before; and Americans generally were at some pains to explain their position in it. Comic books, like other products of mass culture, comprised one vehicle for explanation." Bradford Wright makes a similar argument in *Comic Book Nation: The Transformation of Youth Culture in America* (Baltimore: Johns Hopkins press, 2001) xii. For more on the history of comic books at this time see Jean-Paul Gabillet, *Des comics et des hommes: Histoire culturelle des comic books aux Etats-Unis* (Nantes: Edition du temps, 2005); Mike Benton, *The Comic Book in America: An Illustrated History* (Dallas: Taylor, 1993); Les Daniels, *Comix: A History of Comic Books in America* (New York: Outerbridge & Dienstfrey, 1971); Randy Duncan and Matthew J. Smith, *The Power of Comics: History, Form and Culture* (New York: Continuum, 2009); Gerard Jones and Will Jacobs, *The Comic Book Heroes: From the Silver Age to the Present* (New York: Crown, 1985), Martin Winkler, *Super Heroes* (Paris: EPA, 2003), Mike Benton, *Superhero Comics of the Silver Age* (Dallas: Taylor, 1991).

2. Numerous commentators have tried to analyze the attraction and meaning of Superman. See, for example, Umberto Eco, "The Myth of Superman," in *The Role of the Reader* (Bloomington: Indiana University Press, 1979); Antonio Altarriba, "Superman: le mythe," in Viviane Alay & Danielle Coraddo, eds., *Mythe et bande-dessinée* (Clermont-Ferrand: Presses Universitaires Blaise Pacal, 2000); Dennis Dooley and Gary Engle, eds, *Superman at Fifty* (New York: Macmillan, 1987); Glenn Yeffeth, ed. *The Man from Krypton: A Closer Look at Superman* (Dallas: Ben Bella/Smart Pop Books, 2005); Thomas Andrae, "From Menace to Messiah: The History and Historicity of Superman," in Donald Lazere, ed., *American Media and Mass Culture: Left Perspectives* (Berkeley: University of California Press, 1987); Danny Fingeroth, *Superman on the Couch: What Superheroes Really Tell Us about Ourselves and Our Society* (New York: Continuum, 2004); Mark Waid, "The Real Truth about Superman," in Tom Morris and Matt Morris, eds., *Superheroes and Philosophy* (Peru, IL: Open Court Publishing, 2005).

3. Regaldo, Aldo, "Modernity, Race and the American Superhero." Jeff McLaughlin, ed. *Comics as Philosophy* (Jackson: University of Mississippi Press, 2005), 91.

4. Engle, Gary, "What Makes Superman So Darned American?" Dennis Dooley and Gary Engle, eds. *Superman at Fifty* (New York: Macmillan, 1987), 90.

5. Wright, Bradford, *Comic Book Nation: The Transformation of Youth Culture in America* (Baltimore: Johns Hopkins press, 2001), 10.

6. Gary Grossman, *Superman: From Serial to Cereal* (New York: Popular Library, 1976), 139, has even called him "a symbol of ever lasting democracy." Lawrence Watt-Evans points out in "Previous Issues" from Yeffeth, op cit; p. 1: "Superman has powers and abilities far beyond those of mortal men; he can make himself ruler of the world, take anything he wants or kill anyone who gets in his way — but he doesn't. He's a good guy, the *ultimate* good guy, because he apparently isn't even *tempted* to abuse his powers. He's wholesome and noble and selfless. His foster parents raised him that way, and he's true to his upbringing."

7. The early 1950s is not considered a high point in the history of the Superman comics. After the departure of its creators, Jerry Siegel and Joe Shuster, the stories often became rather silly. Mort Weisinger took over as editor, believing that Superman was "invulnerable" and that "even bad scripts can't hurt him." Quoted in Ron Goulart, *The Comic Book Reader's Companion* (New York: Harper, 1993), 161.

8. The Korean War did, however, form the basis of a number of realistic comic books though. For more on this see Wright, 131–4.

9. Mila Bongco, *Reading Comics: Language, Culture and the Concept of the Superhero*

in Comic Books (New York : Garland, 2000), 21, observes that: "The representation of enemies and villains in these comic books is highly dependent on the social and cultural relations of the United States at any one time."

10. "The Imagination of Disaster" published in *Against Interpretation* (New York: Farrar, Straus & Giroux, 1966). See also Brian Murphy, "Monster Movies: They Came from Beneath the Fifties," in *Journal of Popular Film*, 1:1 (Winter 1972) 31–44; Lori Maguire, "The Destruction of New York City: A Recurrent Nightmare of American Cold War Cinema," *Cold War History* (Nov. 2009) 9:4, 513–524; Joyce Evans, *Celluloid Mushroom Clouds: Hollywood and the Atomic Bomb* (Boulder, Col: Westview Press, 1998); Toni Perrine, *Film and the Nuclear Age: Representing Cultural Anxiety* (New York: Garland, 1998) and Paul Boyer, *By the Bomb's Early Light: American Thought and Culture at the Dawn of the Atomic Age* (New York: Pantheon Books, 1985).

11. For more on Luthor see Bob Batchelor, "Brains vs. Brawn: The Many Lives (and Minds) of Lex Luthor, the World's Greatest Villain," in Yeffeth, *op cit.*

12. Siegel, Jerry (w), and Joe Shuster (a). "Europe at War, Part II." *Action Comics #23* (April 1940). New York: DC Comics.

13. Siegel, Jerry (w), and John Sikela (a). "Powerstone." *Action Comics #47* (April 1942). New York:DC Comics.

14. Hamilton, Edmond (w), and Wayne Boring (a). "Superman's Super-Magic Show." *Action Comics #151* (Dec. 1950). New York:DC Comics.

15. For more on this, see Robert Divine, *Blowing in the Wind: The Nuclear Test Ban Debate* (Oxford: Oxford University Press, 1978) and Richard Miller, *Under the Cloud: The Decades of Nuclear Testing* (New York: The Free Press, 1986). For its impact on popular culture see Joyce Evans, *Celluloid Mushroom Clouds: Hollywood and the Atomic Bomb* (Boulder, Col: Westview Press, 1998). Also Toni Perrine, *Film and the Nuclear Age: Representing Cultural Anxiety* (New York: Garland, 1998) and Paul Boyer, *By the Bomb's Early Light: American Thought and Culture at the Dawn of the Atomic Age* (New York: Pantheon Books, 1985).

16. Finger, Bill (w), and Al Plastino (a). "Superman Returns to Krypton." *Superman #61* (Nov.-Dec. 1949). New York: DC Comics.

17. Engle, Gary, "What Makes Superman So Darned American?" Dennis Dooley and Gary Engle, eds. *Superman at Fifty* (New York: Macmillan, 1987), 94.

18. Eisenhower warned: "In the councils of government, we must guard against the acquisition of unwarranted influence, whether sought or unsought, by the military-industrial complex. The potential for the disastrous rise of misplaced power exists and will persist." "Farewell Address," 17 January 1961; americanrhetoric.com.

19. Schwartz, Alvin (w), and Wayne Boring (a). "Luthor's Secret Weapon." *Action Comics #141* (Feb. 1950). New York: DC Comics.

20. Binder, Otto (w), and Al Plastino (a). "The Kryptonite Man." *Action Comics #249* (Feb. 1959). New York: DC Comics.

21. Having created his own personal rocketship, Luthor asserts that: "The air force can't shoot down my special armored ship."

22. Binder, Otto (w), and Al Plastino (a). "The Curse of Kryptonite." *Superman #130* (July 1959). New York: DC Comics.

23. As Clark Kent explains at one point: "Those radiations can destroy me in time!"

24. Binder, Otto (w), and George Papp (a). "The Boy of Steel vs. the Thing of Steel." *Superboy #68* (Oct. 1958); New York: DC Comics.; Otto Binder (w), Al Plastino (a) "The Battle with Bizarro." *Action Comics #254* (July 1959). New York: DC Comics.

25. As Engle has observed on page 94: "It is finally his own power he fears, as much as the power of his enemy of the moment. One slip, one super-thrust when he should have parried and he himself might bring about the destruction of Metropolis."

26. Bernstein, Robert (w), and Al Plastino (a). "The Menace of Metallo." *Action Comics #252* (May 1959). New York: DC Comics.

27. Woolfolk, William (w), and Al Plastino (a). "Three Supermen from Krypton." *Superman #65* (July-Aug. 1950). New York: DC Comics.

28. Anonymous (w), and Wayne Boring (a). "The Menace from the Stars." *World's Finest Comics #68* (Jan.-Feb. 1954). New York: DC Comics.

29. Binder, Otto (w), and Wayne Boring (a). "The Super-Sergeant." *Superman #122* (July 1958). New York: DC Comics.

30. Binder, Otto (w), and Wayne Boring (a). "The Super-Merman of the Sea." *Action Comics #244* (Sep. 1958). New York: DC Comics.

31. Binder, Otto (w), and Dick Sprang (a). "The Three Magic Wishes." *Superman #123* (Aug. 1958). New York: DC Comics.

32. The full text of the Gaither Report can be found at *http://www.gwu.edu/~nsarchiv/ NSAEBB/NSAEBB139/nitze02.pdf* (accessed 29 June 2011)

33. Binder, Otto (w), and Al Plastino (a). "The Super-Duel in Space." *Action Comics #242* (July 1958). New York: DC Comics.

34. Binder, Otto (w), and Wayne Boring (a). "Titano the Super Ape." *Superman #127* (Feb. 1959). New York: DC Comics.

35. Finger, Bill (w), and Wayne Boring (a). *Action Comics #248* (Jan. 1959). New York: DC Comics.

BIBLIOGRAPHY

Altarriba, Antonio. "Superman: le mythe." In Viviane Alay and Danielle Coraddo, eds., *Mythe et bande-dessinée.* Clermont-Ferrand: Presses Universitaires Blaise Pacal, 2000.

Andrae, Thomas. "From Menace to Messiah: The History and Historicity of Superman." In Donald Lazere, ed., *American Media and Mass Culture: Left Perspectives.* Berkeley: University of California Press, 1987.

Anonymous (w), and Wayne Boring (a). "The Menace from the Stars." *World's Finest Comics #68* (Jan.-Feb. 1954). New York: DC Comics.

Batchelor, Bob. "Brains vs. Brawn: The Many Lives (and Minds) of Lex Luthor, the World's Greatest Villain." In Glenn Yeffeth, ed., *The Man from Krypton: A Closer Look at Superman.* Dallas: Ben Bella/ Smart Pop Books, 2005.

Benton, Mike. *The Comic Book in America: An Illustrated History.* Dallas: Taylor, 1993.

_____. *Superhero Comics of the Silver Age.* Dallas: Taylor, 1991.

Bernstein, Robert (w), and Al Plastino (a). "The Menace of Metallo." *Action Comics #252* (May 1959). New York: DC Comics.

Binder, Otto (w), and Wayne Boring (a). "The Super-Merman of the Sea." *Action Comics #244* (Sep. 1958). New York: DC Comics.

_____. "The Super-Sergeant." *Superman #122* (July 1958). New York: DC Comics.

_____. "Titano the Super Ape." *Superman #127* (Feb. 1959). New York: DC Comics.

Binder, Otto (w), and George Papp (a). "The Boy of Steel vs. The Thing of Steel." *Superboy #68* (Oct 1958); New York: DC Comics.

Binder, Otto (w), and Al Plastino (a). "The Battle with Bizarro." *Action Comics #254* (July 1959). New York: DC Comics.

_____. "The Curse of Kryptonite." *Superman #130* (July 1959). New York: DC Comics.

_____. "The Kryptonite Man." *Action Comics #249* (Feb. 1959). New York: DC Comics.

_____. "The Super-Duel in Space." *Action Comics #242* (July 1958). New York: DC Comics.

Binder, Otto (w), and Dick Sprang (a). "The Three Magic Wishes." *Superman #123* (Aug. 1958). New York: DC Comics.

Bongco, Mila . *Reading Comics: Language, Culture and the Concept of the Superhero in Comic Books*. New York: Garland, 2000, 21.

Boyer, Paul. *By the Bomb's Early Light: American Thought and Culture at the Dawn of the Atomic Age*. New York: Pantheon Books, 1985.

Daniels, Les. *Comix: A History of Comic Books in America*. New York: Outerbridge & Dienstfrey, 1971.

Divine, Robert. *Blowing in the Wind: The Nuclear Test Ban Debate*. Oxford: Oxford University Press, 1978.

Dooley, Dennis, and Gary Engle, eds. *Superman at Fifty*. New York: Macmillan, 1987.

Duncan, Randy, and Matthew J. Smith. *The Power of Comics: History, Form and Culture*. New York: Continuum, 2009.

Eco, Umberto. "The Myth of Superman." In Eco, Umberto, *The Role of the Reader*. Bloomington: Indiana University Press, 1979.

Eisenhower, Dwight. "Farewell Address." 17 January 1961, accessed at http://americanrhetoric.com.

Engle, Gary. "What Makes Superman So Darned American?" Dennis Dooley and Gary Engle, eds. *Superman at Fifty*. New York: Macmillan, 1987.

Evans, Joyce. *Celluloid Mushroom Clouds: Hollywood and the Atomic Bomb*. Boulder, Col: Westview Press, 1998.

Finger, Bill (w), and Wayne Boring (a). *Action Comics #248* (Jan. 1959). New York: DC Comics.

Finger, Bill (w), and Al Plastino (a). "Superman Returns to Krypton." *Superman #61* (Nov.-Dec. 1949). New York: DC Comics.

Fingeroth, Danny. *Superman on the Couch: What Superheroes Really Tell Us About Ourselves and Our Society*. New York: Continuum, 2004.

Gabillet, Jean-Paul. *Des comics et des hommes: Histoire culturelle des comic books aux Etats-Unis*. Nantes: Edition du temps, 2005.

Goulart, Ron. *The Comic Book Reader's Companion*. New York: Harper, 1993), 161.

Grossman, Gary. *Superman: From Serial to Cereal*. New York: Popular Library, 1976.

Hamilton, Edmond (w), and Wayne Boring (a). "Superman's Super-Magic Show." *Action Comics #151* (Dec. 1950). New York: DC Comics.

Jones, Gerard, and Will Jacobs. *The Comic Book Heroes: From the Silver Age to the Present*. New York: Crown, 1985.

Maguire, Lori. "The Destruction of New York City: A Recurrent Nightmare of American Cold War Cinema." *Cold War History* 9:4 (Nov. 2009), 513–524.

Miller, Richard. *Under the Cloud: The Decades of Nuclear Testing*. New York: The Free Press, 1986.

Murphy, Brian Murphy. "Monster Movies: They Came from Beneath the Fifties" in *Journal of Popular Film*, 1:1 (Winter 1972), 31–44.

Perrine, Toni. *Film and the Nuclear Age: Representing Cultural Anxiety*. New York: Garland, 1998.

Regaldo, Aldo. "Modernity, Race and the American Superhero." In Jeff McLaughlin, ed., *Comics as Philosophy*. Jackson: University of Mississippi Press, 2005.

Savage, William W., Jr. *Comic Books and America 1945–1954*. Norman: University of Oklahoma Press, 1990.

Schwartz, Alvin (w), and Wayne Boring (a). "Luthor's Secret Weapon." *Action Comics #141* (Feb. 1950). New York: DC Comics.

Siegel, Jerry (w), and Joe Shuster (a). "Europe at War, Part II." *Action Comics #23* (April 1940). New York: DC Comics.

Siegel, Jerry (w), and John Sikela (a). "Powerstone." *Action Comics #47* (April 1942). New York: DC Comics.

Sontag, Susan. "The Imagination of Disaster" published in *Against Interpretation*. New York: Farrar, Straus & Giroux, 1966.

Waid, Mark. "The Real Truth about Superman." In Tom Morris and Matt Morris, eds., *Superheroes and Philosophy*. Peru, IL: Open Court Publishing, 2005.

Winkler, Martin. *Super Heroes*. Paris: EPA, 2003.

Woolfolk, William (w), and Al Plastino (a). "Three Supermen from Krypton." *Superman #65* (July-Aug. 1950). New York: DC Comics.

Wright, Bradford. *Comic Book Nation: The Transformation of Youth Culture in America*. Baltimore: Johns Hopkins University Press, 2001.

Yeffeth, Glenn, ed. *The Man from Krypton: A Closer Look at Superman*. Dallas: Ben Bella/ Smart Pop Books, 2005.

Kryptonite, Radiation, and the Birth of the Atomic Age

Peter Lee

The Atomic Age exploded on to the world stage on August 6, 1945. Not content with bringing down the curtain on the Pacific theater and ending a five-year world tour engagement, atomic power returned to the headlines the following year at the Bikini Atoll. The first test, "Able," was an atmospheric bomb, but "Baker" was detonated underwater and brought down the house by going up in a mushroom cloud, blanketing spectators and fishermen with radiation. By the decade's end, the Cold War was heating up on both sides of the Iron Curtain.

Atomic power played a prominent role in postwar American culture. Before Little Boy descended on Nagasaki, Pocket Books capitalized on public wariness about the possibilities and pitfalls of fission, positing that atomic energy gave "the world but two alternatives: *the end of war or the end of humanity*."[1] Between these two extremes, Americans needed to cope with the introduction of an all-mighty power. One work even suggested that atomic energy was akin to lightning bolts from the Mount: "God has permitted science to unlock the ultimate forces locked in the atom, thirty million times as powerful as dynamite. Now scientists are frightened lest men may use this awful power to destroy the world."[2]

Up in the Sky!

Comic books had long featured mad men wanting to rule or ruin the planet, and atomic energy fit into tales of worldwide catastrophes. Titles such as *Atomic War* depicted the destruction of American cities.[3] As early as *Captain Marvel Adventure #66* (Oct. 1946), the titular superhero found himself in a global atomic war. Searching for survivors, the captain learns that everyone is dead: "...radioactive rays came even out to the remotest farms and villages!" Thankfully, the atomic war and search for survivors were merely a radio broadcast and the issue ends with a moral: "I guess we'd all better learn to live and get along together — one nation with all other nations and one person with all other persons — so that the terrible atomic war will never occur!"[4]

Nevertheless, atomic power was here to stay. One scholar notes that the strengthening of the Comics Code in 1954 toned down crime magazines, "but it said nothing about atomic weapons."[5] Indeed, in the kid-friendly *Dennis the Menace #37* (Aug. 1959) a simulated atomic blast dwarfs anything that the titular troublemaker can muster.[6] In *Lassie #51* (Oct.-Nov. 1960), young Timmy finds a radioactive isotope and government officials confiscate his belongings for fear of contamination; the faithful collie can do nothing.[7] Atomic Age comics even imperiled the embodiment of truth, justice, and the American way: Superman.

In the 1950s, Superman stories were exciting, yet rarely controversial. Nevertheless, even Superman could not stay silent about the newly discovered power that could level Metropolis. Superman was impervious to nuclear weapons; however, he was not immune to the then-mysterious effects of radiation that emerged from atomic detonation. *Action Comics #101* (Oct. 1946), revealed that during the Bikini tests, the intense radiation awakened a brainwashed Superman and he filmed the mushroom cloud for posterity.[8] A year later, Superman recalled the deed as one of his finest feats.[9]

Superman's association with atomic energy predated the United States entrance into World War II. For the first broadcast of Superman's radio program in 1940, writers were already splitting the atom: Superman's father, Jor-El, explains that his experimental rocket runs on atomic forces. By 1945, the program broadcasted a multi-part saga featuring Superman battling the "Atom Man." The plot thickens with the inclusion of a radioactive substance called "kryptonite," which weakens Superman.[10] DC saw green in the radioactive element and integrated it into the comics. The Man of Steel's relationship with kryptonite, and atomic radiation in general, grew complex as the 1950s progressed, ultimately becoming a metaphor for Americans grappling with the realities of nuclear energy in everyday society.

Kryptonite quickly became Superman's constant nemesis. In 1939, the Man of Steel's newspaper strip chronicled simply that an "internal cataclysm" destroyed Krypton.[11] For Superman's tenth anniversary, writers detailed Krypton's fate. In *Superman #53* (July-Aug. 1948), Jor-El informs Krypton's scientific community that "the core of Krypton is composed of a substance called *uranium* [...] which, for untold ages has been setting up a cycle of chain-impulses, building in power every moment! [...] Gentlemen, *Krypton is one gigantic atomic bomb*!"[12] Jor-El recommends a mass evacuation, but his leaders are dubious; the writers' own government officials had deemed flight from nuclear explosions impractical.[13] On his own, Jor-El sends his son to Earth. The infant survives Krypton's destruction, but atomic energy would shadow Superman into adulthood.

In 1949, the same year that the Soviets detonated their own atomic warhead, Superman met his own Promethean element. In *Superman #61* (Nov.-Dec. 1949), Superman encounters glowing green fragments that weaken him. Superman deduces that the pieces are "particles of Krypton, flung into space! When Krypton exploded, all the atomic elements fused to become one deadly compound!" Superman disposes the kryptonite into the ocean, which would become a favorite dumping ground. However, Superman muses, "Somewhere out in trackless space, there must be more particles of kryptonite!"[14] In *Superman #130* (July 1959), Superman explains that radiation "penetrate[s] my otherwise invulnerable skin and change the red corpuscles of my bloodstream to green! I'll become a victim of blood-poisoning." Concerning this "Kryptonite fever," one doctor explains, "He's afflicted just like people over-exposed to *radium* rays! But we can't inject any drugs ... the hypodermic needles only bend against his skin!" Superman sole recourse is lead because "lead is a dense metal that stops *all* radiations."[15] Unfortunately, Superman can't don a cumbersome lead suit all the time. *Adventure Comics #261* (June 1959) adds that "kryptonite meteors do not burn when falling to Earth because, unlike ordinary meteors, they cannot combine with oxygen."[16] Thus, kryptonite bombarded the Earth with impunity.

To Superman's woe, such kryptonite fragments were consistently attracted to Earth, especially the United States. From a storytelling standpoint, by endangering the protector of the "American Way," writers empowered Superman's co-stars to defend their hero. Comic books stressed that kryptonite did not harm Earthlings, giving average Americans (save for subversives and scum) stakes in safeguarding their country. In *Jimmy Olsen #6* (July-Aug. 1955), kryptonite fragments rain down on Metropolis and Superman reluctantly retreats into a shelter. As Superman sequesters himself, the citizens gather the kryptonite for disposal, except for the crooked "Angles" Archibald, who offers kryptonite for sale for a thousand dollars a piece.[17] In *Superboy #51* (Sep. 1956), kryptonite threatens Superboy's dog, Krypto; thankfully, the military responds and saves the Boy of Steel's canine companion.

More Fun with Fission

Despite the fretting over fission, more enterprising Americans saw potential uses in atomic energy. The historian Paul Boyer argues that while naysayers had the most accurate predictions concerning atomic power, many optimists predicted bright futures.[18] DC Comics also posited that nuclear power was limitless. In *Adventure Comics #121*, a boy enters a contest to display "the most valuable mineral." Superboy thinks, "I'll win the prize for Teddy and do my country a service at the same time!" Superboy flies to the North Pole, and unearths some black rock. An impressed judge identifies it as "*pitchblende,* greatest source of our two most needed elements—*radium* ... and *uranium* ... principal raw material for *atomic energy!*"[19] Teddy wins and Superboy vows to harness the nation's new source of atomic strength.

Between the adventures depicted on the comics pages, advertisements marketed atomic power as appropriate playthings for budding scientists. One book publisher had a surefire sales pitch ("boys — it's *free!*") for an "exciting new book on *atomic energy* and *The Wonders of Chemistry*." "Don't miss it, fellows! Introduces you to the miracles of Atomic Energy ... and lets you in on secrets of the mysterious Atomic World [...] Tells about the fun, thrills, adventure and big future opportunities awaiting boys who know chemistry." The result: "...safe *atomic energy experiments!*"[20]

Superman stories also toyed with the potential of atomic marvels. In *Jimmy Olsen #9* (Dec. 1955), Olsen's landlord accidentally rubs Olsen's new atomic fuel on his bald pate and discovers that the subatomic particles make a useful hair growth tonic. Unfortunately, the effects don't last.[21] In *Jimmy Olsen #29* (March 1958), Superman reveals a secret: "kryptonite rays react peculiarly on certain rare mineral waters!" The process is "an amazing chemical reaction [that] converted that mineral water into a *fountain of youth!*" However, Superman pulls the plug on exploiting the waterworks, telling Olsen, "I can't tell the world ... or else crooks would hear of those *kryptonite* mountains! They could dig some of it out to use against me!"[22]

As Olsen learned, despite the potential profits from radioactive resources, darker clouds loomed over all things nuclear. In *Jimmy Olsen #27* (March 1958), Olsen decides to create a news hoax, he eats kryptonite-tainted fruit. "The *kryptonite* fruit's turned my skin and hair *green* all over!" He poses as a Martian, but everyone suspects that he's an alien spy.[23] In *Jimmy Olsen #16* (Oct.-Nov. 1956), Superman shields the cub reporter with his body during an atomic test. Superman realizes, "The super bomb evidently cast strange atomic radiations around Jimmy," giving the youngster invulnerability. Superman consults some "scientific facts" and learns that "such radiation effects seldom last more than twenty-four hours."[24] In *World's Finest Comics #87*, a thief acquires and swallows Jor-El's radioactive capsules "to be used only if needed to renew our super-powers on Earth."[25] Fortunately, Batman does the same. Less fortunately, three issues later, the vigilante Batwoman does likewise and proceeds to uncover Batman's identity.[26]

Despite the clear and present danger radiation and kryptonite poses in every story, DC posited that atomic science could still provide beneficial use for humanity. Well into the 1960s, the U.S. Atomic Energy Commission maintained that while radiation was a "hazard," the Commission asserted that "within limits we can live with this problem so that we can obtain the benefits of the atomic age [...] the conclusion is clear: *We can enjoy the benefits of the nuclear age with safety to employees and to the public.*"[27]

Atomic Adversaries

That even benign uses for radiation could result in grave consequences underscored the growing pessimism concerning radiation. As Boyer demonstrates, popular perception concerning fatal fall-out led to the decline of scientists' prestige in the public sphere.[28] Even J. R. Oppenheimer, a central figure in nuclear physics, would be tainted "red" in Congressional-sanctioned name-calling.[29] Ironically, this backlash against the scientific community backfired in 1957, when the Soviet Union's *Sputnik* sailed overhead, causing social panic. Educators called for a revamping of the educational curriculum to emphasize science, to produce, as one congressman stated, "eggheads, not fatheads."[30]

Caught in the cultural change to emphasize science was Superman's arch foe, Lex Luthor, whose cranium rendered him a literal "egghead." Luthor had long menaced Superman; however, in the postwar decade, Luthor underwent a revision. As Superboy's friend, Luthor devotes his genius to battle kryptonite. An experiment goes awry and his hair and morals disappear. A vengeful Luthor vows to use his brainpower to kill Superboy. In the context of the emerging space race, Superboy considers Luthor's villainy a loss for American science. In *Superboy #86* (Jan. 1961), Jonathan Kent laments, "About Lex Luthor ...! What a shame his brilliant mind has been warped by a mad, unreasoning hatred for you!" Superboy agrees, "He could become a great scientist except for his evil ambition!" Indeed, while they converse, Luthor constructs "kryptonite men" which later overwhelm Superboy and Krypto.[31] In *Action Comics #249* (Feb. 1959), Luthor concocts a liquid kryptonite, drinks it, and becomes a "Kryptonite Man."[32]

Luthor is not alone in his exploitation of radiation. Since hoarding kryptonite is not illegal (Olsen and Lane have their own stashes), other knowledgeable knaves easily acquired it. In *Superboy #69* (Dec. 1958), a renegade scientist constructs a "kryptonite flamethrower" that "multiplies *kryptonite* to 1000 times its usual strength!"[33] After Superboy throws it into the sea, some thugs salvage the weapon. In *Adventure Comics #216* (Sep. 1955), Superboy uncovers "Krypton City," an uninhabited urban center spared Krypton's fate, but has turned to kryptonite and "with great sorrow," Superboy destroys the city.[34] In *Action Comics #252* (May 1959), a scientist places a criminal's brain in a robot body powered by a uranium capsule which lasts twenty-four hours. A stronger element is kryptonite: "its energy will last you forever!" Thus was born "Metallo," another kryptonite-powered adversary.[35]

Less evil but no less dangerous was the cultural obsession with radiation. With advertisements calling for youngsters to explore the atomic world, uranium mining emerged as a cottage industry for profiteers.[36] Popular culture cashed in with feature films such as *Dig That Uranium* (1957), starring the Bowery Boys. DC responded with its own thick-headed teenagers in *Jimmy Olsen #7* (Sep. 1955). Olsen wants "to save the headstrong juvenile prospectors from their own foolhardy adventure." With their parents' blessings, having learned about uranium at school, and equipped with a Geiger counter, the youths rush to strike it rich. After several false starts, running low on water, and meeting snakes, mirages, and body aches, the boys learn that uranium mining is not easy.[37]

Nevertheless, Metropolis is apparently a center of radioactive research and nuclear testing. The results of contact with nuclear radiation were frequently absurd. In *Superboy #54* (Jan. 1957), Superboy wraps his "super-suit" around a warhead to prevent "radiation burns" from injuring workers. Unfortunately, his costume is contaminated, forcing Superboy to work in normal fabrics prone to tearing.[38] Later that issue, an H-bomb damages Superboy's voice, leaving him to communicate through visual cues.[39] In *Jimmy Olsen #33* (Dec. 1958), in a nuclear dumping ground outside Metropolis, "a lightning bolt strikes a glass prism which had been contaminated by radium," which bringing to life television broadcasts of Jack Frost and the Pied Piper.[40] In *Jimmy Olsen #26* (Feb. 1958), "x-rays cause an atomic change" in Olsen's wristwatch, causing him to gain "superweight."[41] That same issue, a "zany scientist" gives Olsen a tablet infused with "nuclear radiations" and he physically enlarges while his mental prowess shrinks.[42] In *Showcase #10* (Sep.-Oct. 1957), Lane acquires superpowers but Superman reasons that "an impetuous Lois, plus dangerous powers, may add up to *super-trouble!*" Superman uses kryptonite to rob Lane's powers to prevent that potential "super trouble."[43]

Equally worrisome were near-misses from atomic disasters. Metropolis had frequent nuclear meltdowns. In *Action Comics #198* (Nov. 1954), an atomic generator with a "faulty coil" threatens an industrial plant. The manager orders an evacuation because "the atomic generator may turn radioactive." The explosion takes out a wall, showing Metropolis unharmed in the background. The industrialist muses, "Perhaps it's just as well we had this near-disaster. It will cause us to be more careful with experimental models in the future!"[44] In *Jimmy Olsen #34* (Jan. 1959), Olsen watches technicians pump "a new atomic fuel" into a guided missile. Unfortunately, a tech shouts, "The touchy fuel started a wild chain-reaction! It'll blow up! *Run!*" Olsen lives, but the danger to mere mortals is clear.[45]

While DC shied away from depicting the radioactive effects of atomic power on normal people, anything having to do with kryptonite endangered Superman, including Kent's secret identity. In *Superman #125* (Nov. 1958), Kent's college professor tries to uses the substance to reveal his student's secret.[46] In *Jimmy Olsen #12* (April 1956), an archaeologist unmasks Kent's alter ego when the reporter succumbs to kryptonite. Kent concedes, "All right — you've got me! Please ... drag me out of range *gasp* of the rays!" The archaeologist dies, but that his secret is compromised remained a source of worry.[47] In *Jimmy Olsen #27* (March 1958), an evil duplicate of Olsen uses kryptonite and exposes Kent's alter ego.[48] In *Adventure Comics #261* (June 1959), Lois Lane is shocked that Lana Lang would use the stuff to expose Clark Kent's secret identity: "How could you think of such a thing?"[49]

Despite the evident dangers, even Superboy thinks of using radiation. In *Superboy #89* (June 1961), he errs in believing that a super-powered youth, Mon-El, harbors sinister intentions and exposes him to lead, not knowing that lead is fatal to Mon-El's race. A guilt-ridden Superboy places Mon-El in limbo while he searches for an antidote ("Life may be hard ... but at least you'll be alive!" Superboy informs him).[50] One thousand years later, the inter-galactic Legion of Superheroes finally cures Mon-El. However, as *Adventure Comics #267* (Dec. 1959) informs readers, even in the future, a radioactive element, Sigellian, endangers the Legionaries. Superboy converts it into a stable isotope, but the threat of radiation remains.[51]

Even friends, family, and well-intentioned folks imperiled the Man of Steel. In *Adventure Comics #265* (Oct. 1959), a careless Jonathan Kent plays with Superboy's robot, releasing "super-radiations" that age Superboy. Kent also exposes his son to kryptonite that same issue.[52] In *Adventure Comics #266* (Nov. 1959), superhero Green Arrow fashions some green metal into his trade-marked weapon. Superman rebuffs him: "If any of your kryptonite arrows fell into criminal hands, there was a chance it could be used against me!" A chas-tised Green Arrow dumps his remaining stock into a lake.[53]

As a story motif, kryptonite's success spawned imitations. While the green form was the "pure" version of the element, tampering resulted in new varieties to plague the Man of Steel. In *Adventure Comics #252* (Sep. 1958), a red rock falls to Earth, making Superboy weak. Superboy analyzes it and learns, "The substance is *red kryptonite*— a refined alloy of regular *kryptonite* which has *ten times* the radiation power of regular *kryptonite*!"[54] This sample was artificially created; however, red kryptonite was a natural phenomenon, namely kryptonite that passes through a red cloud in space, changing its molecular structure.

Red kryptonite, unlike the green variety's one-way relationship with Superman, opened a window to imaginative story-telling. In *Lois Lane #36* (Aug. 1962), Lane explains that "each variety of *red kryptonite* has an unpredictable effect on the survivors of the planet *Krypton!*" Unfortunately, a thirteen billion volt cyclotron next door explodes, sending "a powerful beam of neutrons" into Lane's red kryptonite sample. She mutates into a wrathful hairy creature, not unlike the radioactive tarantulas, blobs, behemoths, and "*Them!*" concurrently rampaging across American cinema. Another thirteen billion volt jolt into another red kryptonite restores her.[55] *Action Comics #290* (July 1962) proclaimed on the cover, "By popular demand: another all 'Red Kryptonite' issue" and the red stuff depowers half of Superman's body.[56] In *Adventure Comics #290* (April 1962), red kryptonite renders Superboy amnesic, but his heroic personality still shined through.[57]

Red kryptonite also opened a floodgate for more tinted varieties, although not all held dire consequences for the Man of Steel. In *Adventure Comics #279* (Dec. 1960), Superboy encounters white kryptonite. Superboy learns "it was green kryptonite first until it met a space cloud and turned into something I never knew existed ... white kryptonite!" The white stuff only affected plant life, however.[58] *Adventure Comics #299* (Aug. 1962) introduces gold kryptonite, which "has the delayed effect of stealing any of your superpowers *permanently.*"[59] Blue kryptonite, a corrupt version of green kryptonite, harms "Bizzaros," imitations of Superman also created by radiation. In *Jimmy Olsen #70*, rumors of silver kryptonite surface and Superman panics. The rumors are false; nevertheless, the glowing rocks kept the Man of Steel, and his readers, on his toes.[60]

Imaginary Stories, Real Death

With kryptonite the only fatal threat to Superman, writers emphasized the lethal dangers to spike their stories' excitement. Like contemporary science fiction writers dwelling upon apocalyptic doomsdays, comic book scribes imagined worse case scenarios as the likelihood of nuclear war intensified as the 1950s progressed.[61] In *Action Comics #253* (June 1959), an Olsen doppelganger attempts to kill Superman with kryptonite. Superman acts out a death scene: "The radiation — is — too — strong ... this ... is ... murder!"[62] Although Superman defeats Olsen's lookalike, radiation proved too enticing a motif to keep writers away. In "imaginary stories" — scenarios that take place outside of DC's continuity — comic books toyed with the darker side of radiation under the pretense of fantasy. Even Jerry Siegel envisioned the death of his creation "which may or may not ever happen." In *Superman #149* (Nov. 1961), Luthor bombards the Man of Steel with kryptonite rays. As Lane and Olsen watch, Superman turns green, writhes in pain ("Owww!"), and dies ("Ohh-hhhhh"). As gangsters gloat about the Man of Tomorrow becoming history, people of all nations pay their final respects: in death, Superman creates a united world.[63]

Similarly, in *Jimmy Olsen #29* (June 1958), Olsen writes his own book envisioning a renegade scientist who concocts a "helium bomb," described as "equal to 1,000,000 H-bombs! Some foreign power will pay me plenty for this!" Superman escapes with Olsen, but they learn that "radioactive fall-out of that super-bomb spread all around the world! Did it kill every living thing?" The answer is affirmative; in a lifeless Metropolis, Superman chokes that "we're the only two people left alive!" Olsen then hits a writing block: "If all people on Earth were wiped out, *Superman* and I would have *nothing* left to do! [...] I'll need a whole new plot! Jeepers!"[64]

As Olsen stressed over make-believe tales, DC Comics continued to explore the darkest plots of all: radiation induced annihilation. Superman was immune to all Earthly elements, but his supporting cast was not. While readers and the Comics Code prohibited Olsen or Lane from perishing, Superman was helpless to aid those who flirted too closely with fission. In *Lois Lane #27* (Aug. 1961), Lane attends an atomic demonstration at an "Atoms for Peace-time" project to "advance the peaceful interests of science!" After a follow-up examination, Lane looks at her prognosis: "Exposure to radiation complete" and "death within a week. No measures can prevent change." Thankfully, the "Lois Lane" file concerned a guinea pig being subjected to experiments.[65] In *Showcase #10* (Sep.-Oct. 1957), Lane is blinded during a nuclear demonstration.[66]

Another fall-guy from fall-out was Jimmy Olsen. While covering a new atomic plant in Metropolis, Olsen brushes up against an "atomic pile" that houses the "deadly radiations." The risk of contamination was slim: "unless there happens to be a fine crack in the brick, letting the rays escape! But ... ha, ha, ha, the chances are one in a million!" Olsen beats the odds, as plants wither, birds die, and he leaves glowing footprints. Olsen exiles himself but realizes, "Scientists say anybody getting an overdose of atomic radiations could only live ... (gasp!) *a few hours!*" Superman visits Olsen but is unable to help: "For once, I am unable to save you, Jimmy! Oh, Jimmy ... my pal." Superman cries while Olsen arranges his last will and testament. Olsen ultimately survives and although Superman did not dwell on such tragic outcomes, his inability to save those contaminated by radioactive exposure was apparent.

While Lane and Olsen survived, the casualty rates for one-issue characters were much higher. In *Adventure Comics #276* (Sep. 1960), Superboy is stranded on a meteor encircled by kryptonite rings. With him is his old Kryptonian robot nanny, who self-destructs so that Superboy can use its lead innards to fashion a containment suit.[67] In *Superman #125* (Nov. 1958), Superman acquires the ability to conjure a miniature version of himself. The tiny Superman shifts a kryptonite meteor out to sea, but dies. Superman observes, "It's fading to nothingness ... the *kryptonite* disintegrated it forever! It *sacrificed* itself for me!"[68] In *Superman #123* (Aug. 1958), kryptonite kills the first "Supergirl," although DC introduced a permanent Supergirl as Superman's cousin.[69] In *Action Comics #252* (May 1959), Supergirl explains that her city was spared Krypton's fate, but a subsequent kryptonite shower killed everyone save her: "All the people are dying! I'm an *orphan* of space now ... *sob!*"[70]

A Nuclear Now

In *Superboy #77* (Dec. 1959), DC printed a promotion lauding atomic science. "The Atom: Servant of Man" praised the atomic particles for stopping yellow fever and providing cancer treatments. However, the announcement was juxtaposed next to a story in which Krypto rules a planet of dog worshippers. Krypto's reign abruptly ends when he encounters the "planet's richest prize," kryptonite. Radioactive energy served man, but was deadly to man's best friend.[71]

Such was the contradictory portrayals of atomic energy. While comics posited the wonders of a nuclear lifestyle, hazards abounded. In *Lois Lane #61* (Nov. 1965) Lane witnesses a new device that "can instantly neutralize the shock and radiation of an atom bomb! It will make all nuclear weapons obsolete!" Unfortunately, an explosion turns her into a humanoid reptile. Public pity follows, since Lane was "one of the most beautiful girls in *Metropolis*! How tragic!"[72] Lane regains her looks, but the dangers of radiation remained.

In *Superman #233* (Jan. 1971), DC shook up Superman's status quo. Kent becomes a television reporter and, as a break from an overused plot device from the previous two decades, becomes immune to kryptonite.[73] Ironically, a nuclear explosion makes Superman impervious to Krypton's remnants. However, even in this period of political deterrence, nuclear menaces shadowed the Man of Steel. The same incident also spawns a villain who siphons power from him; by the story's conclusion, Superman lost one third of his strength.

Nevertheless, kryptonite varieties were still essential plot devices. In *Lois Lane #112* (Aug. 1971), for instance, Lane uses white kryptonite to kill a malevolent tree.[74] Superman's immunity faded and he realized that kryptonite was here to stay. In *Superman #130* (July 1959), Superman admits that after 855,019 attempts, "*There is no antidote!*"[75] David Lilienthal, chairman of the Atomic

Energy Commission from 1946 to 1950, recognized the cultural and social power that atomic energy had in postwar America. Lilienthal placed Americans on an unstable stockpile that could strengthen their nation if they seized the opportunity. "We are all participants in that future chain of events that these epochal discoveries have set off," he wrote in 1949. "There are no supermen to solve these problems for us."[76]

The stories in Superman comics have a diverse representation of nuclear power. Its effects can be positive or negative, permanent or fleeting, tremendous or trivial. At a time when Americans were coming to grasp with nuclear power and all it meant, the comic book adventures of the Man of Steel reflected the real-world uncertainty about just how life changing or life threatening nuclear power could be.

CHAPTER NOTES

1. *The Atomic Age Opens.* Ed. Donald Porter Geddes. (New York: Pocket Books, 1945), 48.

2. Laubrach, Frank C., *Prayer: The Mightiest Force in the World.* (New York: Fleming H. Revell Company, 1946), 94.

3. Wright, Bradford, *Comic Book Nation: The Transformation of Youth Culture in America.* (New York: Johns Hopkins University Press, 2001), 120–121.

4. Binder, Otto (w), and C.C. Beck (a). "Captain Marvel and The Atomic War," *Captain Marvel Adventures #66* (Oct. 1946). New York: Fawcett Publications.

5. Szasz, Ferenc M., "Atomic Comics," *Atomic Culture: How We Learned to Stop Worrying and Love the Bomb.* Ed. Scott C. Zeman and Michael A. Amundson. (Boulder: University of Colorado, 2004), 18.

6. Toole, Fred (w), and Al Wiseman (a). "Dennis vs. the U.S. Army," *Dennis the Menace #37* (Aug. 1959). New York: Hallden.

7. Fujitani, Bob (a), "The Hot Car," *Lassie #51* (Oct-Nov. 1960). New York: Dell Publications.

8. Siegel, Jerry (w), and Win Mortimer (a), "Crime's Paradise!" *Action Comics #101* (Oct. 1946). New York: DC Comics.

9. Siegel, Jerry (w), and Sikela, John (a). "The Confessions of Superman!" *World's Finest Comics #26* (Jan.-Feb. 1947). New York: DC Comics.

10. See *The Superman Radio Scripts. Vol. 1: Superman vs. the Atom Man.* (New York: Watson-Guptill Publications, 2001).

11. Siegel, Jerry, and Joe Shuster, *Superman: the Dailies, 1939–1940.* (Northampton, Ma: Kitchen Sink Press, 1999), 13–17.

12. Finger, Bill (w), and Wayne Boring (a), "The Origin of Superman," *Superman #53* (July-Aug., 1948), New York: DC Comics.

13. See Kenneth D. Rose, *One Nation Underground: The Fallout Shelter in American Culture.* (New York: New York University Press, 2001), 24–28.

14. Finger, Bill (w), and Al Plastino (a), "Superman Returns to Krypton," *Superman #61* (Nov.-Dec. 1949). New York: DC Comics.

15. Binder, Otto (w), and Al Plastino (a). "The Curse of Kryptontie!" *Superman #130* (July 1959). New York: DC Comics.

16. Binder, Otto (w), and George Papp (a). "Superboy Meets Lois Lane," *Adventure Comics #261* (June 1959). New York: DC Comics.

17. Binder, Otto (w), and Curt Swan (a). "100 Pieces of Kryptonite!" *Jimmy Olsen #6* (July-Aug. 1955). New York: DC Comics.

18. Boyer, Paul, *By the Bomb's Early Light: American Thought and Culture at the Dawn of the Atomic Age.* (Chapel Hill: University of North Carolina Press, 1994), 118.

19. Cameron, Don (w), and Al Wenzel (a). "The Great Hobby Contest!" *Adventure Comics #121* (Oct. 1947). New York: DC Comics.

20. Advertisement. *Crime Does Not Pay #58* (Dec. 1957). New York: Lev Gleason Publications.

21. Binder, Otto (w), and Curt Swan (a). "Jimmy Olsen, Cub Inventor!" *Jimmy Olsen #9* (Dec. 1955). New York: DC Comics.

22. Binder, Otto (w), and Curt Swan (a). "Jimmy Olsen's Super Pet!" *Jimmy Olsen #29* (June 1958). New York: DC Comics.

23. Binder, Otto (w), and Curt Swan (a). "The Boy from Mars," *Jimmy Olsen #27* (March 1958). New York: DC Comics.

24. Binder, Otto (w), and Curt Swan (a). "The Boy of Steel!" *Jimmy Olsen #16* (Oct.-Nov. 1956). New York: DC Comics.

25. Finger, Bill (w), and Curt Swan (a). "The Reversed Heroes," *World's Finest Comics #87* (March-April 1957). New York: DC Comics.

26. Hamilton, Edmond (w), and Dick Sprang (a). "The Super-Batwoman!" *World's Finest Comics #90* (Sep.-Oct. 1957). New York: DC Comics.

27. Brannigan, Francis L., *Radiation in Perspective.* (Washington DC: U.S. Printing Office, 1963), 16.

28. Boyer, 243–265.

29. See David Caute, *The Great Fear: The Anti-Communist Purge under Truman and Eisenhower.* (New York: Simon and Shuster, 1978), 462–479.

30. Quoted in Ryan Boyle, "A Red Moon over the Mall: The *Sputnik* Panic and Domestic America." *The Journal of American Culture.* 31:4 (Dec. 2008), 373–382, quote on 379.

31. Siegel, Jerry (w), and George Papp (a). "The Army of Living Kryptonite Men!" *Superboy #86* (Jan. 1961). New York: DC Comics.

32. Binder, Otto (w), and Al Plastino (a). "The Kryptonite Man!" *Action Comics #249* (Feb. 1959). New York: DC Comics.

33. Finger, Bill (w), and George Papp (a). "The Indestructible Robot!" *Superboy #69* (Dec. 1958). New York: DC Comics.

34. Finger, Bill (w), and Curt Swan (a), "The Wizard City," *Adventure Comics #216* (Sep. 1955). New York: DC Comics.

35. Bernstein, Robert (w), and Al Plastino (a). "The Menace of Metallo!" *Action Comics #252* (May 1959). New York: DC Comics.

36. Amundson, Michael A., "Uranium on the Cranium," *Atomic Culture,* 49–63.

37. Binder, Otto (w), and Curt Swan (a)."The Amazing Mirages," *Jimmy Olsen #7* (May 1955). New York: DC Comics.

38. Binder, Otto (w), and Curt Swan (a). "Superboy's Substitute Suits," *Superboy #54* (Jan. 1957). New York: DC Comics.

39. Binder, Otto (w), and John Sikela (a), "The Silent Superboy," *Superboy #54.*

40. Binder, Otto (w), and Curt Swan (a) "Images that Came to Life!" *Superman's Pal, Jimmy Olsen #33* (Dec. 1958). New York: DC Comics.

41. Binder, Otto (w), and Curt Swan (a). "The World's 'Heavyweight' Champ," *Jimmy Olsen #26* (Feb. 1958). New York: DC Comics.

42. Binder, Otto (w), and Curt Swan (a). "The Human Skyscraper," *Jimmy Olsen #28* (April 1958). New York: DC Comics.

43. Binder, Otto (w), and Wayne Boring (a). "The Forbidden Box from Krypton!" *Showcase #10* (Oct. 1957), New York: DC Comics.

44. Boring, Wayne (w), and Stan Kaye (a). "The Six Lives of Lois Lane!" *Action Comics* *#198* (Nov. 1954). New York: DC Comics.

45. Binder, Otto (w), and Curt Swan (a). "Superman's Pal of Steel," *Jimmy Olsen #34* (Jan. 1959). New York: DC Comics.

46. Coleman, Jerry (w), and Al Plastio (a). "Clark Kent's College Days," *Superman* *#125* (Nov. 1958). New York: DC Comics.

47. Binder, Otto (w), and Curt Swan (a). "The Secret of Dinosaur Island!" *Jimmy Olsen* *#12* (April 1956). New York: DC Comics.

48. Binder, Otto (w), and Curt Swan (a). "The Outlaw Jimmy Olsen," *Jimmy Olsen* *#27* (March 1958). New York: DC Comics.

49. Binder, Otto (w), and George Papp (a). "Superboy Meets Lois Lane," *Adventure Comics #261.* New York: DC Comics.

50. Bernstein, Robert (w), and George Papp (a). "Superboy's Big Brother!" *Superboy* *#89,* June 1961). New York: DC Comics.

51. Siegel, Jerry (w), and George Papp (a). "Prisoners of the Super-heroes!" *Adventure Comics #267* (Dec. 1959). New York: DC Comics. "Sigellian" was probably named after the issue's writer.

52. Swan, Curt (w), and Stan Kaye (a). "The First Superman Robot!" *Adventure Comics* *#265* (Oct. 1959). New York: DC Comics.

53. Bernstein, Robert (w), and Lee Elias (a). "The Case of the Vanishing Arrows!" *Adventure Comics #266* (Nov. 1959). New York: DC Comics.

54. Schwartz, Alvin (w), and John Sikela (a). "The Super-Sentry of Smallville!" *Adventure Comics #252* (Sep. 1958). New York: DC Comics.

55. Schaffenberger, Kurt (a). "The Madame Jekyll of Metropolis!" *Lois Lane #36* (Oct. 1962). New York: DC Comics.

56. Curt Swan (a). "Half a Superman!" *Action Comics #290* (July 1962). New York: DC Comics.

57. Finger, Bill (w), and George Papp (a). "The Duel of the Superboys!" *Adventure Comics #295* (April 1962). New York: DC Comics.

58. Binder, Otto (w), and Curt Swan (a). "Superboy Visits the 50th Century!" *Adventure Comics #279* (Dec. 1960). New York: DC Comics.

59. Siegel, Jerry (w), and George Papp (a). "The Unwanted Superbaby!" *Adventure Comics #299.* (Aug. 1962), New York: DC Comics.

60. Swan, Curt (a). "The Secret of Silver Kryptonite!" *Jimmy Olsen #70* (July 1963). New York: DC Comics.

61. See: Thomas D. Clareson, *Understanding Contemporary American Science Fiction: The Formative Period, 1926–1970.* (Columbia: University of South Carolina Press, 1990), 40–127.

62. Schwartz, Alvin (w), and Curt Swan (a). "The War Between Jimmy Olsen and Superman!" *Action Comics #253* (June 1959). New York: DC Comics.

63. Siegel, Jerry (w), and Curt Swan (a). "The Death of Superman!" *Superman #149* (Nov. 1961). New York: DC Comics.

64. Binder, Otto (w), and Curt Swan (a). "The Superman Book That Couldn't Be Finished!" *Jimmy Olsen #29* (June 1958). New York: DC Comics.

65. Binder, Otto (w), and Kurt Schaffenberger (a). "The Last Days of Lois Lane," *Superman's Girl Friend, Lois Lane #27* (Aug. 1961). New York: DC Comics.

66. Coleman, Jerry (w), and Wayne Boring (a). "The Sightless Lois Lane," *Showcase #10.*

67. Binder, Otto (w), and Al Plastino (a). "The Robinson Crusoe of Space!" *Adventure Comics # 276* (Sep. 1960). New York: DC Comics.

68. Coleman, Jerry (w), and Wayne Boring (a). "Superman's New Power!" *Superman* *#125* (Nov. 1958). New York: DC Comics.

69. Binder, Otto (w), and Dick Sprang (a). "The Girl of Steel!" *Superman #123* (Aug. 1958). New York: DC Comics.

70. Binder, Otto (w), and Al Plastino (a). "The Supergirl from Krypton!" *Action Comics #252.*

71. Schiff, Jack (w), and Morris Waldinger (a). "The Atom: Servant of Man"; Jerry Siegel (w), and George Papp (a). "The Space Adventures of Krypto!" *Superboy #77* (Dec. 1959). New York: DC Comics.

72. Dorfman, Leo (w), and Kurt Schaffenberger (a). "The Reptile Girl of Metropolis!" *Lois Lane #61* (Nov. 1965). New York: National Comics Publications [DC Comics.]

73. O'Neil, Denny (w), and Curt Swan (a). "Superman Breaks Loose!" *Superman #233* (Jan. 1971). New York: DC Comics.

74. Bates, Cary (w), and Werner Roth (a). "A Tree Grows in Metropolis!" *Lois Lane #112* (Aug. 1971). New York: DC Comics.

75. Binder, Otto (w), and Al Plastino (a). "The Curse of Kryptonite!" *Superman #130 (Jul 1959).* New York: DC Comics.

76. David Lilienthal, *This I Do Believe.* (New York: Harper & Brothers Publishers), 153.

BIBLIOGRAPHY

Advertisement. *Crime Does Not Pay #58* (Dec. 1957). New York: Lev Gleason Publications.

Amundson, Michael A. "Uranium on the Cranium." *Atomic Culture,* 49–63.

Bates, Cary (w), and Werner Roth (a). "A Tree Grows in Metropolis!" *Lois Lane #112* (Aug. 1971). New York: DC Comics.

Bernstein, Robert (w), and Lee Elias (a). "The Case of the Vanishing Arrows!" *Adventure Comics #266* (Nov. 1959). New York: DC Comics.

Bernstein, Robert (w), and George Papp (a). "Superboy's Big Brother!"

Bernstein, Robert (w), and Al Plastino (a). "The Menace of Metallo!" *Action Comics #252* (May 1959). New York: DC Comics.

Binder, Otto (w), and C.C. Beck (a). "Captain Marvel and the Atomic War." *Captain Marvel Adventures #66* (Oct. 1946). New York: Fawcett Publications.

Binder, Otto (w), and Wayne Boring (a). "The Forbidden Box from Krypton!" *Showcase #10* (Oct. 1957), New York: DC Comics.

Binder, Otto (w), and George Papp (a). "Superboy Meets Lois Lane." *Adventure Comics #261* (June 1959). New York: DC Comics.

Binder, Otto (w), and Al Plastino (a). "The Curse of Kryptonite!" *Superman #130* (July 1959). New York: DC Comics.

_____. "The Kryptonite Man!" *Action Comics #249* (Feb. 1959). New York: DC Comics.

_____. "The Robinson Crusoe of Space!" *Adventure Comics # 276* (Sep. 1960). New York: DC Comics.

_____. "The Supergirl from Krypton!" *Action Comics #252.*

Binder, Otto (w), and Kurt Schaffenberger (a). "The Last Days of Lois Lane." *Superman's Girlfriend, Lois Lane #27* (Aug. 1961). New York: DC Comics.

Binder, Otto (w), and Dick Sprang (a). "The Girl of Steel!" *Superman #123* (Aug. 1958). New York: DC Comics.

Binder, Otto (w), and Curt Swan (a). "The Amazing Mirages." *Jimmy Olsen #7* (May 1955). New York: DC Comics.

_____. "The Boy from Mars." *Jimmy Olsen #27* (March 1958). New York: DC Comics.

_____. "The Boy of Steel!" *Jimmy Olsen #16* (Oct.-Nov. 1956). New York: DC Comics.

_____. "The Human Skyscraper." *Jimmy Olsen #28* (April 1958). New York: DC Comics.

_____. "Images that Came to Life!" *Superman's Pal, Jimmy Olsen #33* (Dec. 1958). New York: DC Comics.

_____. "Jimmy Olsen, Cub Inventor!" *Jimmy Olsen #9* (Dec. 1955). New York: DC Comics.

_____. "Jimmy Olsen's Super Pet!" *Jimmy Olsen #29* (June 1958). New York: DC Comics.

_____. "100 Pieces of Kryptonite.' *Jimmy Olsen #6* (July-Aug. 1955). New York: DC Comics.

_____."The Outlaw Jimmy Olsen." *Jimmy Olsen #27* (March 1958). New York: DC Comics.

_____. "The Secret of Dinosaur Island!" *Jimmy Olsen #12* (April 1956). New York: DC Comics.

_____. "The Silent Superboy." *Superboy #54.*

_____. "Superboy Visits the 50th Century!" *Adventure Comics #279* (Dec. 1960). New York: DC Comics.

_____. "Superboy's Substitute Suits." *Superboy #54* (Jan. 1957). New York: DC Comics.

_____. "The Superman Book That Couldn't Be Finished!" *Jimmy Olsen #29* (June 1958). New York: DC Comics.

_____. "Superman's Pal of Steel." *Jimmy Olsen #34* (Jan. 1959). New York: DC Comics.

_____. "The World's 'Heavyweight' Champ." *Jimmy Olsen #26* (Feb. 1958). New York: DC Comics.

Boring, Wayne (w), and Stan Kaye (a). "The Six Lives of Lois Lane!" *Action Comics #198* (Nov. 1954). New York: DC Comics.

Brannigan, Francis L. *Radiation in Perspective.* Washington D.C.: U.S. Printing Office, 1963.

Boyer, Paul. *By the Bomb's Early Light: American Thought and Culture at the Dawn of the Atomic Age.* Chapel Hill: University of North Carolina Press, 1994.

Boyle, Ryan. "A Red Moon over the Mall: The *Sputnik* Panic and Domestic America." *The Journal of American Culture.* 31:4 (Dec. 2008), 373–382.

Cameron, Don (w), and Al Wenzel (a). "The Great Hobby Contest!" *Adventure Comics #121* (Oct. 1947). New York: DC Comics.

Caute, David. *The Great Fear: The Anti-Communist Purge under Truman and Eisenhower.* New York: Simon and Shuster, 1978.

Clareson, Thomas D. *Understanding Contemporary American Science Fiction: The Formative Period, 1926–1970.* Columbia: University of South Carolina Press, 1990.

Coleman, Jerry (w), and Wayne Boring (a). "The Sightless Lois Lane." *Showcase #10.*

_____. "Superman's New Power!" *Superman #125* (Nov. 1958). New York: DC Comics.

Coleman, Jerry (w), and Al Plastino (a). "Clark Kent's College Days." *Superman #125* (Nov. 1958). New York: DC Comics.

Dorfman, Leo (w), and Kurt Schaffenberger (a). "The Reptile Girl of Metropolis!" *Lois Lane #61* (Nov. 1965). New York: DC Comics.

Finger, Bill (w), and Wayne Boring (a). "The Origin of Superman." *Superman #53* (July-Aug., 1948), New York: DC Comics.

Finger, Bill (w), and George Papp (a). "The Duel of the Superboys!" *Adventure Comics #295* (April 1962). New York: DC Comics.

_____. "The Indestructible Robot!" *Superboy #69* (Dec. 1958). New York: DC Comics.

Finger, Bill (w), and Al Plastino (a). "Superman Returns to Krypton." *Superman #61* (Nov.-Dec. 1949). New York: DC Comics.

Finger, Bill (w), and Curt Swan (a). "The Reversed Heroes." *World's Finest Comics #87* (March-April 1957). New York: DC Comics.

_____. "The Wizard City." *Adventure Comics #216* (Sep. 1955). New York: DC Comics.

Fujitani, Bob (a). "The Hot Car." *Lassie #51* (Oct-Nov. 1960). New York: Dell Publications.

Geddes, Donald Porter, ed. *The Atomic Age Opens.* New York: Pocket Books, 1945.

Hamilton, Edmond (w), and Dick Sprang (a). "The Super-Batwoman!" *World's Finest Comics #90* (Sept-Oct. 1957). New York: DC Comics.

Laubrach, Frank C., *Prayer: The Mightiest Force in the World*. New York: Fleming H. Revell Company, 1946.

Lilienthal, David. *This I Do Believe*. New York: Harper & Brothers Publishers.

O'Neil, Denny (w), and Curt Swan (a). "Superman Breaks Loose!" *Superman #233* (Jan. 1971). New York: DC Comics.

Rose, Kenneth D. *One Nation Underground: The Fallout Shelter in American Culture*. New York: New York University Press, 2001.

Schaffenberger, Kurt (a). "The Madame Jekyll of Metropolis!" *Lois Lane #36* (Oct. 1962). New York: DC Comics.

Schiff, Jack (w), and Morris Waldinger (a). "The Atom: Servant of Man"

Schwartz, Alvin (w), and John Sikela (a). "The Super-Sentry of Smallville!" *Adventure Comics #252* (Sep. 1958). New York: DC Comics.

Schwartz, Alvin (w), and Curt Swan (a)."The Death of Superman!" *Superman #149* (Nov. 1961). New York: DC Comics.

_____."The War Between Jimmy Olsen and Superman!" *Action Comics #253* (June 1959). New York: DC Comics.

Siegel, Jerry (w), and Win Mortimer (a). "Crime's Paradise!" *Action Comics #101* (Oct. 1946). New York: DC Comics.

Siegel, Jerry (w), and George Papp (a). "The Army of Living Kryptonite Men!" *Superboy #86* (Jan. 1961). New York: DC Comics.

_____."The Space Adventures of Krypto!" *Superboy #77* (Dec. 1959). New York: DC Comics.

_____. "The Unwanted Superbaby!" *Adventure Comics #299* (Aug. 1962), New York: DC Comics

Siegel, Jerry (w), and Joe Shuster (a). *Superman: the Dailies, 1939–1940*. Northampton, Ma: Kitchen Sink Press, 1999.

Siegel, Jerry (w), and John Sikela (a). "The Confessions of Superman!" *World's Finest Comics #26* (Jan.-Feb. 1947). New York: DC Comics.

The Superman Radio Scripts. Vol. 1: Superman vs. the Atom Man. New York: Watson-Guptill Publications, 2001.

Swan, Curt (a). "Half a Superman!" *Action Comics #290* (July 1962). New York: DC Comics.

_____. "The Secret of Silver Kryptonite!" *Jimmy Olsen #70* (July 1963). New York: DC Comics.

Swan, Curt (w), and Stan Kaye (a). "The First Superman Robot!" *Adventure Comics #265* (Oct. 1959). New York: DC Comics.

Szasz, Ferenc M. "Atomic Comics." *Atomic Culture: How We Learned to Stop Worrying and Love the Bomb*. Ed. Scott C. Zeman and Michael A. Amundson. Boulder: University of Colorado, 2004), 18.

Toole, Fred (w), and Al Wiseman (a). "Dennis vs. the U.S. Army." *Dennis the Menace #37* (Aug. 1959). New York: Hallden.

Wright, Bradford. *Comic Book Nation: The Transformation of Youth Culture in America*. New York: Johns Hopkins University Press, 2001.

Truth, Justice, and the American Way in Franco's Spain

Louie Dean Valencia-García

When Superman first arrived to fascist Spain from the planet "Crypton" in 1940, a year after the end of the Spanish Civil War, he was clad in yellow tights and a red and blue cape — the colors of the recently fallen Spanish Republic — and was known as "Ciclón, el Superhombre," or "Cyclone, the Superman." Initially failing to find a fan base in Spain, Ciclón disappeared after three years of sporadic publication. Early attempts by Spanish publishers to print Superman comics were censored for having either attacked Catholic dogma, morality, the church, the regime (or its institutions), or those who had collaborated with the regime,[1] thus leaving publication of such superhero genre comic books primarily to foreign printers. Despite his appearance throughout the 1940s in the less popular Argentine children's magazines *Billiken* and *La Pandilla*, it was not until the regular publication of Superman's 1950's reincarnation, translated and published by the Mexican press Editorial Novaro,[2] that the American icon was broadly popularized in Spain.[3]

While the Spanish importation of the American superhero certainly reflected American cultural imperialism of the post-war era, the fascist regime in Spain was especially aware of the capacity for Superman comics' pluralistic tropes to subvert Francoist constructions of society, sexuality, and gender roles. Spain's heroes were supposed to be José Antonio de Rivera, the founder and martyr of the fascist party in Spain, and the authoritarian dictator Francisco Franco, who ruled Spain from 1939 until his death in 1975[4]; there was no room in that mythology for an American superhero. However, as Walther Bernecker has described, Spaniards of the long 1960s were experiencing a change of *mentalitie*, particularly visible amongst young people, that coincided with political, economic, and cultural changes in the second half of the Francoist dictatorship. In this period Spaniards migrated from rural communities to metropolitan capitals, experienced both a general escalation in standard of living and an increased amount of tourism, a rise in consumerism, and increased contact with foreign popular cultures.[5] The long 1960s in Spain engendered a period of tension between the old guard of the regime and a new generation of young people that had no memory of the Spanish Civil War — a generation that looked toward both Spanish pluralistic traditions of old and to a budding global youth culture. The primary battleground of this threat was found in everyday life; it was the regime's intent to disrupt this invasion of foreign influences, one of these targets being Superman comics that seemed to extol democratic (and capitalist) ideals.

Fearful of these comics, in 1959 the Spanish Ministry of Information and Tourism created the Commission of Information and Child and Youth Publications (CICYP), which was lead by Juan Beneyto Pérez, head of the National Press Council, and the Dominican priest Jesús María Vázquez, as well representatives from the Ministry of Education and Science, the State School of Journalism, the Female Section of the Traditional Spanish Falange, the National Delegation of Youth, and the Episcopal Commission of Communications, amongst others.[6] After several years of censorship the Spanish Ministry of Information and Tourism decided to completely ban Superman comics in 1964 under the advisement of its CICYP because of tropes that threatened to delegitimize the regime through its publication of non-traditional values. Prior to the ban *Supermán* was the top-selling comic book in Spain.[7] However, refusing to give up their favorite comics, young Spaniards continued reading Superman comics despite the prohibition.[8]

Aware of the ineffectuality of the ban, the CICYP consulted with the Institute of Public Opinion, to create a public campaign against Superman comics, headed by Alfonso Alvarez Villar, the director of the Institutes' journal, the *Spanish Journal of Public Opinion (SJPO)*.[9] Alvarez' role in this campaign is significant as his position allowed him to easily inform the highest ranks of the administration of the danger of the American icon. Further, the primary purpose of the journal was to provide the administration of the regime with surveys and analysis of popular opinion for purposes of state control; the fact that Alvarez himself took a lead role in these studies indicates the import of this threat to the regime. Two years after Superman's prohibition, in an attempt to counter this threat, Alvarez wrote one of the most ardent attacks on Superman in the *SJPO*. Most of the readers of the journal were high-ranking Francoist officials (and not curious academics) that would have been interested in public opinion for reasons of propaganda and state control; this governmental report, to which few eyes had access, formed part of the regime's strategy to prevent the inculcation of counter-normative tropes in Spanish youth.

The first forty years of Superman in Spain were tumultuous at best, as censors, religious figures, and sociologists under the dictatorship fought the importation of the American superhero because of the "threat" to Spanish youth that the icon represented, a hero that exalted pluralistic, capitalistic, democratic American ideals. So real was the threat that Superman represented to the regime that Alvarez wrote in 1966, despite two years of prohibition, "Supermán nevertheless continues prowling through the minds of our children, adolescents and even the majority of Spanish adults.... Supermán continues alive in Spain and it is possible that he will never die."[10] Alvarez further cited a survey conducted for the journal, reporting that 148 out of 150 children, ages nine to twelve years old, of "distinct social classes," read Superman comic books, indicating that Superman was indeed still popular despite prohibition. Even as the regime was generally moving toward a less restrictive censorship policy, with the *Ley de la Prensa of 1966,* a provision included mandatory review of children's literature by the CICYP.[11]

Alvarez' assault on Superman was the just one attack in a larger battle against the Man of Steel, as this report was intended to incite a wider campaign against Superman comics. In his detailed 30-page study of the "myth of Superman," Alvarez vehemently attacked Superman. In fact, the CICYP provided Alvarez with their own collection of comics so that to further the campaign against Superman.[12] By the end of the 1960s, numerous articles had been published in Spanish newspapers attacking Superman. Such drastic measures to curtail young people from reading comics was not only indicative of the perceived danger of these comics, but also points to the continued resistance to the prohibition by young people.

Forms and Functions of Superman Comic Books in the 1960s

Understanding Superman comics in Spain first necessitates a look at the social, political, and cultural forces that influenced American comic books published during the McCarthy era from which the Spanish comics were translated. In the 1950s, U.S. congressional inquiries into perceived "communist" and "moral" threats to American youth prompted the creation of the self-regulatory "Comics Code Authority," forcing comic books publishers to sanitize their publications, and conform to the political pressures of the era.[13] As a result, many comic books of the period appeared not only overtly "American" in tone, but skewed toward a representation of the U.S. that viewed its hero as being a "perfect" exemplar for young Americans — an immigrant fully inculcated with the ideology of his adopted homeland, living a puritanical, idealistic existence while extolling ideas of democracy, "truth, justice and the American way."

For young Americans of the 1950s Superman idealized American exceptionalism and puritanical tropes; young Spaniards interpreted these comic books in ways that differed drastically from their U.S. contemporaries. While Superman undeniably represented an extension of "Americanization" and cultural imperialism, the superhero also became representative of implicit everyday dissent against the Francoist regime. The popularity of Superman comics in Spain reflected a desire by Spanish youth to embrace democratic and pluralistic ideals. In the U.S., Superman comics arguably represented normative behavior, however, in Spain, the hero represented an alternative vision of society and politics. These stories that represented a hyper-idealization of democracy and justice, the hyper-modern city of "Metropolis," and the nebulous-yet-hopeful "American way" contained subversive ideas that threatened the dictatorship.

Tebeos, traditional Spanish comics, were lauded as being particularly "Spanish" by the regime; not only did most *tebeos* escape prohibition, but they also played into a national agenda that promoted "Spanishness."[14] Nevertheless, despite Superman's prohibition, according to one 1965 government-conducted survey of some 700 boys and girls, *Supermán* was still the most popular superhero comic book in Spain, and the fifth most popular overall in the *tebeo* category. Further, *Supermán* was the second most favored comic amongst boys, behind *Hazañas Bélicas* (*War Deeds*). While Superman was less popular amongst girls, his adventures still were amongst the top-favored.[15] According to the same survey, Superman held the strongest fan base amongst upper-middle class youth — more than double that of young people from the low-income (*clase baja*) households. Superman was favored by privileged youth, and was even more popular than Capitán Trueno, who was a "Prince Valiant" sort of figure — a gallant Spanish knight set in the 12th century.[16] Superman even remained popular despite the fact that the regime actively tried to promote comics such as Capitán Trueno to displace *Supermán*.[17]

As Michel de Certeau has described in *The Practice of Everyday Life*, tales and legends have a particular role in society, teaching "tactics" to subvert authorities of power.[18] Certeau further argues that everyday life is riddled with ways in which people "poach" ideas and reappropriate them, rather than simply being passive consumers of culture. Through the constructions of figures, alliterations and play on words found in tales and legends, tactics are remembered, taught and incorporated into everyday practices, resulting in the subversion of established order through the use of 'tropes, ordinary languages and ruses, displacements, and ellipses" in order to counter "proper meanings." While these "fables" are indeed, as Certeau states, "fabulous," their cultural currency, in the face of repression, is indicative of their potential to subvert a hegemonic authoritarian system. The personages of Superman, Lois Lane,

Supergirl, Superboy, and even the city of "Metropolis" must be considered through this lens under the Francoist dictatorship. While those characters and situations might now appear conservative and contrived, to the young readers of Superman comics in the 1950s and 1960s, those stories, and even possession of those comics, subverted the dictatorship.

There was something exciting about reading the adventures of a foreign superhero that was strictly forbidden. In fact, despite their illegality, a single Superman comic book was often shared by numerous boys and girls. Faustino R. Arbesú (b. 1939), the founder of Salón Internacional del Cómic del Principado de Asturias, an important Spanish comic book conference begun in 1972, and the comic book journal *El Wendigo* (begun in 1974), recalls not only Ciclón, but remembers Supermán in the 1950s and 60s:

> ... we lived in a fascist state and Superman was public enemy number one. Hitler even gave discourses against Superman. They published him here [referring to Ciclón], but they erased the "S." I didn't have any Superman *tebeos*, but I had a friend that did, and I would go to his house to read them with delirium. In 1952 or 1953 [Supermán comics] finally arrived to Spain, but they came from Mexico and they cost a fortune. With that money you could go to the cinema two times. I never bought them, but I had an advantage.... My wife, who was well-to-do — she was the daughter of a doctor — had them.[19]

Indeed, the eventual supplanting of the Castilian word "*tebeo*" for the anglicized "cómic" by the 1970s further shows the import of American comic books and is demonstrative of their appropriation in form and language by young Spaniards. The imaginary counter-normative world found in Superman comics threatened the regime with: an "asexual," submissive superman; a sexually dominant, professional woman who on occasion dressed as a man and was known for finding trouble in her role as investigative reporter, and for challenging the Man of Steel; and a modern metropolis that exalted the dominance of the modern American democracy and everyday life. In these comics young readers encountered tropes that were both counter-normative and subversive to the regime.

Much like the cheap pamphlets and novels of the nineteenth century, both in the United States and abroad, comic books of the era were generally considered "low culture," the domain of young people and a representation of adolescent agitation against both adults and high culture.[20] While the success and global spread of Superman is reflective of late capitalism, consumerism and American cultural imperialism, these cheap, portable comics were also used as a type of "currency" by young people for trade — which implicitly positioned comic books to counter authority, consequently creating a system of trade that existed to some degree against capitalism and outside of normal consumerism once the comics were acquired by young people. In the Spanish case, once banned by the regime, the dissemination of these comics through illegal channels came to reflect an anti-capitalistic quality, as the youth comic trade would function as a sort of "black market."

Moreover, the "public" nature of these comics is an essential consideration as they were a type of public property traded amongst the youth. As in the United States, young people in Spain frequently wrote their names on the front cover of their comics in hopes that those comics would return to them — a public loan as it were. Of these surviving comics, one often finds nicknames, rather than full names, written on the covers, functioning not only to exclude people from a *peña*, or a small group of intimate friends, but also consequently occluding the identity of the owner of the banned material from authorities.

This public/private proprietorship seen in the copies of those comic books that survive and can be bought in street markets and second hand stores today, with names of the young owners permanently marking the cover. The size of these comics is important to note too, as they were portable and easy to hide from authority figures. Comics were uniquely positioned because of their form, content, and accessibility to act as a place of dissent and tactic against the regime. Children were able to express perhaps more agency than their adult counter parts, as they would not have feared the repercussions of their illegal trading and reading of contraband comics.

Strange Visitor from Another Planet: Myth and the Super-man

Superman comics that circulated in the 1960s were colored by naïve idealism, and adulation of modernity, democracy and futuristic utopianism — told through exciting situations and strange adventures. In the years after the Second World War, particularly because of Superman/Clark Kent's dualistic tropes (rural/urban, extraterrestrial/national icon, flamboyant/stoic, powerful/weak, etc.) and the utopian vision of the modern metropolis, Superman came to fulfill a mythological role of hero/savior for youth around the world — a very "American" hero, indeed. These dualisms, along with Superman's status as mythic American hero, were perceived as a threat to the well-being of Spanish youth by threatening to usurp the folklore that legitimized the patriarchal dictatorship.

Gema Pérez-Sánchez has discussed the Francoist tendency to fear a feminization of Spain. Pérez-Sánchez asserts, "Francoist political, religious, social, and cultural institutions attempted to reconstruct a dominant Spanish identity predicated on nineteenth-century gender roles. Above all, they sought to undo the timidly feminist accomplishments of the Republic."[21] While not a concern to the regime in the 1940s, by the 1950s and 1960s homosexuality and male femininity were perceived as a genuine threat by the regime as new laws such as the Law of Vagrants and Thugs of 1954, and later the Law of Social Danger and Rehabilitation of 1970 attacked what the regime perceived as queer dangers that threatened to destabilize its power.[22]

The regime took advantage of Superman's own "queer" origin in its attack on Superman; the character was a strange visitor who threatened to destabilize Francoist constructions of masculinity and power. Alvarez' attack demonstrated a fear of American democratic and proto-feminist ideals' long-lasting effects on young Spaniards. To counter these threats, Alvarez tried to paint those proto-feminist images as a queer danger to young minds. In his report, Alvarez asserts that Superman demonstrated "a very marked misogyny"—referring to the Spanish meaning of *misoginia* as "an aversion to women." Alvarez further claims that Superman comics omitted vignettes that would have shown kisses and embraces, arguing that Superman was not an "innocent" comic. Alvarez continues, "The relations between the protagonist and Lois reveal a terror on the part of the superman towards an authentic sexual bond," such a relationship, according to Alvarez, "negatively influences the long-term sexual formation of boys and adolescents." For Alvarez, Superman not only avoided women, but that he was an "asexual perversion."[23]

At first glance one would think this "asexuality" reflected the "puritanical" nature of Superman comics of the era. In fact, this "antierotic" Superman was a creation of Francoist censorship. Alvarez' attempt to incite a homophobic fear of Superman becomes more obvious when looking at the General Archives of the Administration, which houses the Francoist regime's censorship records, as one can easily find numerous instances in which censors circled and marked such objectionable material for censorship — specifically kisses and moments of affection between Lois and Superman.[24] As Alvarez had access to these same comics provided by the Commission for his study, which would have included censors' markings and notes, he would have known that this "asexual" Superman was not just the result of American Puritanism, but was exaggerated by Francoist censorship. Moreover, what Alvarez implicitly demonstrates is a fear by the regime of a heroic figure who did not act with the bravado expected of a man of Superman's power in the cultural context of Franco's Spain.

Although the regime did fear Superman's "misogynistic" behavior, what more than likely were the true dangers to Franco's patriarchal hegemony were the examples of "feminine" behavior found in the dual identity of Clark Kent/Superman. A "super-man" was supposed to epitomize masculinity, however, the American superhero did not conform to the *machista* masculine persona glorified by the dictatorship. Superman was not the errant knight Capitán

Trueno who glorified Spanish masculinity. One such example of an inversion of gender roles that escaped censorship can be found the story "El asombroso superniño," published in April 1958 in *Supermán #132*. In the story, Clark Kent finds a child with super-powers and takes the toddler in. To the young reader's surprise, Clark dons a ruffled, white apron and takes to the kitchen to prepare a meal for his new "super-baby."[25] These images of the world's most powerful man dressing as a "woman," preparing breakfast, and acting as a mother figure, were certainly transgressive for young people in the Spain of the 1960s. While not precisely "drag," Superman's assumption of a feminine role, in his secret identity, demonstrates not only a certain level of counternormative behavior, but also taught young readers how both masculine and feminine gender were socially constructed. While Superman might have been the epitome of the perfected male in form, he also had a "feminine" side.[26] While not cross-dressing *per se*, a "feminized," domestic Superman, imitating a woman, challenged young Spaniards perceptions of masculinity. Although it can be argued that this cross-dressing might have been done for comedic effect, the normality of the situation is what is most surprising. In the story, Superman performs the role of "mother" to the orphaned super-toddler in a very natural way.

Alvarez' attack on the Man of Tomorrow was followed by a steady campaign that appeared in magazines and newspapers. Alvarez also wrote numerous articles for newspapers such as *ABC*, the *Heraldo de Aragón* and the *Hoja Del Lunes* on Superman and American comic books. Critics and scholars such as Antonio Martín Martinez, Guillermo Díaz-Plaja, Manuel Vela, Francisco Anson, Luis Gasca (many of whom also wrote for the *SJPO*), along with numerous anonymous writers, plagued the Spanish press with attacks against Superman, including publications in *Arriba*, *La Cordorniz*, *La Gaceta de la Prensa Española*, *Solidaridad Nacional*, *La Voz de Asturias*, *La Vanguardia Española*, *El Correo Español*, *La Voz de España*, amongst others.[27] These numerous attacks during the 1960s on Superman comics generally reflected the regime's fear of how those American ideals would affect young readers, and how seriously the dictatorship took the threat.

Lois Lane: A Super Woman in a Man's World

Further, the regime used gendered heterosexist constructs to demarcate its power, attempting to delegitimize any contending constructions of gender that would challenge the patriarchal power. As deftly discussed by Gema Pérez-Sánchez, the homophobic writings by the Francoist judge Antonio Sabater point to the fears found in the period of transgressive sexualities and queer behavior. In the works of Sabater, lesbians were accused of wearing "manly shoes and clothes" and of displaying "manly ways of behavior."[28] For Sabater, these "manly women," a trope long found in Iberian history in such personages as the Lieutenant Nun, Isabel the Catholic, and Juana la Loca,[29] were dangerous because they had the capacity to perform masculine gender roles that agitated against the patriarchal regime. Not only was the myth of Superman troubling to Falangist critics, but there was also a fear of the character of "Luisa Lane"— or Lois Lane — a woman reporter who challenged gender roles through her profession, her clothing, and her relationship with Superman.

Lois' "manly" actions are demonstrated in numerous comics of the era, and are even more accentuated by the fact that she demonstrated a type of bravado despite her lack of superpowers. In one 1956 adventure, Lois mounts a buoy, uses it to board a ship, pulling herself onto the craft, all in an attempt to capture a band of smugglers. Bursting in on the fiends' plot, Lois is welcomed by a shocked male moustached pirate, "Jeepers! A woman! How did a *woman* make it on board!" Naturally, Lois responds that she too is a smuggler, and is there to help them, as per the suggestion of another smuggler friend, of course. Her timid photographer, Jimmy Olsen, who had already been caught, accidentally gives the reporter away, and they both are captured. Lois then manages to escape, finds a club, and convinces Jimmy that they need to defend themselves, taking the lead in the attack.[30] Lois' acts in this story were transgressive when compared to what most Spanish children in the 1960s would have expected from a woman. She not only was investigating an international plot, she also took on a combative role — a trope rarely seen since the Republican posters of the Spanish Civil War. Once captured, it is Lois that takes a dominant role, persuading her male photographer to fight along side her — all this while dressing like a man, much to the chagrin of the likes of Sabater.

Alvarez remarks with certain disgust that Superman comics presented women as being curious, desiring of "modern men" (as opposed to "traditional" men), bossy (*mandonas*), intuitive, and jealous — as well as other "unsavory" traits.[31] Often, within the pages of the Superman comics, there was confusion as to Lois' profession, which was sometimes translated as "secretary" (the English 'girl reporter' was not much better). However, while she might have been called a secretary, Lois still acted as an investigative reporter. Alvarez even compares Lois to Pandora because of her curiosity, "the true personality of the journalist."[32] Francoist supporters feared Lois' capacity to infect young people with her proto-feminist character — something that once released could not be recaptured.

In the stories published in the 1950s and 1960s, Lois Lane often pursued the Man of Steel, a reversal of the Spanish norms of courtship during that era. In many of these tales it was Superman, not Lois, that would play hard-to-get, another inversion of gender roles at the time. In a highly patriarchal society in which it was the male's role to pursue the female, Lois' hunt to win Superman was extremely aggressive and inappropriate for a woman. While the reader today might read Lois' acts to capture Superman as heteronormative and even demeaning to women, under a considerably more patriarchal regime such as that of Franco, Lois' actions were both counter-normative and even proto-feminist.

In an attempt to delegitimize Superman comics, Alvarez compares Superman and Lois' relationship to that of a father and daughter, made especially "incestuous" as Lois continually attempted to marry an "asexual" Superman. For Alvarez, Superman was a deformation of masculinity, and Lois was a deformity of femininity. While Lois Lane was indeed Superman's "girlfriend," the interactions between the two was antagonistic, as numerous stories revolved around Lois' attempts to discover the mild-mannered man underneath the Man of Tomorrow's flamboyant exterior. Censors, and even young children, could have interpreted this particular search for the man behind the "superman" as a threat to expose the frailty of the weak persona behind the *machista* Spanish man. Indeed, Lois' attempt to discover Superman's identity highlighted the truth of the performative characteristics of masculine bravado that legitimized the Francoist patriarchal order — under the façade of the Superman there was a weakling. Superman was not as "virile" as he would seemingly appear, and certainly was less than all-powerful.

In the patriarchal Francoist era, Lois Lane not only threatened to undermine male dominance, but she also stood as a model for a new sort of independent woman. To young Spaniards, Lois Lane conveyed a message that was subversive to patriarchal norms of the conservative, late-fascist regime. The Francoist regime, which arguably became more authoritarian than fascist by its end, had established its legitimacy through fascist constructions of masculinity, and like Nazi Germany and Fascist Italy, exalted a conception of patriarchal dominance. In the character of Lois Lane young people saw a woman that broke gendered stereotypes.

Imagining "Metropolis": Play and Youth Super-Empowerment

By the late 1960s, despite public attacks, young Spaniards had incorporated the tropes of Superman into their everyday lives — even writing and listening to music that extolled the character. Superman had moved from being strictly "American" to being "Spanish" as well. The 1969 album *Los Ilustrisimos Bravos*, by the Spanish rock and roll group "Los Bravos," featured the song "Como Superman," or "Like Superman"—representing the cultural currency and reappropriation of both American music and Superman.[33] The song with its lyrics about wanting to be like Superman, constructing a happier, better world, and wanting to "volar lejos de aquí" (fly far away from here), pointed to a rejection of Francoism. Young Spaniards wanted to not only imagine a better world for themselves; they wanted to be active creators of that world based upon tropes they had read in Superman comics.

While Superman is indubitably representative of American consumerist culture, for many idealistic young Spaniards the characters found in Superman comics represented an alternative vision of society. Henri Lefebvre, when discussing the French poet Arthur Rimbaud, writes about how a childlike perspective allows children and those with childlike perspectives to see animals, angels and incredible cities where most people just see faces, clouds and landscapes. For children, and or those with young *mentalities* such as Rimbaud, "the word 'image' takes on a new meaning, working on two levels, that of the senses and that of the mind or the dream. In this heightened confusion of the abstract and the concrete, symbol and sensation are no longer distinguishable."[34] Even if young people might consciously know that there is no real-life "Superman," on some level a desire still existed that there were a hyper-modern city protected by a superman, and a "girl reporter" with a nose for trouble. This imaginary world was not passive, but was active and performative; young people would have also imagined themselves as those characters when playing.

La Gaceta de la Prensa Española, the professional news bulletin that funneled official state opinion and information to journalists, attempted to incite popular fear of children pretending to be Superman in the article, "The Pamphlet of the 20th Century, 'Superman': Psychologists accuse this pseudo-children's character of having the power to induce schizophrenic delirium."[35] The article warned of the "danger" of becoming a part of the "religion of Superman" and of young people pretending to be those characters. Taking from Alvarez, Martín also accuses Superman of "*misoginia*" towards Lois Lane. Antonio Martín Martínez writes, "An effect of a consumerist mythology, Superman is acolyte, priest, and god of his own religion. In his particular world he is the owner of Good and Bad ... the result is a dehumanizing drug."[36] The author's fears of capitalism and materialism are indeed understandable; nevertheless, his argument becomes more problematic when he discusses how these democratic ideologies threatened Spanish society, i.e. the stability of the Francoist regime. Martín further argues *Supermán* comics contained messages that taught young readers that they could transcend their "simple human condition." Martín demonstrates a fear of equality and pluralism, and a fear that young readers would want to also be like Superman, that they too might want to live an "American" way of life. Martín feared that Spaniards would look away from religion and patria towards false gods — the double-edged peril of American democracy and capitalism. He writes:

> "Comics" are in fashion. The average man on the street has been reading them since his youth. The adult incorporates [comic books] into everyday urban culture. Children are taken by the multitude of the colored sensations that succeed at a frantic rhythm. Sociologists are worried. Superman is an idol for North America; and more than that, a symbol. A physical and moral symbol of the "American way of life" [quoted in English] and of democracy ... an idol for the millions of readers of all ages and social conditions.[37]

Martín was primarily concerned with the way American ideals were so readily incorporated into individual identity and the quotidian urban life. By acting out these roles in their everyday lives, young people both rejected Francoism and looked toward pluralistic ideas of equality through play and performance.

In "Supermán," Spanish youth had a role model that transcended age. Martín further writes, "Superman is the god of the irresponsible. [Superman] acts subliminally through ideological processes to alienate us from the human condition." He continues, "Supermanism is the escape valve, the impossible dream that a society, such as that of the United States, to fix millions of small, frustrated, repressed men."[38] Indeed, Martín demonstrated a Francoist fear that Superman would alienate young people from the regime, allowing them to imagine an impossible dream that could deliver Superman's followers from "repressed frustration."

Supermán Returns: The Search for Truth, Justice, and the Spanish Way

By 1972 Supermán comics had returned to newsstands in Spain. In that period the regime lessened its attack on comics — perhaps realizing the inevitable arrival of this new global youth culture, that such strict censorship only further piqued young people's interest in prohibited material. This loosening of state control of censorship was in fact starting in the late 1960s, with the passing of new laws that gave more autonomy to publishers, such as the Ley de la Prensa of 1966. Although these comics still had to undergo an extensive process of review, new Superman comics published by Novaro brought even more progressive and transgressive ideas in the years during the years of transition to a parliamentary democracy after the dictator's death in 1975.

The decade would also bring about a more obvious Spanish appropriation of the "cómic" in the production of native Spanish stories that used layouts and stories that were closer to American comics than Spanish *tebeos*.[39] The sudden expansion of the *cómics* of the late 1970s that were both activist and political, and were printed both through official channels and by underground (and often homemade) presses, is further indicative of the importance of these comics of the 1950s and 60s in the inculcation of democratic ideals, and the teaching of new ways of dissent. Many, if not most, of the writers and artists of these political and underground Spanish comics of the 1970s had read Superman comics in their childhood. While the surreptitious reading of Superman comics in late Francoist era is more reflective of the ways in which young people were interested in an alternate vision of society, the comics of the period taught young people new perspectives and tropes that contributed to the inculcation of ideas that better prepared young people to adapt to those drastic changes of the new democracy.

While Superman comics were far from being the impetus of democratic change in Spain, they did reflect ways young people imagined their world and ways in which young people subverted the dictatorship. During the long 1960s young people in Europe and the United States began to exert unprecedented influence on society and culture not only through a new spending power, but also a tiny minority of them that were quickly becoming cultural idols of the period through their music, activism and dissent.[40] In Spain, despite oppression, young people under the dictatorship demonstrated agency in their everyday lives. While these acts of dissent might not have been as obvious as in other parts of Europe, young Spaniards acted against the regime as exemplified through in the quotidian acts of possessing, trading, and reading prohibited, comic books that extolled pluralistic democratic and transgressive tropes.

CHAPTER NOTES

1. See Archivo General de la Administración, Expediente 6694 and 6693 in Signatura 21/10896, 1954. While these records do not identify specifically which of these early "attacks" these Superman comics engaged in, it is possible to say that early on Francoist censors perceived a threat from these comics, censoring many a decade before the eventual ban.

2. For a brief history of Editorial Novaro, with particular attention paid to Spain, see Moliné, Alfons. Novaro: (el globo infinito). Madrid: Sinsentido, 2007.

3. In the later part of the decade the Spanish press, Editorial Dólar, began to produce "graphic novels" that reprinted stories that were originally distributed by the McClure Newspaper Syndicate in the U.S. Dólar had considerable difficulties with censorship when compared with Novaro. See Archivo General de la Administración, Exp. 6697, 6694, 6693 in Sig. 21/10896, 1954.

4. For more on the regime's use of folklore and mythology as a method to legitimize itself see, Ortiz, Carmen. "The Uses of Folklore by the Franco Regime." *The Journal of America Folklore*, Vol. 112, 446 (Autumn, 1999): 479–496.

5. Bernecker, Walther L. "El Cambio De Mentalidad En El Segundo Franquismo." In *España en cambio: el segundo franquismo, 1959–1975*, edited by Nigel Townson, 49–70. Madrid: Siglo XXI, 2009.

6. Vásquez, Jesús María, Manuel Camacho, Jesús María, Félix Madin, Antonio Martín, María Monteserrat Sarto, eds. *Prensa infantil y juvenil: pasado y presente*. Publication. Madrid: Ediciones de la Comisión de Informaciones y Publicaciones Infantiles y Juveniles, 1967. 36, and 121–122

7. *Estudio sobre Superman, sin número.*, Centro de Investigaciones., Archives of the *Instituto de la Opinión Pública*, 1966.

8. Alvarez Villar, Alfonso. "Supermán, mito de nuestro tiempo." *Revista española de la opinión pública*, no. 6 (Oct. 1966): 217.

9. Ibid.

10. Ibid.

11. Vázquez, Jesús María, Félix Madin, Antonio Martín, and María Monteserrat Sarto u Manuel Camacho, eds. *Prensa infantil y juvenil: pasado y presente*. Publication. Madrid: Ediciones De La Comisión De Informaciones Y Publicaciones Infantiles Y Juveniles, 1967. 48.

12. Alvarez Villar, Alfonso. "Supermán, mito de nuestro tiempo.": 235. All of the exemplars published by Novaro from 1958–1964 that would have eventually arrived to the Archivo General de la Administración were "proportioned" by the Comisión de Información y Publicaciones Infantiles and the Hereroteca Nacional to the *Instituto de la Opinión Pública*, which published the *Revista Española de la Opinión Pública*, thus accounting for their disappearance from the general censorship archives. This collaboration further emphasizes the importance of Alvarez' work in understanding the official rationale for the prohibition of the Superman comics. These comics were given to the *Instituto de la Opinión Pública*, and according to the Centro de Investigaciones Sociologicas, the government arm that would have inherited Alvarez Villar's materials, the documents were most likely lost or destroyed during a move from a previous location. One consultant from the Library at the CIS recalled a box of comics from the period, and recounted that two former co-workers argued for years as to what became of those comics.

13. See Wright, Bradford W. *Comic Book Nation: The Transformation of Youth Culture in America*. Baltimore: Johns Hopkins University Press, 2001 and Hajdu, David. *The Ten-Cent Plague: The Great Comic Book Scare and How It Changed America*. New York: Picador, 2009.

14. See, Alary, Viviane. "The Spanish Tebeo." *European Comic Art* 2, no. 2 (Autumn 2009): 253–76.

15. Alvarez Villar, Alfonso. "Encuesta entre los niños y adolescentes." *Revista española de la opinión pública*, no. 2 (Dec. 1965): 212. This survey was done by the Spanish Institute of Public Opinion, but was never publicly distributed. Most of these surveys were secret. The regime gathered this information so that to maintain a general sense of the opinion of the population, and selectively distributed and used that information for purposes of propaganda, etc. Of note is that the sample in this particular survey included a disproportionate number of upper-middle class youth, which generally would have been of more interest to the regime as they were more likely to become dissidents. Also, an average of 15 percent of young male participants responded "no comment." Only 3 percent of young females refused to comment. This refusal to comment is perhaps reflective of the "fear" of possible repercussions for non-conformative responses. Many similar surveys in that Journal of adults of the era were notorious for having up to ninety percent of respondents refusing to answer more polemical questions.

16. Ibid.

17. Vázquez, Jesús María, 42.

18. De Certeau, Michel. *The Practice of Everyday Life.* Berkeley: University of California Press, 2006., 23.

19. Lagar, Eduardo. "Faustino R. Arbesú En La Primera Viñeta." *La Nueva España* (Oviedo, Asturias), February 25, 2007, LXXI ed., Última Página sec.

20. In fact, much of the language found in the archives describes Superman's adventures as "stupid," indicating the disdain for the content of those stories. Archivo General de la Administración, Exp. 7435, Sig. 03228, 1973.

21. Pérez-Sánchez, 21.

22. Ibid., 28–29.

23. Ibid., 218.

24. While the Cultural Archives of the Archivo General de la Administración does not have specific exemplars of any of the Superman comics published by Novaro from the 1958–1964, as they were lent to the Alvarez Villar and subsequently lost, there are several examples of censored Superman comics published by Novaro from after the general ban on Superman comics was lifted in 1972 that demonstrate what might have been censored. Comics that showed affection between Superman and Lois, portrayed Lois as a "modern" woman, that portrayed Superman as too "godlike", or counter-Catholic, or that did not appear "Spanish" enough were frequently marked with the censor's red pencil as dangerous. See: Archivo General de la Administración, *Superman Libro comic II,* Exp. No10789, box 73/04400.

25. Woolfolk, William (w), and Plastino, Al (a). "El asombroso superniño." *Supermán #132.* (Dec. 1958). Madrid: Editorial Novaro. Originally published as "The Amazing Super-Baby," in *Action Comics #217* (June 1956).

26. As Judith Butler has argued, "In imitating gender, drag implicitly reveals the imitative structure of gender itself— as well as its contingency." Butler, Judith. *Gender Trouble: Feminism and the Subversion of Identity.* New York: Routledge, 2006. 187.

27. Also of interest is Luis Gasca's work published for the SJPO that compiled both national, and international bibliographies on comic books and tebeos. The publication of these very extensive bibliographies demonstrates that for the regime the threat present in these comics was very real. These bibliographies would have been used to provide material with which to combat American comic books. See, Gasca, Luis. "Bibliografía Mundial Del "Comic"" Revista Española De La Opinión Pública, no. 14 (Oct. 1968): 365–90.

28. Sabater, Tomás Antonio. *Gamberros, homosexuales, vagos y maleantes; estudio jurídico-sociológico* Barcelona: Editorial Hispano Europea, 1962. 209.

29. The Lieutenant Nun, Catalina de Erauso, was a transgendered man of the 16th century, and is a personage much lauded in Spanish literature as being a "pure", and "manly" woman, for more see "From Convent to Battlefield: Cross-Dressing and Gendering the Self in the New World of Imperial Spain." In *Queer Iberia: Sexualities, Cultures, and Crossings from the Middle Ages to the Renaissance,* edited by Josiah Blackmore and Gregory S. Hutcheson, by Mary Elizabeth Perry. Durham, NC: Duke University Press, 1999. Also, powerful women, such as Queen Isabel the Catholic and her daughter, Queen Juana "la Loca," were also considered "manly women." For more discussion on the masculine traits of Isabel and Juana, see Aram, Bethany. *Juana the Mad: Sovereignty and Dynasty in Renaissance Europe.* Baltimore: Johns Hopkins University Press, 2005. 6.

30. Unknown (w), and Wayne Boring (a). "El Diario International 'El Planeta'." *Supermán #75.* (April 1956). Madrid: Editorial Novaro. Originally published as "The International Daily Planet," in *Action Comics #203* (April 1955).

31. Alvarez Villa, Alfonso. "Supermán, mito de nuestro tiempo.": 244.

32. Ibid., 232.

33. Los Bravos. "Como Superman." Released 1969. *Ilustrisimos Bravos.* 1969, Vinyl recording.

34. Lefebvre, Henri. *Critique of Everyday Life.* Vol. 1. London: Verso, 2008, 109.

35. Martín, Antonio. "Un folletín del siglo XX: 'Superman': Los psicólogos acusan a este personaje seudoinfantil de "poder inducir al delirio esquizofrénico." *Gaceta De La Prensa Española*, no. 196 (Oct. 1967): 17.

36. Ibid., 17–18.

37. Ibid., 18–19.

38. Ibid., 20.

39. For more on the underground and independent Spanish comics of the period, see Lladó, Francesca. *Los comics de la transicion: El boom del comic adulto 1975–1984.* Barcelona: Ediciones Glénat, 2001.

40. Schildt, Axel. *Between Marx and Coca-Cola: Youth Cultures in Changing European Societies, 1960–1980.* New York: Berghahn Books, 2007. 43.

BIBLIOGRAPHY

Alary, Viviane. "The Spanish Tebeo." *European Comic Art* 2, no. 2 (Autumn 2009): 253–76.

Alvarez Villar, Alfonso. "Encuesta entre los niños y adolescentes." *Revista española de la opinión pública*, no. 2 (Dec. 1965).

_____. "Supermán, mito de nuestro tiempo." *Revista española de la opinión pública*, no. 6 (Oct. 1966).

Aram, Bethany. *Juana the Mad: Sovereignty and Dynasty in Renaissance Europe.* Baltimore: Johns Hopkins University Press, 2005.

Bernecker, Walther L. "El Cambio de Mentalidad en el Segundo Franquismo." *España en cambio: el segundo franquismo, 1959–1975.* Madrid: Siglo XXI, 2009.

Butler, Judith. *Gender Trouble: Feminism and the Subversion of Identity.* New York: Routledge, 2006.

De Certeau, Michel. *The Practice of Everyday Life.* Berkeley: University of California Press, 2006.

Estudio sobre Superman, sin número. Centro de Investigaciones. Archives of the *Instituto de la Opinión Pública*, 1966.

Gasca, Luis. "Bibliografía mundial del 'comic.'" *Revista Española de la Opinión Pública*, no. 14 (Oct. 1968): 365–90.

Hajdu, David. *The Ten-Cent Plague: The Great Comic Book Scare and How It Changed America.* New York: Picador, 2009.

Lagar, Eduardo. "Faustino R. Arbesú en la primera viñeta." *La Nueva España.* (Oviedo, Asturias), February 25, 2007, LXXI ed., Última Página sec.

Lefebvre, Henri. *Critique of Everyday Life.* vol. 1. London: Verso, 2008.

Lladó, Francesca. *Los comics de la transición: El boom del comic adulto 1975–1984.* Barcelona: Ediciones Glénat, 2001.

Los Bravos. "Como Superman." *Ilustrisimos Bravos.* Vinyl recording, 1969.

Martín, Antonio. "Un folletín del siglo XX 'Superman': Los psicólogos acusan a este personaje seudoinfantil de "poder inducir al delirio esquizofrénico." *Gaceta De La Prensa Española*, no. 196 (Oct. 1967): 17.

Moliné, Alfons. *Novaro: El globo infinito.* Madrid: Sinsentido, 2007.

Ortiz, Carmen. "The Uses of Folklore by the Franco Regime." *The Journal of American Folkore*, Vol. 112, 446 (Autumn, 1999): 479–496.

Sabater, Tomás Antonio. *Gamberros, homosexuales, vagos y maleantes: Estudio jurídico-sociológico.* Barcelona: Editorial Hispano Europea, 1962. 209.

Schildt, Axel. *Between Marx and Coca-Cola: Youth Cultures in Changing European Societies, 1960–1980.* New York: Berghahn Books, 2007.

Unknown (w), and Wayne Boring (a). "El Diario International 'El Planeta.'" *Supermán #75* (April 1956). Madrid: Editorial Novaro. Originally published as "The International Daily Planet" in *Action Comics #203* (April 1955).

Vázquez, Jesús María, Félix Madin, Antonio Martín, and María Monteserrat Sarto u Manuel Camacho, eds. *Prensa infantil y juvenil: pasado y presente.* Madrid: Ediciones de la Comisión de Informaciones y Publicaciones Infantiles y Juveniles, 1967.

Woolfolk, William (w), and Plastino, Al (a). "El asombroso superniño." *Supermán #132* (Dec. 1958). Madrid: Editorial Novaro. Originally published as "The Amazing Super-Baby" in *Action Comics #217* (June 1956).

Wright, Bradford W. *Comic Book Nation: The Transformation of Youth Culture in America.* Baltimore: Johns Hopkins University Press, 2001.

The Inflexible Girls of Steel

Subverting Second Wave Feminism in the Extended Superman Franchise

Thomas C. Donaldson

In the early 1970s, DC Comics seemed to embrace second wave feminism within its superhero line. At the beginning of the decade, the company expanded the number of features with female characters in leading roles. DC creators also appeared to shift away from the industry convention of modeling their female characters on an archetype of femininity that resonated with the values of domestic containment, moving toward a vision of womanhood that was more powerful, confident, and less dependent on male support. DC Comics made these changes at the same time when second wave feminism gained national prominence, suggesting the company was responding to changing social values as well as to pressure from advocates of feminism, such as the editors of *Ms. Magazine*. DC made the extended Superman franchise a major vehicle for presenting this new attitude toward women, since it was home to two female characters that had been well-established as leading features, Lois Lane and Supergirl.

From its beginning, the comic book industry can be seen as anti-feminist in its orientation: women should play a subordinate and subservient role, largely limited to that of lover, wife, and mother. However, creators were willing to experiment with the medium's gender values, even in the early phase of development. During the Golden Age (1935–1951), DC Comics and other companies created several leading female superheroes, most notably Wonder Woman, and stories featuring these characters can be considered nominally feminist. The comic industry's adoption of the 1954 Comics Code, in large measure because of the work of psychiatrist Fredric Wertham, reinforced — in fact, codified — the industry's anti-feminist orientation. When creating the Comics Code, industry leaders responded directly to Wertham's criticisms that Wonder Woman as a character, in addition to being strong and independent, encouraged sexual deviance — lesbianism — in readers because the character did not seek to marry or raise children. By establishing rules which mandated that creators portray marriage and family life as the ideal outcomes of romantic plots, as well as forbidding portraying any sexual perversion, the comic industry reinforced domestic containment within American society, which sought to limit women's roles in public life and idealized homemaking. The rules encouraged creators to imbue female characters with a narrowly defined vision of femininity that could not be seen as threatening to male power. In demonizing the character of Wonder Woman, Wertham, in essence, created an alternative and antithetical archetype for future female superheroes. As Wonder Woman was strong and stoic, aloof from "normal" male-female relations and a leading character, future heroines, like Marvel Comics' Invisible Girl, would be weak, emotional, devoted to the heterosexual and patriarchal order and marginal members of team books.

At the dawn of the 1970s, as second wave feminism was gaining greater attention in the American media, DC Comics made small efforts to reduce the marginalization of women in the superhero genre, focusing their efforts on the Superman franchise, which included not only the *Superman* and *Superboy* titles, but *Action Comics, Adventure Comics* (home of the Legion of Superheroes — a team of super-buddies for Superboy and Supergirl), *Superman's Pal, Jimmy Olsen, Superman's Girl Friend, Lois Lane,* and *World's Finest Comics.* DC moved Supergirl from being a secondary feature in *Action Comics* to the lead (cover) feature in *Adventure Comics,* replacing the Legion of Superheroes as of issue *#381* (June 1969).[1] As *Adventure Comics* was then an anthology title, the company also devoted many of the secondary features to female characters as well. Often, the company reprinted stories which focused on superheroines, but also created a number of new stories featuring female leads, most notably the sorceress Zatanna. The company also developed a new character, the Thorn, as a secondary feature in *Superman's Girl Friend, Lois Lane,* beginning in issue *#105* (Oct. 1970).[2]

In July 1972, the editors of *Ms. Magazine,* including iconic feminist leader Gloria Steinem, launched a series of editorials celebrating the original feminist virtues of the industry's most prominent female character, Wonder Woman. This editorial campaign celebrating Wonder Woman's feminist virtues served to appropriate the character as an icon of liberal feminism, a fact that comic industry leaders could not help but notice. Soon after the *Ms.* editorial campaign, both DC and Marvel quickly developed lines of comics starring female characters. DC Comics launched *Supergirl* in November 1972, moving the heroine out of *Adventure Comics* and into the first comic DC had published with a female title character since the creation of the Wonder Woman series. Shortly after developing this eponymous comic, creators developed an entirely new character, the Black Orchid, to replace Supergirl as *Adventure Comics*' lead feature.[3]

In addition to decreasing their marginalization of women within the superhero genre, creators also developed female superheroes who served as avatars of liberal feminism. First, these characters were empowered as the leading characters in the comics and features in which they appeared, a reversal of the trend regarding female characters from the previous decade, playing off of liberal feminists' key concerns: equality of opportunity in the job market and equality of pay for women. Companies made the eponymous comic books and features represent an opportunity for female characters that had for many years been enjoyed almost exclusively by male superheroes. As lead characters, creators showed these heroines as the decisive actors: a woman stopped the villain; a woman rescued the bystander; a woman saved the day. This was significantly different from the female who grew worried when faced with a threat and who fainted prior to the final battle with the villain.

Creators used the theme of equality of opportunity in another manner by empowering these heroines professionally; they had careers as well as being superheroes. Prior to this, creators rarely depicted female superheroes having any sort of a job. This development could be construed as an acceptance of feminist principles because it shows a woman both pursuing a vocation other than wife and mother, and obtaining a job that was traditionally held by men. For example, from *Adventure Comics #406* (Dec. 1970) to *Adventure Comics #424* (Oct. 1972), creators had Supergirl hold a job as an assistant television news camera operator.[4] Creators suggest the liberal feminist concern of equality in the workplace with the scenes in which they depict Linda Danvers (Supergirl's civilian identity) searching for work prior to obtaining her position as camera operator. Danvers meets with a series of three personnel officers at three unidentified businesses, each with disappointing results. At the first business, as Danvers receives her first rejection the officer informs her that "things are sort of tight right now."[5] The second officer shows Danvers more sympathy, telling her that "your resume looks good — but..." Danvers completes the thought for the officer: "I know — things are tight right now," suggesting that she has heard this explanation several times.[6] Up to this point, creators have suggested that Supergirl might be a victim of a downturn in the economy. The third panel in the sequence cements the feminist orientation of the scene. A third personnel officer, a balding, older man in a rumpled suit, leers over Danvers with a smile on his face: "We don't have any positions right now — but — if you'd have dinner with me tonight — perhaps..."[7] Creators assert the feminist subtext by subjecting Supergirl to sexual harassment.

Although portrayed as a mild and largely annoying transgression, the scene nevertheless suggests that the officer is promising a job, or the possibility thereof, for Danvers in exchange for an evening of "romantic companionship." In a genre that casts all action in the moral absolutes of good and evil, creators make the officer's advance morally reprehensible. This helps burnish Supergirl's heroic nobility, because Danvers, being Supergirl, has the moral strength to resist the advance: "No thanks — things aren't *that* tight, right now!"[8]

Lastly, creators made these superheroines physically more powerful than their 1960s counterparts. In this manner, creators showed the liberal feminist heroines of the 1970s to be dependent on no man, able to stand toe-to-toe with most any male character in direct combat because of their raw physical strength. Thus, they were able to engage directly and effectively in the genre's primary mode of conflict resolution, personal combat. By endowing these female characters with physical toughness, creators gave them the ability to act decisively to bring resolution to the story plots.

Additionally, creators made "women's lib" a motif within the stories of these female adventurers. For example in the Thorn feature published in *Superman's Girl Friend, Lois Lane #123* (June 1972), creators open the story with Rose Forrest, alter-ego of the Thorn, encountering a group of women protesting at an employment agency while she is out looking for work. Carrying signs that read "How About Women," and "Equal salaries for equal work," the group storms the agency offices, yelling their demands:

WOMAN 1: We want equal rights — your agency doesn't employ enough women!
WOMAN 2: More jobs for women! And more pay!
WOMAN 3: You can't shut us out any longer!
WOMAN 1: We demand equal opportunity![9]

From there, the creators literally have Rose stumble onto a crime down the street, a crime which happens to be perpetrated by men against a wealthy woman, but has no other tangible link to feminist principles or direct link to the protest at the beginning of the story. The creative team seemed to use this opening scene to demonstrate that feminism was a social fact worth acknowledging rather than using it to help advance the plot in any significant way.

In spite of the ways that they attempted to validate second wave feminism textually and metatextually, creators never really called masculine hegemony in to question with these characters because they, like their counterparts in television, were negotiating between "liberal feminism and anti-feminism." Where producers of the adventure heroine shows of the 1970s "virtually [ignored] radical feminism altogether," the comic industry confronted radical feminism in a manner similar the way it was depicted in the wider media.[10] According to Tricia Jenkins, the two forms of feminism differed from one another in that radical feminism

... was most closely associated with thinkers such as Germaine Greer, Shulamith Firestone, and Kate Millet, whose work collectively called for the cultural transformation of patriarchy and even the eradication of marriage and the traditional family. Liberal feminism was most closely associated with Gloria Steinem and the concepts of reformist feminism, which work to elevate women's status in the family, though work place, the media and the education system within the confines of established superstructures.[11]

The news media, Jenkins argues,

... tended to encourage liberal feminist tenets while ridiculing those of radical feminists. As Susan Douglas writes, the media in the early- and mid–1970s were careful to document inequities in employment and champion liberal feminist reforms, but neither the print media nor television devoted news time to inequities in marriage, divorce, and child rearing since "critiques of marriage and the family were much too explosive. Instead, these concerns, which were primarily articulated by radical feminists, were dismissed as "loony and bizarre," and, in general the media depicted radical feminists as ugly, humorless, and "disorderly man-haters in desperate need of some Nair."[12]

Comic book creators essentially maintained hegemonic masculinity as the ideal gender order through the creation of logical flaws that served to subtly undermine the feminist content and allowed men to symbolically retain dominant social authority. Essentially, creators expanded occupational opportunities for female characters, and conferred greater public agency to them, but did so in such a way that hegemonic masculinity was never fully repudiated. For example, creators may have been seeking to evoke feminism with Supergirl's job search harassment scene, but they quickly undermine the feminist content by the heroine's response to the officer's advance. Danvers does not become morally outraged by the third officer's proposition, nor does the character take any action against the officer, either in her civilian or heroic identity. Supergirl simply continues her job search, turning to her male cousin, Superman, for assistance. Presumably, Danvers has both the power and moral authority conferred to her by her heroic status to confront the harassing officer, and prevent him from inflicting this type of injustice on women who do not possess her power. Yet, creators depict her doing nothing whatsoever to rectify the injustice, suggesting that the officer's behavior is not a problem to be stamped out.

The manner in which creators have Supergirl obtain the job as camera operator further undermines the feminist message of this character development. Prior to having her begin her job search, Danvers is depicted graduating from Stanhope College, which she had been attending since *Action Comics #318* (Nov. 1964).[13] Despite being educated, Danvers gets the job at K-SFTV in San Francisco due to nepotism, using Clark Kent's connections within the field to bypass the hiring process. Additionally, it is suggested that Kent's actions are perceived by other characters as arising from something other than familial concern. In the scene where Danvers initially arrives at K-SFTV to meet her soon-to-be superiors, Geoffrey Anderson and Johnny Drew, who are not aware that Danvers and Kent are secretly related, seem to intimate that Kent might have a sexual relationship with their applicant. When Danvers introduces herself to the two, Anderson replies "Clark's friend? Why, the *dog!*" to which Drew follows with "Hiding you from us all this time!"[14] This suggests that they are employing their male gaze to make their initial assessment of Danvers, seeing her as a sexual object rather than a potential employee. Whether it is because Kent is acting on behalf of a lover (as the Anderson and Drew's response could imply) or a family member (as the audience knows), as far as the reader can tell, Supergirl gets the job solely due to nepotism, rather than being more qualified than any other candidate. This undermines the feminist principle of equality of opportunity and that women can do the same work as any man.

Also, by making Supergirl pursue a career in journalism, creators put the character deeper in the shadow of her iconic male counterpart. In fact, it was at this time that creators in the *Superman* franchise moved Clark Kent from his long-held position of reporter for the Daily Planet newspaper, to a position as a television news anchorman as part of an effort to keep the character current. Therefore, creators on the Supergirl feature placed the character in the same sector of the journalism industry that Superman worked. The juxtaposition of their two roles further undermines the feminist subtext of this development, as creators placed Superman/Clark Kent a position of greater esteem. He works in front of a camera, while she is behind the camera, reinforcing the idea that a good woman confines herself to the background in order to support a man.

As the decade progressed, creators at DC Comics developed a career arc for Supergirl that is highly problematic with regard to feminism. At the end of the character's run in *Adventure Comics*, creators have Supergirl quit her job in journalism, and, in the Supergirl series that begins in 1972, they enroll Danvers in graduate school. While this could be read as validating the feminist concern that women should have more opportunities to pursue advanced education, creators have the character pursue a degree in acting, a profession that has limited call for advanced education and in which women have historically had a presence.

When the character was moved to *Superman Family,* creators had Supergirl obtain a job as a guidance counselor at the New Athens Experimental School, beginning in issue *#165* (July 1974).[15] While they portrayed the character as a working professional, this development is problematic with regard to liberal feminism for two reasons. First, the character became involved in the education industry, which has been a field traditionally open to women, and, therefore, does not represent a new area of opportunity for female labor. Second, despite the fact that creators have the school's dean tell a board member (and the audience) that Linda Danvers "comes with excellent qualifications," the character's history suggests otherwise. In terms of education, Supergirl has an undefined Bachelor's degree, and a graduate degree in acting (logically, a Masters in Fine Arts). In regard to work experience, the character worked in television journalism. It is hard to see how this history would give Supergirl "excellent qualifications" to work as a school guidance counselor. In *Superman Family #208* (July 1981), Supergirl changes careers again, this time pursuing a career in acting, an area in which she had clearly established credentials. However, creators made this career move problematic with regard to feminism because they made Supergirl become a cast member of the fictional daytime soap opera "Secret Hearts."[16] Feminist scholars of late have been reevaluating the soap opera as a cultural artifact; for example, sociologist Danielle Blumenthal argues in *Women and Soap Opera: A Cultural Feminist Perspective* that soap opera viewing is "purposeful, transformative, and empowering for women."[17] But in the era in which *Superman Family #208* was produced, many feminist scholars were "simply hostile" to soap operas, according to feminist film studies scholar Charlotte Brunsdon. To feminists, these "programs were one instance of the brainwashing project of the mass media, the project to keep women thinking all they could do was be housewives."[18]

Even though Lois Lane had a long history of being depicted as a woman working in a profession, creators felt the need to alter her professional status to amplify the feminist imagery projected by the character. In *Superman's Girl Friend, Lois Lane #121* (April 1972), creators decided to make a small change in the character's professional status. They have Lois decide to give up her position as a staff reporter at the Daily Planet, opting instead to work as a freelance journalist. Creators explained this action as means for Lois to exert more control over her labor, better enabling her to promote social justice: "No one tells me what to write about—I pick my own stories.... I have a responsibility to [the] people! There's far too much injustice all around to be ignored any longer!"[19] Creators contradict feminist principles as much as they embrace them with the underlying logic of this action. Creators imply that Lane has more creative control over her work; however, rather than strengthening her status at the Daily Planet her position is more tenuous and she is more beholden to the newspaper's male leadership. In fact, the creative team acknowledges this within the story, when they have Lois search for roommates with whom she can share living expenses: "Now that I'm a free-lancer," the reporter thinks to herself, "the money won't be steady ... so I can't afford [my] luxury apartment!"[20]

Another problematic aspect of the portrayal of feminism was that creators continued to portray the movement in a negative light. Before the editorial campaign by the Steinem-led *Ms. Magazine*, creators developed a number of stories that implied that radical feminism was the be all and end all of the women's liberation movement. In these stories, creators equated matriarchy, violent man-hatred, and/or male subjugation with feminism. By doing so, they used symbolic condemnation to portray the second-wave feminism as an illegitimate, spurious, and dangerous movement. DC Comics creators developed such a Supergirl story in *Adventure Comics #417* (March 1972), "All Men are But Slaves." In the story, Supergirl journeys to another planet in pursuit two male acquaintances who have mysteriously disappeared. Upon reaching the alien planet, the heroine finds that the world is, as one reader later described it, "a matriarchal society full of female chauvinists," and that men, including her acquaintances, are enslaved.[21] When Supergirl attempts to free the imprisoned Earth men, she finds herself fighting the planet's female population, who has branded her a "male sympathizer" and a "traitor to her sex!"

Ultimately, the planet's queen demands that Supergirl and her male acquaintances to be brought before her in order to resolve the conflict. The queen grants the three leave to return to Earth, because the planet's "laws firmly state that only our own men shall be enslaved!"[22] Supergirl is incredulous: "Why make slaves of anyone? A society cannot truly proper when one group is enslaved! This is absolute insanity, if you ask me!"[23] The queen explains the origins of her society: "Once men ruled here! And there were wars among our many cities! Our atmosphere was choked with pollution! Finally we revolted! And since then there has been no wars, and very, very little pollution!"[24] Supergirl ponders the adventure upon returning home, musing "If the male leaders here continue to promote wars and help produce pollution, will the women here someday revolt, just as they did there?"[25] DC creators make clear that there are problems with patriarchal society, but that a matriarchal society, as a possible consequence of second wave feminism if taken to an extreme, is as problematic, if not more so. "I'm certainly glad that's over!" Supergirl says to herself, implying that she prefers to be on patriarchal Earth, despite all of its flaws.[26]

In the letter column addressing "All Men are But Slaves" as few issues later, one reader stated: "I don't think that the Earth will become a Utopia if the female sex takes over. Sorry, girls."[27] As the reader implies, creators before the *Ms.* editorial campaign seemed to believe that gender politics was a zero-sum issue, that one gender would garner dominant power and the other would be reduced to minority status, that no equitable power sharing arrangement was conceivable. The story essentially suggested that feminism was not a form of progressive thought, but rather a regressive gender ideology. Creators, in effect, told cautionary tales, warning that the pendulum of gender power could (and very likely would) swing too far, leading to the oppression of men.

In addition to suggesting that feminism would doom men to a life of servitude if allowed to gain power, creators made portrayed radical feminism as a high-minded, but ultimately hollow ideology. Creators showed the ideology being used by ambitious opportunists to give them the veneer of intellectual and moral legitimacy, when, in reality, they were only truly interested in personal power. For example, in the two issues of *Adventure Comics* that followed "All Men Are But Slaves," issues *#418* (May 1972) and *#419* (June 1972), creators had the superheroine Black Canary take a job as a martial arts instructor for a feminist organization called the Women's Resistance League.[28] According to its president, the organization's purpose is "to make women equal to men in every respect, including physically! We're tired of being dominated by male strength!"[29] Much to her surprise, the heroine learns that the League also intends to aid a female criminal (revealed to be Batman's foe, Catwoman, at the end of the story) escape from prison. As part of their plan, the League members disguise their gender using disheveled men's suits and hideous fright masks. The League attacks the police escorting Catwoman to prison with guns and grenades waging war, albeit one with no casualties, with the duly constituted authorities of patriarchal society. The choice of Catwoman particularly reinforces the implication that feminism is a false ideology used to legitimize personal aggrandizement, as the character had been portrayed as a bored wealthy socialite turned thief.

While creators moderated the practice of negatively portraying feminism after the *Ms. Magazine* editorial campaign, they never completely abandoned it. In "World Without Men," published in *World's Finest #233* (Oct. 1975), Superman and Batman travel to Belton, a "ghost town" with an ominous reputation[30] Upon entering Belton, the two heroes (in their civilian identities) discover it is "a town of females only," in which they have recreated patriarchal society minus the men, with women performing any and all jobs, including construction, auto repair, sanitation, police service and even the anachronistic profession of black-smithing.[31] The pair quickly get in trouble with Belton's authorities; "Men have few rights in Belton," the female mayor informs them:

> MAYOR: Big Sister has shown us our female rights to live in dignity without men dominating us!
> BRUCE WAYNE: Real heavy Women's Lib stuff! But ... without men, how will you have lovers ... husbands ... families?
> MAYOR: Big Sister Sybil has promised us that when men give up their domineering ways ... we shall allow them to touch us ... again. Meantime, our strength is living apart ... in freedom and sisterhood! Diana, take them to jail![32]

Just as the police chief is about to imprison Clark Kent and Bruce Wayne, creators present a scene that serves to call into question the notion of women's equality, and that they can do any job that men are able to do. A construction worker loses her footing while working on a nearby rooftop, and clings for her life to the buildings rain gutter. While the police chief holds Kent and Wayne, men who could have quickly and easily rectified the situation, at bay with her gun, other town residents rush to the worker's rescue, only to arrive as she plunges to her death. When in jail, Superman and Batman discover several men who have likewise been unjustly imprisoned by Belton's authorities, one of whom passes on his suspicion that other men have been murdered by the town's female population.

The pair break out of jail and proceed to track down the town's spiritual leader, Big Sister Sybil, an extraterrestrial monster, a giant serpentine creature, with tentacle-like limbs and a giant unblinking eye above fanged mandibles for a head. Sybil reveals to the heroes that she was "exiled from my own world for being hideous!" Having been discovered, Sybil reveals that she is simply using the "foolish women" of Belton, in order to salve her own ego wounded by her ugliness; she is "changing them into ugly things," like herself, by means of poisoning the town's water supply with alien chemicals. After Sybil reveals that "the only antidote to the serum was a male's touch," the heroes quickly dispatch the monster, returning her to outer space from whence she came. Ultimately, creators serve justice to Sybil by having the creature jailed in a mirrored prison by another extraterrestrial society, forcing her to see her "hideous self reflected for eternity!"[33]

Thus, in "World Without Men," the creative team employed all of the elements of symbolic condemnation of radical feminism established by previous creators: unconstrained matriarchal authority combined with irrational man-hatred to create an environment of male subjugation; a leader with little real interest in the betterment of women's condition, using feminism as a convenient ploy to mask a hidden agenda of personal aggrandizement; and women who are easily seduced by the high-minded, but ultimately false ideology. They enhanced the dangerous nature of feminism by depicting the spiritual leader of Belton's feminists as a monster, a grotesque. With this, creators suggested that feminism is not only dangerous, but a corrupt concept. Also, creators implied that feminism is not a natural outgrowth of western civilization by making Sybil an alien. Worse, feminism is a toxic presence; by having Sybil poison the Belton feminists the creative team suggests that feminism is not just dangerous to men. If women subscribe to feminism they will be cursed, doomed to become hideously deformed as they are deprived of "lovers ... husbands ... families," because they will deny themselves the salvation of a "man's touch" in the pursuit of their monstrous ideology. DC creators made

Sybil the epitome of a "loony and bizarre" avatar of radical feminism with her monstrous appearance, on the one hand, and her completely illogical plan of self-gratification on the other.

In addition to the continued symbolic condemnation of radical feminism, creators occasionally expressed overt hostility to the women's movement. DC Comics ran a second, separate letters page in *Superman's Girl Friend, Lois Lane*, for three issues (*#124–126*; Jul.-Sep. 1972), published in the immediate wake of the *Ms.* editorial campaign.[34] Series editors told readers that the feature was due "to the tremendous reader response to the 'new' Lois Lane," and that they felt the need for a second columnist "...who can deal specifically with the new image of Lois. Since issue *#121*, the mail that has poured in has been both pro and con. We feel that if the subject is so important to you and so controversial, it warrants its own special page..."[35] The "mystery columnist," who was given the pseudonym "Alexander the Great," wrote with an exaggerated, bombastic voice, decrying the effort to invest the Lois Lane character with any sense of feminism, deriding the women's movement as both ludicrous and unnatural, and addressing any reader who seemed to approve of the series' new direction with contempt, as shown in the following exchange from *Lois Lane #125* (Aug. 1972):

> Dear Editor:
>
> About the subject of Women's Lib, Lois is carrying it too far and Superman not far enough. He must realize that "woman power" means more than fisticuffs and inane clichés, and that being loved and needed doesn't mean being enslaved. Her actions in the last two issues show that she must believe this. Her crack about "cooking in the kitchen" is the reason that some of the women I know hate the movement. It makes the woman who wants to fulfill herself "just" as a wife and mother feel worthless. What Women's Lib should boil down to is the right of every woman to choose the life she wants for herself and to be able to live it. I hope Lois and [Superman] both wake up.[36]

To which "Alexander" replied:

> What's the matter, kid. Have you fallen for Lois or something? There is only one way to do things, and that's the man's way. Can you imagine women in key roles of history? If it had been a woman instead of Moses, we'd have ten THOUSAND Commandments, instead of ten. And the Alamo? It would've fallen in ten minutes! "Florence" of Arabia would never have made it, and "Georgia" Washington would've drowned in the Delaware River. How can any girl in her right mind refute what I've made plain?? Forget Women's Lib. If we gave them the world, they'd ruin it![37]

Likely, the company intended the column to be read as a tongue-in-cheek gag, casting "Alexander" in the role of male chauvinist curmudgeon. However, given the timing of this feature, its exclusive focus on the incorporation of feminism into the superhero genre, the vindictive tone of the column, and the need for anonymity, it is also likely that DC staffers were using this as an opportunity to publicly vent their frustration at the editors of *Ms.* for demanding that the company conform to their gender values.

The extended *Superman* franchise acted as a microcosm of the problematic manner in which the larger comic book industry was approaching second wave feminism in the 1970s. The industry may have attempted to incorporate second wave feminism into the genre's gender values following the editorial attack on industry policies by *Ms. Magazine*, but the effort was half-hearted at best. Both DC and Marvel promptly abandoned the experiment. They both canceled all of the new eponymous titles featuring female superheroines as leading characters; DC's *Supergirl* had the best showing with nine issues published in just over a year. DC likewise canceled *Superman's Girl Friend, Lois Lane* after issue *#137* (Sep. 1974) and relegated both Lois Lane and Supergirl to a new anthology comic in April 1974, the very title of which suggests submission to patriarchal authority, *Superman Family*. While the company would maintain Zatanna and Black Canary in *Justice League of America*, creators would not use The Thorn for several years after the cancellation of *Lois Lane*. The company also replaced Black Orchid as lead feature of *Adventure Comics* with the male hero, the Spectre, briefly maintaining the heroine as the star of a backup feature in *Phantom Stranger* in issues *#31* through *#41* (June 1974–March 1976).

The *Ms.* campaign accelerated the move away from using female superheroes as avatars of domestic containment, as dictated by much-reviled Wertham and therefore represented a triumph of second wave feminism. However, the editors of *Ms.* also cultivated hostility toward their effort and toward the women's movement in general among comic industry workers. The industry had already been through a public controversy regarding the gender values projected through its products, and harbored a grudge against Fredric Wertham ever since. Given this history, it is logical that this hostility may have contributed to the comparatively quick cancellation to the early feminist superhero series, as well as the continued condemnation of the women's movement through the vilification of radical feminism. Creators moved away from using female superheroes as avatars of domestic containment, a symbolic repudiation of Wertham's conservative vision of gender, but otherwise failed to develop a truly pro-feminist vision of heroic womanhood. Because they only made a nominal commitment to the ideology, creators effectively subverted the moral authority of feminism, rendering it into little more than a plea for better or treatment of women within a gender order in which male domination went unchallenged.[38]

Chapter Notes

1. Bates, Cary (w), and James Winslow Mortimer (a). "The Supergirl Gang." *Adventure Comics (1938) #381* (June 1969). New York: DC Comics.

2. Kanigher, Robert (w), and Ross Andru (a). "Night of the Thorn." *Superman's Girlfriend, Lois Lane (1958) #105* (Oct. 1970). New York: DC Comics.

3. Mayer, Sheldon (w), and Tony DeZungia (a). "Black Orchid." *Adventure Comics (1938) #428* (July 1973). New York: DC Comics.

4. Sekowsky, Mike (w, a). "Suspicion." *Adventure Comics (1938) #406* (May 1971). New York: DC Comics; Skeates, Steve (w), and Tony DeZungia. "Crypt of the Frozen Graves." *Adventure Comics (1938) #424* (Oct. 1972). New York: DC Comics.

5. "Suspicion." *Adventure Comics (1938) #406* (May 1971).

6. Ibid.

7. Ibid.

8. Ibid.

9. Kanigher, Robert (w), and Don Heck (a). "The Richest Girl In The World!" *Superman's Girlfriend, Lois Lane (1958) #123* (June 1972). New York: DC Comics.

10. Jenkins, Tricia. "Nationalism and Gender: The 1970s, *The Six Million Dollar Man*, and *The Bionic Woman*," *Journal of Popular Culture* (Feb. 2011). 102.

11. Ibid., 96.

12. Ibid., 102.

13. Dorfman, Leo (a) and Jim Mooney (a). "Supergirl Goes to College!," *Action Comics #318* (Nov. 1964). New York: DC Comics.

14. Sekowsky, Mike (w), and (a). "Suspicion." *Adventure Comics (1938) #406* (May 1971).

15. Maggin, Elliot S. (w), and Art Saaf (a). "Princess Of The Golden Sun!" *Superman Family (1974) #165* (July 1974). New York: DC Comics.

16. Harris, Jack C. (w), and James Winslow Mortimer (a). "The Super-Switch To New York." *Superman Family (1974) #208* (July 1981). New York: DC Comics.

17. Blumenthal, Dannielle. *Women and Soap Opera: A Cultural Feminist Perspective*, (1997). Westport, CT: Praeger, 5.

18. Brunsdon, Charlotte. "The Role of Soap Opera in the Development of Feminist Scholarship." *To Be Continued...: Soap Operas Around the World* (1995). New York: Routledge, 58.

19. Bates, Cary (w), and Werner Roth (a). "Everything You Wanted To Know About Lois Lane — But Were Afraid To Ask!" *Superman's Girlfriend, Lois Lane (1958) #121* (April 1972). New York: DC Comics.

20. Ibid.

21. Skeates, Steve Name (w), and Bob Oskner (a). "All Men are But Slaves." *Adventure Comics (1938) #417* (March 1972). New York: DC Comics.

22. Ibid.

23. Ibid.

24. Ibid.

25. Ibid.

26. Ibid.

27. Orlando, Joe (ed.). "Super Fe-Mail" (Letter Column). *Adventure Comics (1938) #421* (July 1972). New York: DC Comics.

28. O'Neil, Dennis (w), and Alex Toth (a). "Black Canary." *Adventure Comics (1938) #418* (May 1972). New York: DC Comics; O'Neil, Dennis (w), and Alex Toth (a). "Black Canary." *Adventure Comics (1938) #419* (June 1972). New York: DC Comics.

29. Ibid.

30. Technically, this story featured Superman Jr. and Batman Jr., character who DC Comics created as part of a quasi-regular series running in *World's Finest*, called "The Super-Sons." Other than the fact that they are supposed to be the children of Superman and Batman, and therefore are portrayed as younger, these characters are virtually indistinguishable from their iconic forebears. Therefore, they are herein referred to as "Superman" and "Batman" to avoid confusing explanation of metatextual minutiae of the DC Comic superhero universe.

31. Haney, Robert (w), and Dick Dillin (a). "World Without Men." *World's Finest Comics (1940) #233*. New York: DC Comics.

32. Ibid.

33. Ibid.

34. Woolfolk, Dorothy (ed.). "Letters to Lois and Rose" (Letter Column). *Superman's Girlfriend, Lois Lane (1958) #123* (July 1972). New York: DC Comics.

35. "Here He Is.... As Promised.... Your Mystery Columnist" (Letter Column). *Superman's Girlfriend, Lois Lane (1958) #124* (July 1972).

36. Woolfolk, Dorothy (ed.). "Here He Is... As Promised.... Your Mystery Columnist" (Letter Column). *Superman's Girlfriend, Lois Lane (1958) #125* (Aug. 1972).

37. Ibid.

38. For more on the comic book industry and the feminist movement, please see the following: Aurther Asa Berger, *The Comic-Stripped American* (New York: Walker and Company, 1973); Hal Blythe and Charlie Sweet, "Superhero: The Six Step Progression." *The Hero in Transition.* Ed. Browne, Ray B. (Bowling Green, OH: Bowling Green Popular Press, 1983), 180–187; R. W. Cornell, *Gender and Power: Society, the Person and Sexual Politics* (Cambridge: Blackwell, 1987); Les Daniels, *Superman: The Complete History* (San Francisco: Chronicle Books, 2000; Les Daniels, *Wonder Woman: The Complete History* (San Francisco: Chronicle Books, 2000); Joanne Edgar, "Wonder Woman Revisited." *Ms.*, July, 1972: 50–55; Susan Faludi, *Backlash: The Undeclared War Against American Women* (New York: Anchor Books, 1992); Joanne Hollows, *Feminism, Femininity, and Popular Culture* (Manchester: Manchester University Press, 2000); Maurice Horn, *Women in Comics* (New York: Chelsea House Publishing, 1977); Sherrie A. Innes, *Tough Girls: Women Warriors and Wonder Women in Popular Culture* (Philadelphia, PA: University of Pennsylvania Press, 1999); Susan Jeffords, *The Remasculinization of America: Gender and The Vietnam War.* (Bloomington, IN: Indiana University Press, 1989); Stan Lee, *The Superhero Women.* (New York: Simon & Schuster, NY, 1977); Kenneth MacKinnon, *Representing Men: Maleness, Masculinity in the Media* (London: Arnold Publishers, 2003); Maxine Margolis, *Mothers and Such: Views of American Women and Why They Changed* (Berkley, CA: University of California Press, 1984); Amy Kiste Nyberg, *Seal of Approval: The History of the Comics Code* (Jackson: University of Mississippi Press, 1998); Norma Pecora, "Superman/Superboys/Supermen: The Comic Book Hero as Socializing Agent." *Men, Masculinity, and the Media.* Ed. Steve Craig. (Newbury Park, CA: Sage, 1992), 61–77; Trina Robins, *The Great Women Superheroes* (Northampton, MA: Kitchen Sink Press, 1994); Lillian S. Robinson, *Wonder Women: Feminisms and Superheroes* (New York: Taylor and Francis Group, 2005); Joan Scott, *Gender and the Politics of History.* (New York: Columbia University Press, 1999); Gloria Steinem, "Introduction." *Wonder Woman* (NY; Holt, Reinhart and Winston, 1972), 6–12. Gaye Tuchman, Arlene K. Daniels, James Benet, *Hearth and Home: Images of Women in the Mass Media.* (New York: Oxford University Press, 1978); Fredric Wertham, *Seduction of the Innocent.* (New York: Rinehart and Company, 1954); Bradford Wright, *Comic Book Nation: The Transformation of Youth Culture in America.* (Baltimore: Johns Hopkins University Press, 2001).

BIBLIOGRAPHY

Bates, Cary (w), and James Winslow Mortimer (a). "The Supergirl Gang." *Adventure Comics (1938) #381* (June 1969). New York: DC Comics.

Bates, Cary (w), and Werner Roth (a). "Everything You Wanted To Know About Lois Lane-But Were Afraid To Ask!" *Superman's Girlfriend, Lois Lane (1958) #121* (April 1972). New York: DC Comics.

Berger, Aurther Asa. *The Comic-Stripped American.* New York: Walker and Company, 1973.

Blumenthal, Dannielle. *Women and Soap Opera: A Cultural Feminist Perspective.* Westport, CT: Praeger, 1997.

Blythe, Hal, and Charlie Sweet. "Superhero: The Six Step Progression." In Ray B. Browne, ed., *The Hero in Transition.* Bowling Green, OH: Bowling Green Popular Press, 1983.

Brunsdon, Charlotte. "The Role of Soap Opera in the Development of Feminist Scholarship." In Robert C. Allen, ed., *To Be Continued..: Soap Operas Around the World.* New York: Routledge, 1995.

Cornell, R. W. *Gender and Power: Society, the Person and Sexual Politics.* Cambridge, England: Blackwell, 1987.

Daniels, Les. *Superman: The Complete History.* San Francisco: Chronicle Books, 2000.

_____. *Wonder Woman: The Complete History.* San Francisco: Chronicle Books, 2000.

Dorfman, Leo (w), and Jim Mooney (a). "Supergirl Goes to College!" *Action Comics #318* (Nov. 1964). New York: DC Comics.

Edgar, Joanne. "Wonder Woman Revisited." *Ms.* (July 1972): 50–55.

Faludi, Susan. *Backlash: The Undeclared War Against American Women.* New York: Anchor Books, 1992.

Haney, Robert (w), and Dick Dillin (a). "World Without Men." *World's Finest Comics (1940) #233.* New York: DC Comics.

Harris, Jack C. (w), and James Winslow Mortimer (a). "The Super-Switch To New York." *Superman Family (1974) #208* (July 1981). New York: DC Comics.

Hollows, Joanne. *Feminism, Femininity, and Popular Culture.* Manchester: Manchester University Press, 2000.

Horn, Maurice. *Women in Comics.* New York: Chelsea House Publishing, 1977.

Innes, Sherrie A. *Tough Girls: Women Warriors and Wonder Women in Popular Culture.* Philadelphia: University of Pennsylvania Press, 1999.

Jeffords, Susan. *The Remasculinization of America: Gender and the Vietnam War.* Bloomington: Indiana University Press, 1989.

Jenkins, Tricia. "Nationalism and Gender: The 1970s, *The Six Million Dollar Man,* and *The Bionic Woman.*" *Journal of Popular Culture* (Feb. 2011): 102.

Kanigher, Robert (w), and Ross Andru (a). "Night of the Thorn." *Superman's Girlfriend, Lois Lane (1958) #105* (Oct. 1970). New York: DC Comics.

Kanigher, Robert (w), and Don Heck (a). "The Richest Girl in The World!" *Superman's Girlfriend, Lois Lane (1958) #123* (June 1972). New York: DC Comics.

Lee, Stan. *The Superhero Women.* New York: Simon & Schuster, 1977.

MacKinnon, Kenneth. *Representing Men: Maleness, Masculinity in the Media.* London: Arnold Publishers, 2003.

Maggin, Elliot S. (w), and Art Saaf (a). "Princess of the Golden Sun!" *Superman Family (1974) #165* (July 1974). New York: DC Comics.

Margolis, Maxine. *Mothers and Such: Views of American Women and Why They Changed.* Berkley: University of California Press, 1984.

Mayer, Sheldon (w), and Tony DeZungia (a). "Black Orchid." *Adventure Comics (1938) #428* (July 1973). New York: DC Comics.

Nyberg, Amy Kiste. *Seal of Approval: The History of the Comics Code.* Jackson: University of Mississippi Press, 1998.

O'Neil, Dennis (w), and Alex Toth (a). "Black Canary." *Adventure Comics (1938) #418* (May 1972). New York: DC Comics

O'Neil, Dennis (w), and Alex Toth (a). "Black Canary." *Adventure Comics (1938) #419* (June 1972). New York: DC Comics.

Orlando, Joe, ed. "Super Fe-Mail" (Letter Column). *Adventure Comics (1938) #421* (July 1972). New York: DC Comics.

Pecora, Norma. "Superman/Superboys/Supermen: The Comic Book Hero as Socializing Agent." In Steve Craig, ed., *Men, Masculinity, and the Media.* Newbury Park, CA: Sage, 1992.

Robins, Trina. *The Great Women Superheroes.* Northampton, MA: Kitchen Sink Press, 1994.

Robinson, Lillian S. *Wonder Women: Feminisms and Superheroes.* New York: Taylor and Francis Group, 2005.

Scott, Joan. *Gender and the Politics of History.* New York: Columbia University Press, 1999)

Sekowsky, Mike (w, a). "Suspicion." *Adventure Comics (1938) #406* (May 1971). New York: DC Comics.

Skeates, Steve (w), and Tony DeZungia (a). "Crypt of the Frozen Graves." *Adventure Comics (1938) #424* (Oct. 1972). New York: DC Comics.

Skeates, Steve (w), and Bob Oskner (a). "All Men are But Slaves." *Adventure Comics (1938) #417* (March 1972). New York: DC Comics.

Steinem, Gloria. "Introduction." In William Moulton Marston, *Wonder Woman.* New York; Holt, Reinhart and Winston, 1972.

Tuchman, Gaye, Arlene K. Daniels, and James Benet, *Hearth and Home: Images of Women in the Mass Media.* New York: Oxford University Press, 1978.

Wertham, Fredric. *Seduction of the Innocent.* New York: Rinehart and Company, 1954.

Woolfolk, Dorothy (ed.). "Here He Is.... As Promised.... Your Mystery Columnist" (Letter Column). *Superman's Girlfriend, Lois Lane (1958) #125* (Aug. 1972.

_____. "Letters to Lois and Rose" (Letter Column). *Superman's Girlfriend, Lois Lane (1958) #123* (July 1972). New York: DC Comics.

Wright, Bradford. *Comic Book Nation: The Transformation of Youth Culture in America.* Baltimore: Johns Hopkins University Press, 2001.

Black Like Lois

Confronting Racism, Configuring African American Presence

CHRISTOPHER B. ZEICHMANN

The impact of the Civil Rights movement inevitably extended far beyond the spheres that saw its most intense focus, those of law and politics. Indeed, the increased stature of African Americans throughout popular culture began in the decades following World War II. Sidney Poitier's Academy Award for Best Actor in *Lilies of the Field* (1963) further marked the mainstreaming of African Americans in the mass media.[1] Comic books were no exception on the matter. Marvel's creation of Black Panther (1966, preceding the formation of the organization), the Falcon (1969), and Joe Robertson at the *Daily Bugle* (1967) evince the editorial direction to incorporate high profile, enduring African American characters that stood as exemplary for the readers in some capacity — either as heroes or as supporters thereof. Similar consciousness regarding racial issues is transparent throughout the early run of the *X-Men* and the *Fantastic Four*, though in the more dubious tradition of the "tragic mulatto."[2]

For whatever reason, DC's superhero comics lagged a few years behind Marvel in this regard.[3] Even by the early 1970s, few important black characters existed, the exception being John Stewart as Earth's backup Green Lantern in 1971.[4] Stewart was initially depicted as a confrontational, jive-talking architect, who proved that he was worthy of the Green Lantern's power ring by saving a police officer's life and exposing a conspiracy mastered by a racist politician. Minor supporting and one-shot African American characters began to appear in DC's superhero titles, rarely missing an opportunity to make some sort of comment on state of race-relations in the process. Though Superman had rarely encountered African Americans in the previous three decades of his existence, the Man of Tomorrow's ongoing corpus soon underwent similar shifts.

However, as the Silver Age transitioned into Bronze Age, the former's allegorization of real-world social ills (X-Men) and tendency to locate such problems in fictional nations (Black Panther's Wakanda) were exchanged for more specific and direct means of addressing such matters. It was during this early period of the Bronze Age that Superman comic books depicted their first African American characters. Consequently, we will see that the characters in these stories often express the opinions of their writers on contemporary political issues verbatim and that their lessons map unambiguously onto the social matrices of the early 1970s in a manner typical of Bronze Age comics.[5] These stories situate Superman and his supporting cast in a society that was still in the process of negotiating how to practice race relations after the close of the Civil Rights era, but amidst the Black Power movement.

Above all else, we will see that Superman stories of the early 1970s assert an integrationist message of mutual respect between African Americans and Caucasians. This point may sound entirely benign, even if the creators often expressed this in a shrill tone. There was, however, a frequent emphasis on the need for African Americans to embrace Caucasian allies, as well as other fixations upon black separatism that ultimately placed the onus of reconciliation on racial minorities. These preoccupations reflect the common perception among Caucasians that the Black Power movement was just as unethical as white supremacist ideologies. This disposition ultimately rendered the force of the writers' anti-racist message impotent.

Vathlo Island and the Implementation of a Multi-Racial Krypton

The first notable black character in a Superman comic occurred in the back-up story to *Superman #234* (Feb. 1971).[6] After losing contact with an orbiting space-prison-cell, Jor-El was contacted by an employee from the tracking station at Vathlo. This man assured Jor-El that the prison was orbiting on schedule, which eventually arrived on schedule. The employee at Vathlo, however, had the skin tone of an African American, making this the first appearance of a black Kryptonian. His skin color was unmentioned during the single panel in which he appeared, as well as the remainder of the story. This silence may have resulted from a remarkable instance of colorblindness by *Superman*'s entire creative team or an independently-minded (and unnamed) colorist. Curt Swan's pencils and inking have rendered this man's physical features indistinguishable from lighter-skinned individuals in the story. An unnamed delegate from the United Nations had similar skin coloration in the issue's lead feature, despite Swan's art being consistent with a Caucasian in all other respects for the character.[7] Regardless, neither story displays any concern over these characters' ethnicity.

This appearance of the (seemingly) sole black individual on Krypton proceeded unmentioned for several months. A map of Krypton was eventually printed in *Superman #238* (June 1971),[8] elucidating this matter. In the "Old World" hemisphere of Krypton, artist Sal Amendola describes "Vathlo Island," which was home for the planet's "highly developed black race." Assistant Editor E. Nelson Bridwell further suggested that the dearth of black Kryptonians in the Superman stories be understood in relation to the United States' imperial legacy: "Remember — you see blacks in the U.S. because their ancestors were brought here as slaves. That never happened in Krypton."[9]

While clarifying the geographic makeup of Krypton, Amendola did little to rectify the perception of a highly-segregated planet. The map is ambiguous and offers itself to divergent interpretations; it can be easily construed as something with progressive intent (a world where race-relations did not share Earth's history of brutality and domination) or crypto-segregationist (a world where race-relations were peaceful due to continued separation). A number of factors suggest that the truth lies closer to the former, though tainted by problematic aspects of the sociology of race from the 1960s.

First, the description of Vathlo Island's inhabitants as a "highly developed black race" is clearly *intended* as a positive characterization. However, this wording suggests that the inhabitants of Vathlo were a sort of novelty worth noting insofar as black advancement was peculiar. Second, this serves as an editorial explanation for the previous absence of black Kryptonians that evinces no attempt to exonerate DC's silence on ethnicity in earlier Superman stories.[10] Third, despite the description of Vathlo Islanders as "highly advanced," they are nonetheless a non-dominant race; they are ultimately confined to a single island. Finally, Mark Waid offers a helpful explanation for the ethnic homogeneity of Krypton in terms of the history of science fiction.

> A lack of ethnicity was an error of omission and I'm not sure given the time that it's fair to call that "racist." [Jerry] Siegel and all those who followed in crafting the Superman legend were, indeed, simply following the traditions of the Golden Age of Science Fiction, when one world always equalled one culture, *maybe* two if they were at war because the plot demanded it.... The gradual recognition of all races and ethnicities across all of pop culture, comics included, really didn't start to blossom until the late 1960s. Yes, Superman was weirdly late to that party ... but again, and not to make excuses, that delay was just creative inertia in action.[11]

Thus, the mythology associated with Krypton had never required conflict extending beyond that generated from Jor-El's predictions of destruction. But the same literary tradition that spawned Krypton's racial uniformity spread to Clark Kent's city of residence as well. Metropolis lacked the racial diversity one would expect of an American city its size and Bridwell's aforementioned appeal to the importation of Africans to America as an explanatory device for the absence of black Kryptonians does not elucidate Metropolis' ethnic homogeneity. We will see similar themes and apprehensions regarding African American social presence emerge in one of the most bizarre Superman stories of all time.

Lois Lane's Experience of the African American Plight

Lois Lane was subject to numerous physical transformations in the Golden and Silver Ages,[12] but one of her most significant occurred at the dawn of the Bronze Age in *Superman's Girl Friend Lois Lane #106* (Nov. 1970),[13] written by Robert Kanigher. The story begins with Lois' description of her idea for a Pulitzer-worthy article about Metropolis' district named Little Africa. She searches for people to interview, but finds herself snubbed by every African American she encounters, even a blind woman who detects Lois' ethnicity by her voice. Now exasperated, Lois becomes subjected to accusations of racism, opposition to integration, and other taunts by an activist named Dave Stevens, who addresses a small crowd of interested locals. Superman approaches her and suggests a solution: that she enter his Plastimold and change her skin color for 24 hours in order that she find acceptance among black locals.

Lois Lane's perspective on the world is radically altered as a result, not only gaining recognition among the locals of Little Africa that had previously rejected her, but also scorned by her Caucasian taxi-driver friend. But tragedy strikes when drug dealers shoot Dave Stevens, with whom she just began conversing again. The doctor at the hospital informs Lois that they lack the blood reserves to give Stevens the necessary transfusion. She agrees to donate her own in order to save Stevens' life. Following the procedure, the effects of the Plastimold wear off prematurely. Lois expresses reservations about visiting Stevens while he recovers: "He called me Whitey! His enemy! Wh-what will he say now?" She ultimately agrees to do so at Superman's insistence. In a dialogue-free conclusion, Stevens becomes visibly shocked when Lois enters, though delight and gratitude quickly replace it. They seal their friendship in a handshake.[14]

John Howard Griffin's popular memoir *Black Like Me*, written a decade prior, served as the literary model for Kanigher's story.[15] Griffin was a Caucasian journalist who artificially changed his skin color, approximating that of African Americans, in order to experience first-hand the racism of the U.S. South for a publication he was writing. *Black Like Me* proved quite influential in both popular culture and in the academy, where it sits as an early study in the sociology of race.[16] The book was an immediate bestseller and even won the Saturday Review Ansfield-Wolf Award.[17] It provoked innumerable threats on Griffin's life, but nonetheless generated Caucasian awareness of— and subsequently, support for —Civil Rights issues.[18] When researching the book, Griffin encountered certain individuals multiple times and found that their reactions were entirely dependent on his skin tone. Themes of African American impoverishment, communal support, and social exclusion by Caucasians likewise feature prominently in both stories. But the similarities between the two stories ran deeper than the protagonists' temporary experience as an African American.

More significantly, both works have an implied audience of Caucasian Americans, though Griffin and Kanigher address this audience quite differently. Kanigher's and Griffin's respective modes of address reflect their respective contexts midst African American political activism. Foremost among these is the way "I Am Curious (Black)" adjusts Griffin's narrative for the Black Power era, since the Civil Rights movement that Griffin addressed had disintegrated after Martin Luther King, Jr.'s assassination in 1968. While the phrase "Black Power" never appears in the Lois Lane story, its presence as a subtext is unmistakable: dashikis, the slogan "black is beautiful," an allusion to James Brown's hit single "Say It Loud — I'm Black and I'm Proud," and unequivocal statements asserting the oppression of African Americans as a foundational component of American culture.

Moreover, historian Gayraud S. Wilmore writes:

> The most important contribution of the black power concept was the recognition of the crucial importance of the political and economic control of the land, and that for those who lived on this increasingly blackenized terrain, which whites had declared ... unfit for white habitation — retreating to the suburbs — racial integration was an idle dream.[19]

Wilmore's primary components of Black Power (i.e., importance of African American land ownership, as well as skepticism of integrationist politics and sympathetic Caucasians) are the principal points of reference in "I Am Curious (Black)" and to a lesser extent the map of Krypton that featured Vathlo Island. The most obvious instance in the former occurs in Dave Stevens' initial polemic against Lois. As she walks by, he accuses Lois — representing all Caucasians — of attempting to quarantine all African Americans in "rat-infested slums," along with opposition to the presence of landed blacks in better parts of Metropolis. "That's why she's our enemy!" Stevens' message is presented as an angry and self-contradictory ideology that is deeply misdirected. Lois contemplates, "He's wrong about me, but right about so many others!"

Lois also encounters an all-black "improvised pre-kindergarten" in an alley wherein children are taught that "black is beautiful." Insofar as this gathering is even necessary, the story further implies African Americans' doubts regarding authorized educational institutions. This sentiment is pervasive in *Superman's Girl Friend Lois Lane #106.* No black character willingly interacts with Lois until after her transformation, with nineteen characters rebuffing her over the course of three pages. Once she changes, Lois is consistently met with hospitality despite the meager means of the people she encounters. One woman — having slammed the door in Lois' face earlier — offers her help, identifying Lois as "sister." The reader cannot help but notice the woman's drastic alteration in friendliness in connection with Lois' skin color. Vathlo Island similarly presumes a narrative of black flourishing midst absolute self-determination and property ownership; the depiction of an inhabitant with an Afro, its isolation as island, and status as the only advanced city in Krypton's Old World hemisphere lend further credence to this interpretation.[20]

In fact, this was a relatively common portrayal of the Black Power movement among Caucasian publications and news outlets at this time.[21] It is difficult to assess how much this representation results from governmental provocation on the one hand and general Caucasian unease with any movement that actively rejected their input on the other.[22] Regardless, the Black Power movement was imagined to be violent, revolutionary, and black supremacist at its core. Superman's words to Lois before she reveals her Caucasian identity to Stevens, "If he still hates you with your blood in his veins, there may never be peace in this world!" echo standard and high-profile denunciations of black racism that identify it as a social evil no less significant than that of Caucasian prejudice. One might compare, for example, President Lyndon B. Johnson's 1966 statement, "we are not interested in Black Power and we're not interested in white power, but we are interested in American democratic power, with a small *d*."[23] Kanigher and others evidently found this rhetoric helpful for thinking about race relations. Both Superman and President Johnson took "Black Power" as semantically parallel with "white power"; they are movements that inspire the same anti–American values of division and unreason.

None of these points, though, cohered very well with the reality of Black Power. First, the word "power" in both the white power and Black Power ideologies denoted significantly different concepts.[24] To summarize, Stokely Carmichael developed the concept of Black Power to articulate an African American lifestyle that was not predicated upon the fear of Caucasian authority and also engendered self-esteem among blacks. This distinction — one accounting for the unspoken privileges that continue to benefit whites — receives no attention in the rhetoric espoused above. Second, and related, is that Black Power was a more diverse movement than Kanigher's story suggests. Dave Stevens was certainly not portrayed as militant, but his aggressive speech nonetheless locates him within a quasi-separatist sphere of activity to which most other black characters in the story implicitly adhere as well. Of course, key terms of the Black Power movement were subject to the same authenticity politics that plague all social formations, including the meaning of "Black Power" itself.[25] Finally, Black Power was nowhere near as popular as portrayed throughout "I Am Curious (Black)." A survey of African American males in Chicago in 1967 regarding the best spokesperson for the black community showed that 3 percent selected Stokely Carmichael, compared to 57 percent supporting Martin Luther King, Jr.[26] Despite the marginal support Black Power received in African American society, mass-media — such as paperback novels, television reports, and news magazine articles — picked up on the Caucasian obsession with its potential as a threat to existing social structures. In the wake of their city's 1967 race riot, one study found that 60 percent of Detroit whites surveyed believed Black Power advocated "violence, destruction, racism, and black domination." In reality, the elements of Black Power that proved most influential among African Americans were those that could be lived with the least disruption in their daily lives: clothing, musical, culinary, and other lifestyle preferences.

To be sure, black rights movements underwent large discursive and structural changes following the assassination of Martin Luther King, Jr. Organizations quickly became more vocal in their autonomy with respect to financing, relationship to the governmental establishment, ability to redefine "success" in black-centric terms, and political ambitions. But again, these changes were largely outcomes of the increased self-worth and "psychological well-being" among African Americans that exceeded the boundaries of the Black Power movement.[27] Most urban and suburban Caucasians (and thus Superman-family creative teams) felt these rhetorical shifts more than those concerning ways of life, resulting from the disproportion of attention the former received in various white-run media.

There is no doubt that Kanigher and his creative team self-identified as Caucasian allies in the struggle for black rights. But one sees evidence that they perceived their sympathy for African American struggles as unappreciated after the close of the Civil Rights era. One might attribute this portrayal to the influence of any number of real-world events. The numerous race riots in metropolitan New York — where Kanigher lived and DC held its offices — are particularly appealing candidates for the source of the story's "can't we all just get along?" sentiment.[28]

Thus, while presenting itself as an adamantly *non*-political message against racism in all its forms, "I Am Curious (Black)" vigorously contests the parameters of the Black Power movement on several fronts. This target, however, was misguided not only because Kanigher was poorly informed as to both the tenets and spread of Black Power, but also because this story reinforced dubious stereotypes of African Americans that ran counter to the well-meaning moral of the story. With the sole exception of the hospital staff, African Americans are uniformly portrayed as impoverished, urban-dwelling, angry individuals that are entirely uninterested in interaction with compassionate Caucasians.

The Legacy of "I Am Curious (Black)"

The story proved to be a large success; fan letters even hailed it as "the story of the year."[29] It comes as little surprise that it generated sequels in the pages of that same series. "Indian Death Charge!" was published in *Superman's Girl Friend Lois Lane #110* (May 1971), wherein Lois temporarily adopts a Pueblo baby after his mother dies.[30] Dave Stevens reappeared in the "I Am Curious (Black)" follow-up entitled "The Foe of 100 Faces" in *Superman's Girl Friend Lois Lane #114* (Sep. 1971)[31]; he became the first African American columnist for the *Daily Planet* in that issue. *Superman's Girl Friend Lois Lane #121* (April 1972) gave the titular character an African American roommate named Julie Spence.[32] Perhaps attempting to capitalize on the success of their precursor, the stories in which these characters appear often have a certain thematic kinship with "I Am Curious (Black)."

Some of these stories display a similar fixation upon radical minorities and their prejudice against Caucasian sympathizers. The splash page of "Indian Death Charge!" features a Pueblo man chastising Lois Lane: "Go back, Lois Lane! This is the red man's last charge to fight for his own land! ... We do ot want a white woman to fight our battle!" Lois objects, "You're wrong, Johnny Lone Eagle! Your fight is mine! No matter what the cost, I'm staying — till the end!" Upon public revelation of Lois' adoption of "Little Moon," two opposing groups protest outside of her apartment. The first are feminists whose message is unclear and the others — somewhat predictably — are Native Americans who protest her actions as another example of Caucasians seizing what is rightfully theirs. The American Indians' objection, despite its sincerity, is presumptuous insofar as they were unaware of the mother of the boy's dying request: that Lois raise Little Moon as her own. "The Foe of 100 Faces" also overlaps and gives the most obvious formulation of the lesson running throughout; Lois tells a black woman who rejects her aid at a protest: "Funny — I thought I was just another human being! If you don't believe that we're all sisters under the skin — then hate has already won the battle!" The woman challenging her immediately sees the error of her ways and welcomes Lois into her fold.[33]

Superman stories in other series treated race with greater tact in the early 1970s. Numerous black characters were introduced in the pages of these publications, even if they lasted only a few issues.[34] Even Dave Stevens and his girlfriend Tina Ames appeared in *Superman's Girl Friend Lois Lane* throughout the 1970s, eventually losing the highly-racialized characterization Kanigher initially provided them. In addition, allegorical tales of anti-racism occasionally appeared. "The Day Krypton Didn't Die!" in *Superman #251* (May 1972) detailed the dangers of prejudice based through a story occurring on Krypton[35]; a mute alien is attacked by Kryptonians for his strange appearance, only to find out that his bodily fluids react explosively with Krypton's soil. If the alien had been seriously injured, his wounds would have killed many. It takes several more years for African American characters to be thoroughly integrated into Superman's world to the point where their presence could pass without comment or recurrence to one or another stereotype, therein reflecting the increasingly settled repercussions of the Civil Rights movement.

"I Am Curious (Black)" and Vathlo Island presently sit as idiosyncratic attempts to redress a perceived racial divide in the United States. Though the former is particularly conspicuous in its sincerity, the ideological criticisms that Superman's creative teams put forth were ultimately marred in both their uncritical acceptance of the dominant (white) conception of African Americans as bigoted and their failure to reflect the opinions and worldview of real-world blacks. The resulting disproportion of emphasis on Black Power and black separatism is thus problematic by contemporary standards, in effect defining "racism" as a form of individual-attitudinal prejudice that could exist among members of all races; this understanding of racism did not consider the roles of societal power dynamics or the institutional disadvantages for ethnic minorities prevalent in America — the preferred interpretation today. Such portrayals, however, were ubiquitous among progressive Caucasians at the time and should be understood as reflecting cultural dispositions more than personal racism; any attempt to account for the niceties of these stories must therefore understand them within the stated policies and opinions of the U.S. government officials at the highest levels. This discourse functioned as an attempt to re-situate Caucasian allies into the development of black rights movements — movements with decreasing reliance on white assistance, as the African American body politic achieved greater social independence.

CHAPTER NOTES

1. However, "in a number of films [from 1950–1965] African Americans were cast in token roles to highlight the racial liberalism of directors, producers and fellow actors."

Verney, Kevern. *African Americans and US Popular Culture*. New York: Routledge, 2003. Print. P. 57.

2. Both Marvel's mutants in general and the Thing's attempts to "pass" in particular stand out as examples. On the tragic mulatto, see Sollors, Werner. *Neither Black Nor White Yet Both: Thematic Explorations of Interracial Literature*. (Cambridge, MA: Harvard UP, 1999), 220–245.

3. For a comprehensive history of African American characters in DC comic books until 1979, see Wells, John. "The Racial Justice Experience: Diversity in the DC Universe: 1961–1979," *Fanzing* 32 (2001): Web. [*http://www.fanzing.com/mag/fanzing32/feature1.shtml*].

4. O'Neil, Dennis (w), and Neil Adams (a). "Beware My Power!" *Green Lantern Vol. 2 #87 (Dec.* 1971). New York: DC Comics. The issue's Green Arrow backup story centers on a race riot in Star City; Broome, John (w), and Gil Kane (a). "What Can One Man Do?" *Green Lantern Vol. 2 #87* (Dec. 1971). New York: DC Comics.

5. Throughout this essay, it is assumed the relationship of an individual to their culture is one that social theorist Pierre Bourdieu terms *habitus*, which provides a useful model for an individual's internalization of their social world and the pre-conscious dispositions to which this leads. For a concise discussion of the concept, see Swartz, David. *Culture and Power: The Sociology of Pierre Bourdieu*. (Chicago: University of Chicago Press, 1997), 95–142. This concentration on the role of social context in the formation of literature will hopefully avoid an accusatory tone and insinuations of personal racism by the creative teams involved in the Superman stories discussed below.

6. O'Neal, Dennis (w), and Curt Swan (a). "How to Tame a Wild Volcano!" *Superman #234* (Feb. 1971). New York: DC Comics.

7. The natives of "Mount Boki," a fictional island in the Pacific Ocean, also appear to have Caucasian features in the lead story, despite an olive skin tone.

8. Binder, Otto (w), and Wayne Boring (a). *Superman #239* (July 1971). New York: DC Comics.

9. Ibid.

10. Vathlo Island proved to be of little mythological import for subsequent Superman tales. Its only other notable occurrence before the *Crisis on Infinite Earths* was a throwaway reference in Moore, Alan (w), and Dave Gibbons (a). "For the Man Who Has Everything." *Superman Annual #11,* (1985). New York: DC Comics.

11. Quoted in Brady, Matt. "Supermen of Color: The Non-White Kryptonians." *Newsarama* 6 Jan 2009. [*http://www.newsarama.com/comics/010906-Supermen-Color.html*]. Emphasis original.

12. E.g., Berstein, Robert (w), and Kurt Schaffenberger (a). "The Cry-Baby of Metropolis." *Superman's Girl Friend Lois Lane #10* (July 1959). New York: DC Comics; Dorfman, Leo (w), and Kurt Schaffenberger (a). "The Reptile Girl of Metropolis!" *Superman's Girl Friend Lois Lane #61* (Nov. 1965). New York: DC Comics.

13. Kanigher, Robert (w), and Ross Andru (a). "I Am Curious (Black)." *Superman's Girl Friend Lois Lane #106* (Nov. 1970). New York: DC Comics.

14. Ibid.

15. Griffin, John Howard. *Black Like Me*. (New York: Houghton Mifflin, 1961). It was developed into a feature film soon after; *Black Like Me*. Dir. Carl Lerner. Perf. James Whitmore. Rhino/WEA, 1964. Film.

16. Numerous other forms of entertainment used Griffin's book as a template, see Sollors 493–495. The title of the Lois Lane story, "I Am Curious (Black)," modifies that of the 1967 art-house film *I Am Curious (Yellow)*, which gained some notoriety for its X rating. The Lois Lane story has no obvious literary connections to this film; Wells states that the late Kanigher never even watched it.

17. Browder, Laura. *Slippery Characters: Ethnic Impersonators and American Identities.* (Chapel Hill: University of North Carolina Press), 213.

18. Ironically, much of this support resulted from Griffin's authority as a white man to the horrors of racism. Browder 213–215.

19. Wilmore, Gayraud S. *Black Religion and Black Radicalism: An Interpretation of the Religious History of African Americans.* 3rd ed. (Maryknoll, NY: Orbis, 1998), 224.

20. On the Afro as symbol of Black pride in the late 1960s, see Byrd, Ayana D., and Lori L. Tharps. *Hair Story: Untangling the Roots of Black Hair in America.* (New York: St. Martin's Press, 2001), 50–71.

21. Van Deburg, William L. *New Day in Babylon: The Black Power Movement and American Culture, 1965–1975.* Chicago: University of Chicago Press, 1992. Print. Pp. 11–28. Cf. Haines, Herbert H. *Black Radicals and the Civil Rights Mainstream, 1954–1970.* (Knoxville: University of Tennessee Press, 1988), 46–74.

22. See Hoover, J. Edgar. "Memorandum to Special Agent in Charge," in *Modern Black Nationalism: From Marcus Garvey to Louis Farrakhan.* Ed. William L. Van Deburg. (New York: New York University Press, 1997), 133–135. The directive was issued in 1967: "The purpose of this new counterintelligence endeavor is to expose, disrupt, misdirect, discredit, or otherwise neutralize the activities of black nationalist, hate-type organizations and groupings, their leadership, spokesmen, membership, and supporters, and to counter their propensity for violence and civil disorder."

23. Ogbar, Jeffrey O. G. *Black Power: Radical Politics and African American Identity.* Reconfiguring American Political History. (Baltimore: Johns Hopkins UP, 2004), 60–67.

24. To be sure, Stokely Carmichael intended the language of "Black Power" to be provocative. "Now we are now engaged in a psychological struggle in this country, and that is whether or not black people will have the right to use the words they want to use without white people giving their sanction to it; and that we maintain, whether they like it or not, we gonna use the word 'Black Power'—and let them address themselves to that; but that we are not going to wait for white people to sanction Black Power." Carmichael, Stokely. *Black Power.* Berkley, CA, 29 October 1966. Keynote Address.

25. McCartney, John T. *Black Power Ideologies: An Essay in African-American Political Thought.* (Philadelphia: Temple University Press, 1992), 111–132.

26. Van Deburg, 16–19. He cites Aberbach, Joel D., and Jack L. Walker. "The Meanings of Black Power: A Comparison of White and Black Interpretations of a Political Slogan." *American Political Science Review* 64 (1970): 367–388.

27. Van Deburg, 292–308.

28. Eds. Rucker, Walter, and James Nathaniel Upton. *Encyclopedia of American Race Riots.* Greenwood Milestones in African American History. 2 vols. (Westport, CT: Greenwood, 2007). This work lists eight major race riots in or near New York City between 1965 and 1971; this does not include the numerous ones resulting from the assassination of Martin Luther King, Jr.

29. Bridwell, E. Nelson. "Letters to Lois and Rose." *Superman's Girl Friend Lois Lane #110 (May 1971).* New York: DC Comics.

30. Kanigher, Robert (w), and Werner Roth (a). "Indian Death Charge!" *Superman's Girlfriend, Lois Lane #110* (May 1971). New York: DC Comics.

31. Kanigher, Robert (w), and Werner Roth (a). "The Foe of 100 Faces." *Superman's Girlfriend, Lois Lane #114* (Sep. 1971). New York: DC Comics.

32. Bates, Carey (w), and Werner Roth (a). "Everything You Wanted to Know About Lois Lane." *Superman's Girl Friend Lois Lane #121* (April 1972). New York: DC Comics.

33. Kanigher, Robert (w), and Werner Roth (a). "Indian Death Charge!" *Superman's Girlfriend, Lois Lane #110* (May 1971). New York: DC Comics.

34. Wells, John. Excluding backups in Superman titles that did not relate to the Super-

man family, Wells lists Johnny Dee and Roxie Thompson in Sekowsky, Mike (w/a). "Johnny Dee — ~~Hero~~ Bum!" *Adventure Comics #399* (Nov. 1970). New York: DC Comics; Jonathan Slaughter and Frank Jackson in Wein, Len (w), and Curt Swan (a). "Danger — Monster at Work!" *Superman #246* (Dec. 1971). New York: National Periodical Publications , DC Comics; Jim Corrigan in Albano, John (w), and José Delbo (a). "The Unseen Enemy!" *Superman's Pal Jimmy Olsen #149* (May 1972). New York: National Periodical Publications, DC Comics; Terry Blake in Bates, Cary (w), and Art Saaf (a). "The Trail of the Madman!" *Supergirl #1* (Nov. 1972). New York: DC Comics.

35. Maggin, Elliot S. (w), and Ruch Buckler (a). "The Day Krypton Didn't Die!" *Superman #251* (May 1972). New York: DC Comics.

BIBLIOGRAPHY

Aberbach, Joel D., and Jack L. Walker. "The Meanings of Black Power: A Comparison of White and Black Interpretations of a Political Slogan." *American Political Science Review* 64 (1970): 367–388.

Bates, Carey (w), and Werner Roth (a). "Everything You Wanted to Know About Lois Lane." *Superman's Girl Friend Lois Lane #121* (April 1972). New York: DC Comics.

Berstein, Robert (w), and Kurt Schaffenberger (a). "The Cry-Baby of Metropolis." *Superman's Girl Friend Lois Lane #10* (July 1959). New York: DC Comics.

Binder, Otto (w), and Wayne Boring (a). *Superman #239* (July 1971). New York: DC Comics.

Black Like Me. Dir. Carl Lerner. Perf. James Whitmore. Rhino/WEA. Film, 1964.

Brady, Matt. "Supermen of Color: The Non-White Kryptonians." *Newsarama*, 6 Jan. 2009.

Bridwell, E. Nelson. "Letters to Lois and Rose." *Superman's Girl Friend Lois Lane #110* (May 1971). New York: DC Comics.

Browder, Laura. *Slippery Characters: Ethnic Impersonators and American Identities.* Chapel Hill: University of North Carolina Press.

Broome, John (w), and Gil Kane (a). "What Can One Man Do?" *Green Lantern Vol. 2 #87* (Dec. 1971). New York: DC Comics.

Byrd, Ayana D., and Lori L. Tharps. *Hair Story: Untangling the Roots of Black Hair in America.* New York: St. Martin's Press, 2001.

Carmichael, Stokely. *Black Power.* Berkley, CA, Keynote Address. 29 October 1966.

Dorfman, Leo (w), and Kurt Schaffenberger (a). "The Reptile Girl of Metropolis!" *Superman's Girl Friend Lois Lane #61* (Nov. 1965). New York: DC Comics.

Griffin, John Howard. *Black Like Me.* New York: Houghton Mifflin, 1961.

Haines, Herbert H. *Black Radicals and the Civil Rights Mainstream, 1954–1970.* Knoxville: University of Tennessee Press, 1988.

Hoover, J. Edgar. "Memorandum to Special Agent in Charge." In William L. Van Deburg, ed., *Modern Black Nationalism: From Marcus Garvey to Louis Farrakhan.* New York: New York University Press, 1997.

Kanigher, Robert (w), and Ross Andru (a). "I Am Curious (Black)." *Superman's Girl Friend Lois Lane #106* (Nov. 1970). New York: DC Comics.

Kanigher, Robert (w), and Werner Roth (a). "The Foe of 100 Faces." *Superman's Girlfriend, Lois Lane #114* (Sep. 1971). New York: DC Comics.

_____. "Indian Death Charge!" *Superman's Girlfriend, Lois Lane #110* (May 1971). New York: DC Comics.

Maggin, Elliot S. (w), and Ruch Buckler (a). "The Day Krypton Didn't Die!" *Superman #251* (May 1972). New York: DC Comics.

McCartney, John T. *Black Power Ideologies: An Essay in African-American Political Thought.* Philadelphia: Temple University Press, 1992.

Moore, Alan (w), and Dave Gibbons (a). "For the Man Who Has Everything." *Superman Annual #11,* (1985). New York: DC Comics.

Ogbar, Jeffrey O. G. *Black Power: Radical Politics and African American Identity.* Baltimore: Johns Hopkins UP, 2004.

O'Neil, Dennis (w), and Neil Adams (a). "Beware My Power!" *Green Lantern Vol. 2 #87* (Dec. 1971). New York: DC Comics.

O'Neil, Dennis (w), and Curt Swan (a). "How to Tame a Wild Volcano!" *Superman #234* (Feb. 1971). New York: DC Comics.

Rucker, Walter, and James Nathaniel Upton, Eds. *Encyclopedia of American Race Riots.* Greenwood Milestones in African American History. 2 vols. Westport, CT: Greenwood, 2007.

Sollors, Werner. *Neither Black Nor White Yet Both: Thematic Explorations of Interracial Literature.* Cambridge, MA: Harvard University Press, 1999.

Swartz, David. *Culture and Power: The Sociology of Pierre Bourdieu.* Chicago: University of Chicago Press, 1997.

Van Deburg, William L. *New Day in Babylon: The Black Power Movement and American Culture, 1965–1975.* Chicago: University of Chicago Press, 1992.

Verney, Kevern. *African Americans and U.S. Popular Culture.* New York: Routledge, 2003.

Wells, John. "The Racial Justice Experience: Diversity in the DC Universe: 1961–1979." *Fanzing* 32 (2001).

Wilmore, Gayraud S. *Black Religion and Black Radicalism: An Interpretation of the Religious History of African Americans.* 3d. ed. Maryknoll, NY: Orbis, 1998.

Red, White and Bruised

The Vietnam War and the Weakening of Superman

Jason M. LaTouche

What does it mean to be a superpower? In 1971, the United States was confronting the physical and moral limitations of being a superpower as it struggled to accept the fact that it would not win the war it had been fighting in Vietnam since the early 1960s. The intense confrontation in the United States between supporters and protestors of the Vietnam War over the nature and use of power and the specific ways the United States' had used its power in Vietnam called into question the comforting, if simplistic, viewpoint of the United States' role as an unambiguously benevolent superpower.

These debates about the nature of power spilled onto the pages of the *Superman* comic book series in 1971 through a ten issue long storyline in which Superman reaches a new ultimate level of power before eventually watching helplessly as all his superpowers are slowly drained away. Over the course of this transition, Superman's use of power and his role as a force for good is challenged by his opponents, his previously adoring general public, and ultimately himself. Superman's struggle to find his place in a world where his power cannot always be trusted to solve problems and where people will not always accept that he will help them echoes the struggle within the United States to accept how its military and political failures in Vietnam were changing the relationship of the United States with the world and with itself.

Striding the World Like a Colossus

By the dawn of the 1970s Superman had become a near-omnipotent demi-god. A legacy of over thirty years of writers' embellishments, Superman's immense powers left him striding the Earth unchallenged in his physical supremacy. With pressure to continually create new levels of excitement and drama, over the years Superman's numerous writers and editors had intentionally and unintentionally augmented Superman's abilities in increasingly fantastical ways. Indeed, the Superman of 1970 had evolved to be quick enough to effortlessly soar across galaxies, strong enough to move planets, and invulnerable enough to fly through the heart of a star.

Along with his tremendous growth in powers, the effects of the 1954 Comics Code Authority, which severely limited writers' abilities to deal with mature issues and narrative ambiguity, had worked to strip away any lingering traces of character weakness from Superman.[1] After more than fifteen years of stories under the aegis of the moral censorship of the Comics Code Authority, Superman had grown into a powerful representation of moral certitude, developing into the literal embodiment of the "Truth, Justice, and the American Way" slogan of the 1950's Superman television series. Indeed, the Superman of this era was a veritable Cold War ambassador for democracy. Superman always made the right choices, always used his power to champion the weak, and was hailed by the regular people in his stories as a near-savior figure.

All this was about to change in 1971. With the retirement of Superman's long term editor, Mort Weisinger, a radical new perspective was brought to the character for the first time in decades. In the pages of *Superman*, under the direction of editor Julius Schwartz writer Dennis (Denny) O'Neil set out to create a storyline for Superman that would radically transform the character and signal a new engagement with the modern world.

Superman Unbound

The first issue of O'Neil's run on *Superman*, "Superman Breaks Loose" *Superman #233* (Jan. 1971), begins with Superman trying to stop a pile of Kryptonite being used in an energy experiment from exploding. He does not succeed. However, upon awakening from the blast Superman is surprised to discover that all of the Kryptonite on the planet has been rendered inert. What had once been a deadly poison to him, now is no threat at all. This point is emphasized later in the story when a saboteur brandishes a piece of Kryptonite to keep Superman at bay and Superman walks up, grabs the green rock, and proceeds to eat it, commenting, "Looks good! Mind if I try some? Mmmm, not bad! A trifle stale and it could use a bit of salt but all in all, a nice little snack!"[2]

Superman feels emboldened by the removal of his one weakness. However, others are less sanguine. Morgan Edge, the owner of a media empire and Clark Kent's new boss, responds to a challenge to his critique of the removal of Kryptonite from the world by stating that what he has against Superman is "the same thing I'd have against anyone supremely powerful. I don't trust anyone who can't be stopped! A wise man once said that 'power corrupts and absolute power corrupts absolutely!' How do we know Superman will be an exception?"[3] Superman contemplates Edge's comments later as he captures some saboteurs, thinking, "I've never felt so confident, knowing there's absolutely nothing that can harm me! Morgan Edge was wrong! Power isn't corrupting. It's freeing me to do unlimited good!"[4] In this, we see the classical Superman: the confident, morally sure, and, ultimately, benign hero.

In these early issues of the storyline, Superman is emboldened by his new freedom from weakness. As he streaks from problem to problem successfully dispatching non-super powered crooks and terrorists, Superman basks in the public's adulation. He is the people's hero, even noting as he hands over to the police a group of terrorists who had attempted to blow up an arena that "Everyone in the arena came out to watch the fun!"[5]

However, in addition to rendering Kryptonite inert, the explosion had the less beneficial effect of creating an extra-dimensional being, the Quarrmer, a being that would serve as a parasite on Superman's powers. Over the next several issues of the storyline Superman's powers would diminish and his confidence in himself, as well as the general public's confidence in him, would fade.

In *Superman #238* (June 1971) Superman finds himself weakened to the point of uncertainty. The story begins with him changing to Superman and being only able to jump from a window rather than flying up into the air because his powers are at such a low ebb. He then confronts a group of terrorists. However, in his weakened state he is nervous about the effectiveness of his super powers. As a result, he is tentative and hesitates before finally engaging with and dispatching the terrorists. Lois Lane notices this and questions him about it. Superman thinks, "How can I tell her that I wasn't sure of myself? That I was afraid even my remaining powers would fail!"[6]

His failure to disclose his weakness ultimately results in the failure of the public to trust him. In *Superman #240* (Aug. 1971) Superman's powers have weakened so far he is unable to keep a building from collapsing. Both the general public and Superman seize upon this failure. The press trumpets, "Superman Fails," people on the street mock him, and Superman questions why he does what he does, "I've a right to bitterness. No man has a better right! I've denied myself the comforts of home, family, to continue helping these ingrates! I thought they admired me for myself! I've lived in a fool's paradise!"[7] However, upon hearing of a situation that calls for his help, Superman remembers who he is, declaring, "No, no! I can't change my whole personality, my very identity! Ever since I can remember, I've been fighting crime — and I've got to be what I am!"[8] By the end of the story Superman is completely without super powers and has to resort to physically punching out the criminals he is facing. When the fight is over, Superman concludes, "In every important way, this is my greatest victory! I don't know whether I'll ever regain my powers, and somehow, I'm not sure I care!"[9] Indeed, Superman struggles to define whether or not the superhero role is worth the effort it causes him personally. By *Superman #241* (Aug. 1971) he notes that by remaining mortal as he currently is he is "without the responsibilities, the loneliness of Superman!"[10]

Unfortunately, Superman is now subject to being injured and a fight has left him with a head wound. This head wound has created brain damage which unleashes Superman's id. After having his super powers restored by I-Ching, a Chinese mystic, Superman flies around the city dispatching all manner of crimes declaring, "No crime is too small for Superman's attention!"[11] His focus on his righteousness blinds him to the consequences of his actions, creating all manner of inconveniences for the people he is supposed to be taking care of. He takes a person speeding in their car and flies them, car and all, onto the observation deck of a skyscraper. He captures a purse snatcher by building a jail around him in the middle of a crowded city road.

When I-Ching tries to explain to Superman that he is acting out of control because of his brain damage, Superman punches a wall, railing, "You're just jealous because you're weak ... like everyone else!"[12] Fleeing I-Ching, Superman confronts a gigantic Oriental War-Demon statue that has been animated by the spirit of another being from the Quarrmer's home dimension. The Oriental War-Demon is being controlled and directed by two hoodlums who are excited to see the War-Demon drain away the rest of Superman's power. Seizing upon the opportunity of fighting a mortal Superman, the two hoodlums beat Superman unconscious and then set off on a rampage with the War-Demon.

However, the War-Demon quickly turns upon the hoodlums declaring, "You say my mission is to destroy? You say I am all-powerful? Then I shall not obey you! No, I shall hurt!"[13] As he tosses the broken bodies of the hoodlums aside, the evil of the War-Demon is reinforced by a text panel that is drawn and lettered like a parchment scroll that quotes the Biblical verse Ecclesiastes 8:8, "...neither shall wickedness deliver those that are given it."[14]

Teaming up with the Quarrmer, Superman defeats the Oriental War-Demon only to end up in conflict with the Quarrmer who is fighting to maintain his hold on the power he has taken from Superman. The evenly matched combatants fight a devastating battle that triggers floods, earthquakes, volcanic eruptions, and other disasters all across the Earth. As they wage their senseless battle Superman realizes, "We could go on all year bashing away, accomplishing nothing! Sheer strength won't win. I'll need cunning! I'm not used to using my brains. In any struggle strength has generally been enough!"[15] Ultimately, Superman takes notice of the consequences of the battle and sees that they have destroyed the Earth, leaving it without a sign of life anywhere. Breaking down in tears, Superman pleads, "Oh Dear Lord! What have we done? For our own selfish ends, we've destroyed everything!"[16]

At this point I-Ching reveals that he has put Superman and Quarrmer into a trance so that they could see the cataclysmic outcome if they should use their awesome powers to fight against each other. As a result of this incredible experience Superman decides to let the Quarrmer permanently keep a third of his power as he returns to his inter-dimensional home world. Refusing I-Ching's offer to restore his powers Superman vehemently declares, "No! I've seen the dangers [of] having too much power.... I am human — I can make mistakes! I don't want or need more!"[17]

So by the end of this final issue of the storyline, Superman is a weaker and more humbled character. He has learned that having power does not always mean one should use it, that acting for 'moral' reasons does not always lead to moral outcomes, that force must be tempered with thought and introspection, and that having too much power is a dangerous thing. These were all lessons that the United States was grappling with as a result of the Vietnam War.

Vietnam and Superman

By 1971 the United States was well on its way to realizing that the Vietnam War would not end in a military and political success for the United States. President Nixon and his administration had already accepted that the war could not be won in any traditional sense and had begun to withdraw U.S. troops from Vietnam as the administration pursued a policy of Vietnamization that had the ultimate goal of leaving the South Vietnamese army in charge of administering the war.[18]

To many this turn of events was seen as the unfortunate result of the United States failing to fully unleash its powers for good. As President Nixon had said in a nationally televised address on April 20, 1970, "If, when the chips are down, the world's most powerful nation, the United States of America, acts like a pitiful, helpless giant, the forces of totalitarianism and anarchy will threaten free nations and free institutions throughout the world."[19] In other words, much like Superman in the 1970s, the United States was the preeminent force for good and its position as the most powerful nation in the world was a blessing as it gave the United States the freedom to unleash its beneficence upon the world. Hence, the people of the United States should exult in their country's ability to use its power to spread virtue across the globe.

So what would keep this from happening? In an earlier nationally televised address on November 3, 1969 Nixon made it clear where the danger lay, stating, "North Vietnam cannot defeat or humiliate the United States. Only Americans can do that." In other words, danger did not lie in the United States' use of its immense power but rather in the threat of its power being limited by those within its borders who would question its virtue.

Building on this idea, Nixon's Vice President, Spiro Agnew, called those within the United States who would oppose the United States use of its power in Vietnam and elsewhere, "nattering nabobs of negativism" and "prophets of doom" who revel in the United States' failures and who would "double cross" our allies while "preen[ing] in blatant obsequiousness" before the United States' enemies.[20] So not only were those who opposed the full use of the United States' power undermining the United States' good intentions they were in fact directly working for the benefit of the enemy.

In setting up his radical overhaul of Superman, O'Neil initially parallels these arguments. Superman loses his weakness to Kryptonite and revels in the fact that he is now emboldened to use his power to its fullest ability — to the great benefit of mankind. The removal of restraints is not a danger but a blessing because of his virtuous power.

Even Agnew's critique of corruption from within is echoed in O'Neil's storyline. The Nixon Administration attacked the news media as having biases that undermine the efforts of the United States to do good in the world.[21] The primary initial critic of Superman's new found power, the media mogul Morgan Edge, is revealed to be secretly working for a galactic despot who plans on enslaving the Earth. Morgan Edge's use of his media empire to pillory and raise alarm over Superman's newfound power echoes the Nixon administration's accusations of the media's bias.

Hence O'Neil's first introduction of the Superman character seemingly places the character in alignment with the era's more conservative viewpoint about the role of the United States in using its powers as a force for good in the world. However, this position is ultimately a smokescreen. In this initial introduction of the new Superman, O'Neil is reinforcing the classical viewpoint of the virtues of superpowers as a force for good in the right hands only to heighten the dramatic tension as he subsequently subverts this framework in later issues.

As Superman loses his power, he does not respond by being forthright about his limitations. Instead he attempts to hide his weaknesses. These actions not only undermine public confidence in Superman but they create dangerous consequences for those he is supposed to be protecting. These problems are only magnified when Superman suffers a brain injury and his 'true' nature is revealed. He flies around using his power arbitrarily, using force disproportionate to the situations he is involved in, lashing out at his allies for being weak, and ultimately proving to be a bigger danger than the problems he was attempting to solve.

Again the echoes to Vietnam War era politics come through quite clearly. By the end of the 1960s and early 1970s public opinion to the war in Vietnam was quickly turning. Gallup public opinion polls show that the percentage of people who thought sending troops to fight in Vietnam was not a mistake had fallen from 61 percent in August of 1965 to only 28 percent as of May 1971.[22] In other words, by the time of O'Neil's refashioning of Superman more than two-thirds of Americans believed it was a mistake for the United States to send troops to Vietnam. This decline in support had accelerated in the two years previous to O'Neil's *Superman* storyline, partly as a result of a series of revelations about how the United States was waging the war in Vietnam.

In late 1969, the United States' public learned about the March 1968 My Lai massacre in which U.S. soldiers entered into the village of My Lai and proceeded to execute unarmed women, children, and elderly civilians. By the time of Lieutenant William Calley's conviction for murder in the My Lai Massacre on March 29, 1971, a Harris public opinion poll revealed that the vast majority of Americans, 77 percent of those surveyed, did not believe that Lieutenant Calley was a rogue villain but rather believed that Calley was following orders from higher ups.[23]

This willingness to believe that the moral failings of the war were a more general institutional problem rather than the problem of a few bad individuals had been growing as more and more stories about how the government had deceived the public about the war effort filtered out into the mass media. These disparate stories of deception were brought into stark relief in 1971 when Daniel Ellsberg leaked a study of the war that had been commissioned by Secretary of Defense Robert S. McNamara in 1967. In what came to be known as the Pentagon Papers, it was revealed that successive Presidential administrations had been deliberately misleading the public about the goals of the war and the means by which the war was being prosecuted.

Most starkly, the papers revealed that as early as 1965, only one year after Congress passed the Gulf of Tonkin Resolution that authorized the President to use conventional forces in South Asia, John T. McNaughton, assistant secretary of defense for international security affairs, had drafted a "Plan for Action for Vietnam" which listed the goals of the war as being 70 percent "to avoid a humiliating defeat," 20 percent "to keep [South Vietnam] ... territory from Chinese hands," and only 10 percent "to permit the people of [South

Vietnam] to enjoy a better, freer way of life."[24] The longer the Vietnam War went on the more revelations there were about the disconnection between the rhetoric of the United States being engaged in a morally virtuous use of force to spread peace and the revealed actions of the war in which the United States was engaged. The awareness of this disconnection began within the protestor community in the mid–1960s but by the early 1970s it was becoming a much more commonly held attitude that was damaging public sentiment towards the war and towards the United States' use of its power.

This tension about deception and trust is echoed in O'Neil's Superman. In "Planet of the Angels" *Superman #236* (April 1971), Superman is pulled through a space warp and ends up on a planet populated with a group of pitchfork carrying devils surrounded by fire. Fleeing, Superman discovers three white robed, winged angels, Gabriel, Raphael, and Michael. The angels tell Superman that he is in Heaven and that he must hurry and go break down a gate separating the angels from the devils so that the angels may slay the doomed devils and restore Heaven to its full virtue. Superman rushes to do their bidding thinking "I'm being carried along on a wave of events I don't understand."[25] By the end of the story Superman discovers that the devils are good and the angels are evil. One of the devils tells him that "evil comes in many guises, some of these are even beautiful" which Superman notes as being "worth remembering!"[26]

This can be read as an almost direct commentary on the growing conflict over trust and power that had developed between the government of the United States and the general public in regards to the Vietnam War. In this metaphoric story, O'Neil raises the central question of who one can trust, warning that even those who appear to have virtuous desires may be hiding more harmful intentions.

These parallels between O'Neil's Superman and the political environment of the Vietnam War within the United States are not accidental. While O'Neil has never stated a direct intention that he used these stories to fashion an anti-war commentary he had in fact written such explicit commentary in many previous comic book stories. Indeed, in the year prior to his refashioning of Superman, O'Neil had similarly overhauled DC Comics' Green Lantern character. In that storyline, O'Neil had the Green Lantern character have a crisis of conscience when explicitly confronted with his failure to address such social problems as urban unrest, racial prejudice, poverty, drug use, and political and economic corruption. With a series of stories stretching over a year O'Neil had the character abandon the superhero role to climb in a pickup truck and travel around the country on a vision quest to learn what it means to be a man and a hero by tackling the real problems of real people.

So O'Neil came to the *Superman* series with a recent history of seeing comic books as a medium in which social commentary could be central to the narrative. In fact, O'Neil has noted that at the time he viewed his role as a comic book writer as being that of a journalist.[27] Hence, it is not accidental that during the fractious political era of the Vietnam War that the social issues surrounding the war would find their way into a storyline emphasizing the dangers of power. Indeed, O'Neil has readily described himself as being at the time a "hippie" and a "peacenik" who "walked on the marches to the Pentagon" and was "hanging out with all the radicals."[28]

Given his political orientation it is not a surprise that in ten months he took Superman from being an inviolate force for good whose incredible powers are seen as an unambiguously beneficial source of virtue for the world to a character whose motivations and use of power is doubted not only by the general public but by himself as well. As if to hammer home the Vietnam connection, O'Neil resolves the storyline by having Superman fight an Oriental War-Demon possessed of Superman's leeched power and upon achieving what he believes to be victory only discovers that he is now engaged in a far greater conflict. This conflict, as I-Ching reveals, can only lead to the total obliteration of the world. Here we see the logical conclusion of superpower conflict in the real world of the Vietnam era. Vietnam is a proxy for the larger war between the United States and the Soviet Union, a war that has the possibility of escalating into a nuclear conflagration that would devastate the entire Earth.

As Superman sees the result of such a conflict, he realizes the moral danger and threat of having so much power and does the morally virtuous thing, freely giving away some of his power, not trusting that even he, a man driven by virtuous ends, could be trusted with it. In this Superman becomes a cautionary tale about power that would resonate powerfully for a public enmeshed in Cold War nuclear fears and Vietnam War disillusionment.

Too Much Reality

While it was Schwartz and O'Neil's intent that this version of Superman continue onward as the permanent characterization of the superhero, this interpretation of the Man of Steel did not to last for long. O'Neil only scripted four of the next thirteen issues of *Superman* before leaving the series entirely due to a "vague sense of discomfort, of not fitting with the assignment somehow."[29] This is not surprising. For Superman was an emblem of a particular ideological viewpoint and the changes O'Neil had wrought were challenging this ideology at a fundamental level in much the same way the Vietnam War was forcing Americans to re-examine their relationship with their country and their country's relationship with the wider world.

Given that the audience of Superman comic books was largely comprised of children and that its creators were largely long-term fans and readers of the classic Superman stories themselves, perhaps sustaining the larger Vietnam War era social concerns about power and morality was too much to ask for in the Superman character. As sales declined, DC management quickly put pressure on Schwartz to return to the pre–1971 type of story Mort Weisinger had been doing.[30]

As a result, almost immediately after the end of O'Neil's initial storyline other editors and writers began to restore Superman to his previous role as an unimpeachable moral arbiter and galactic-scale super powered hero. Indeed, because the multiple Superman comic book series were divided among different editors and writers, even while O'Neil was radically transforming Superman in the *Superman* comic book series he remained much more traditional in the other Superman comic book lines.

In spite of this subsequent reversal, the Superman of 1971 nevertheless remains as a legacy to inform future generations about the nature of power and morality. For over the course of a year, Dennis O'Neil created a unique Superman. Superman, the hero who had always been authority's man, the hero who epitomized Mom, apple pie, and baseball, for a brief window of time found himself crossing over to the other side, empathizing with the radicals and the peaceniks of the Vietnam War era as he discovered that the best Superman is one that is less super.

CHAPTER NOTES

1. Wright, Bradford W. *Comic Book Nation: The Transformation of Youth Culture in America.* (Baltimore: Johns Hopkins University Press, 2001), 173.

2. O'Neil, Denny (w), and Curt Swan (a). "Superman Breaks Loose." *Superman #233* (Jan. 1971). New York: DC Comics, 8.

3. Ibid., 5.

4. Ibid., 10.

5. O'Neil, Denny (w), and Curt Swan (a). "Sinister Scream of the Devil's Harp." *Superman #235* (March 1971). New York: DC Comics, 4.

6. O'Neil, Denny (w), and Curt Swan (a). "Menace at 1000 Degrees!" *Superman #238* (June 1971). New York: DC Comics, 15.

7. O'Neil, Denny (w), and Curt Swan (a). "To Save a Superman." *Superman #240* (July 1971). New York: DC Comics, 6.

8. Ibid., 7.

9. Ibid., 15.

10. O'Neil, Denny (w), and Curt Swan (a). "The Shape of Fear." *Superman #241* (Aug. 1971). New York: DC Comics, 2.

11. Ibid., 11.

12. Ibid., 12.

13. O'Neil, Denny (w), and Curt Swan (a). "The Ultimate Battle." *Superman #242* (Sep. 1971). New York: DC Comics, 11.

14. Ibid., 11.

15. Ibid., 18.
16. Ibid., 21.
17. Ibid., 22.
18. Simon, Dennis M. "The War in Vietnam 1969–1973." August, 2002. Accessed at: http://faculty.smu.edu/dsimon/Change-Viet4.html on January 13, 2010.
19. Ibid.
20. "Agnew Calls Demos 'Nattering Nabobs' Among Other Things." *Spartanburg Herald-Journal* (Sep. 12, 1970). Spartanburg, S.C.: Pg. A-1.
21. "On the National Media." Speech delivered by Vice-President Spiro Agnew on November 13, 1969 in Des Moines, IA. Accessed at: *http://faculty.smu.edu/dsimon/Change-Agnew.html* on February 15, 2010.
22. Lunch, William L., and Peter W. Sperlich. 1979. "American Public Opinion and the War in Vietnam." *The Western Political Quarterly*: 32:1. Pgs. 21–44.
23. Louis Harris and Associates Poll. April 1971. Accessed at: *http://law2.umkc.edu/faculty/projects/ftrials/mylai/SurveyResults.html* on February 1, 2011.
24. Correll, John T. February 2007. "The Pentagon Papers." *Airforce Magazine*. Accessed at: http://www.airforce-magazine.com/MagazineArchive/Pages/2007/February%202007/0207pentagon.aspx on January 6, 2010.
25. O'Neil, Denny (w), and Curt Swan (a). "Planet of the Angels" Superman *#236* (April 1971). New York: DC Comics, 6.
26. Ibid., 15.
27. Daniels, Les. *Superman: The Complete History.* (San Francisco: Chronicle Books, 1998), 133.
28. Irving, Christopher. April 27, 2009. "The Political Evolution of Denny O'Neil." *GraphicNYC*. Accessed at: http://graphicnyc.blogspot.com/2009/04/political-evolution-of-denny-oneil.html on February 2, 2010.
29. O'Neil, Dennis. "Afterword." in *Superman: Kyrptonite Nevermore.* New York: DC Comics, 2008.
30. Daniels, Les, 135–139.

BIBLIOGRAPHY

Agnew, Spiro. "On the National Media." November 13, 1969. Accessed at: *http://faculty.smu.edu/dsimon/Change-Agnew.html* on 15 February, 2010.
"Agnew Calls Demos 'Nattering Nabobs' Among Other Things." *Spartanburg Herald-Journal,* Sep. 12, 1970. A-1.
Daniels, Les. *Superman: The Complete History.* San Francisco: Chronicle Books, 1998.
Correll, John T. February 2007. "The Pentagon Papers." *Airforce Magazine.* Accessed at: http://www.airforcemagazine.com/MagazineArchive/Pages/2007/February%202007/0207pentagon.aspx on January 6, 2010.
Irving, Christopher. April 27, 2009. "The Political Evolution of Denny O'Neil." *Graphic NYC.* Accessed at: http://graphicnyc.blogspot.com/2009/04/political-evolution-of-denny-oneil.html on February 2, 2010.
Louis Harris and Associates Poll. April 1971. Accessed at: *http://law2.umkc.edu/faculty/projects/ftrials/mylai/SurveyResults.html* on February 1, 2011.
Lunch, William L., and Peter W. Sperlich. "American Public Opinion and the War in Vietnam." *The Western Political Quarterly*: 32:1 (1979): 21–44.
O'Neil, Dennis. "Afterword." In *Superman: Kyrptonite Nevermore.* New York: DC Comics, 2008.
O'Neil, Denny (w), and Curt Swan (a). "Menace at 1000 Degrees!" *Superman #238* (June 1971). New York: DC Comics, 15.

_____. "Planet of the Angels" Superman #236 (April 1971). New York: DC Comics, 6.
_____. "To Save a Superman." Superman #240 (July 1971). New York: DC Comics, 6.
_____. "The Shape of Fear." Superman #241 (Aug. 1971). New York: DC Comics, 2.
_____. "Sinister Scream of the Devil's Harp." Superman #235 (March 1971). New York: DC Comics, 4.
_____. "Superman Breaks Loose." Superman #233 (Jan. 1971). New York: DC Comics, 8.
_____. "The Ultimate Battle." Superman #242 (Sep. 1971). New York: DC Comics, 11.
Simon, Dennis M. "The War in Vietnam 1969–1973." August, 2002. Accessed at: http://faculty.smu.edu/dsimon/Change-Viet4.html on January 13, 2010.
Wright, Bradford W. Comic Book Nation: The Transformation of Youth Culture in America. Baltimore: Johns Hopkins University Press, 2001.

The Struggle Within

Superman's Difficult Transition into the Age of Relevance

PAUL R. KOHL

Bryan Singer's 2006 film *Superman Returns* caused a stir among conservative critics when the script removed "The American Way" from the Man of Steel's longtime credo of fighting for "Truth, Justice and the American Way." An even greater tumult was caused more recently when writer David S. Goyer wrote a story for *Action Comics #900* (June 2011) in which Superman does the unthinkable and actually renounces his American citizenship. "I'm tired of having my actions construed as instruments of U.S. policy," he announces, "'Truth, justice, and the American way' — It's not enough anymore."[1]

A passionate outcry arose on both sides of these issues, a testament to the vast political gap that exists in 21st century America. The ideological divide of the 2000s is reminiscent of another great cultural divide in American history. In the 1960s they called it the "generation gap," as adults shook their heads at the long hair and loud music of the counterculture and young people were told not to trust anyone over thirty. Rock music critic John Strausbaugh called it "social upheaval on a scale that would not be revisited for the rest of the twentieth century."[2] The struggle played itself out on the radio airwaves in songs by Bob Dylan and Jefferson Airplane, on the television screens during the nightly news, and on the big screen in films like *Easy Rider* and *The Graduate*. It did not, however, play itself out on the comic racks until the turn of the next decade.

In the April 1970 issue of *Green Lantern*, then known as *Green Lantern/Green Arrow*, writer Denny O'Neil introduced the comic book world to the idea of "relevance." It was an attempt, O'Neil said, to combine his journalism background with his fiction writing by drawing on the work of "the new journalists," writers like Hunter S. Thompson, Norman Mailer, and Tom Wolfe, who wrote about current issues with a combination of journalistic truthfulness and fictional artistry. O'Neil asked himself, "What would happen if we put a superhero in a real-life setting dealing with a real-life problem?"[3]

The answer shook the comic world as the cosmic space-faring Green Lantern found he was unable to defend himself against the charges of a ragged, elderly, African-American man:

> I been readin' about you ... how you work for the blue skins ... and how on a planet someplace you helped out the orange skins ... and you done considerable for the purple skins! Only there's *skins* you never bothered with ... the *black* skins! I want to know ... *how come?!*[4]

The hero whose oath promised that "no evil shall escape my sight" was forced to admit that it had, and that often he hadn't been able to recognize it because it looked like a successful businessman. For the next two years *Green Lantern/Green Arrow* followed the title characters as they confronted social issues of the day, from pollution to feminism, from Native American rights to drug abuse.

O'Neil's radical overhaul of Green Lantern and his rescue of Batman from mid–60s campiness with a return to the darkness of his original 1939 incarnation made him the go-to man at DC Comics for character modernization, and in the January 1971 issue of *Superman #233*, he began work on the original superhero. What Denny O'Neil did in his short run on *Superman* was not overtly turn the Man of Steel into a mouthpiece for the counterculture like *Green Lantern/Green Arrow* or a litmus test for one's ideological leanings like *Action Comics #900* (June 2011). What he did was something subtler, creating in his Superman a metaphor for America, an America humbled by newfound weakness.

O'Neil's run on *Superman* has been dubbed "The Sandman Saga" and contained three major changes to the character's mythology: The transformation of all earth's Green Kryptonite into iron, the evolution of Clark Kent from print journalist to TV newsman, and the introduction of a mysterious sand creature who siphons off much of Superman's power when they are near. Each of these new elements makes "The Sandman Saga" a story in which Superman, forty years before renouncing his American citizenship, questioned for the first time his assumptions about "The American Way."

The End of Green Kryptonite

The substance known as Green Kryptonite, remnants of Superman's destroyed home planet Krypton that are deadly to him after only a brief exposure, did not exist yet when Superman made his first appearance in *Action Comics #1* (June 1938). Green Kryptonite was actually created for *The Adventures of Superman* radio program in 1943, but it wouldn't fully appear in the DC comic books until a decade later, in 1949.

The truth is that Superman's writers didn't need Green Kryptonite at the beginning of the Man of Steel's career. In the beginning he could not fly, only leap, and a bursting shell *could* penetrate his skin. A *deus ex machina* weakness was not necessary for a character that was not yet all-powerful.

Superman's powers gradually increased and Superman emerged from the era of the Second World War with new powers, much as his home country did. Victorious and untouched on the home front, and now the world's sole nuclear power, the United States was the unchallenged world superpower in 1945. That soon changed and in a few years a powerful foe would arise with its own version of the unthinkable weapon.

The Cold War begins about the same time that Kryptonite becomes a regular part of the Superman mythos. Thus also began the editorial stewardship of Mort Weisinger. As *The World Encyclopedia of Comics* notes, "Whereas Siegel's concept centered around a superhuman battling an almost equally endowed opponent, Weisinger's concept had a god-like Superman perplexed not by the second strongest man, but by fools (Mr. Mxyzptlk), pranksters (Toyman), and gadgeted mad scientists (Lex Luthor)."[5]

In the 1950s Superman and the U.S.A. had much in common. Both were nearly invulnerable, yet haunted by the one thing that could destroy them forever, Green Kryptonite and nuclear weapons, respectively. With these complementary threats to the nation and one of its cultural symbols, it's fitting that the opening pages of *Superman #233* (Jan. 1971) finds a scientist, Professor Bolden, attempting to find a method of converting Green Kryptonite into a power source. Superman muses: "I'm running a risk being here! If anything goes wrong with Professor Bolden's experiment ... it could be fatal to me! Still, the work's important! The professor's kryptonite engine could supply cheap electricity for virtually every undeveloped area...."[6] Superman's willingness to risk his life to protect others is one of the traits that most represents "The American Way," but the dual nature of kryptonite's real-world corollary, nuclear power, as both a weapon of mass destruction and a world-saving power source also suggests the hidden dangers that may occur.

Professor Bolden's experiment inevitably goes awry and Superman tries to contain the massive explosion with a lead containment shield, lead, of course, being the only metal that can shield Superman from Green Kryptonite's deadly rays. He's too late and the explosion hits Superman full force, but he is not harmed. The explosion causes a chain reaction that somehow turns the kryptonite into harmless iron; and not just the kryptonite in the experiment, but all the green kryptonite in the world. As a headline in the *Daily Planet* reads "NOW HE'S REALLY INVULNERABLE!"[7]

Thus was the first big change in O'Neil's Superman. A curious choice, given that O'Neil's goal on the character was to make him more human, creating "a greater similarity between Superman and his flawed human readers."[8] The cover of *Superman #233* (Jan. 1971), a Neal Adams work showing Superman bursting chains of green metal over the words "Kryptonite Nevermore!," and the story's title, "Superman Breaks Loose," suggested that the character would be more powerful than ever.

With Green Kryptonite now gone, Superman, as Jimmy Olsen notes "has nothing to be afraid of—except magic ... and that's rare — real rare!"[9] Like Superman, the United States' true vulnerability had always come from the outside, such as the threats of foreign militaries, or the political threats of fascism and communism. Even the "red scare" of the 1950s was perceived at the time as the product of Soviet agents infiltrating the government.

At the end of the Second World War the United States was "super power" among nations, just as the Man of Steel was a superhero among mortals. As Gabriel Partos writes, "With America acquiring the nuclear bomb in 1945, there seemed no limits to its military and political power."[10] Partos then quotes Noam Chomsky: "1945 was an historic moment in which there was one country with such extraordinary wealth and power that it could in fact organize the whole world."[11] And Superman had been on the front lines, both on the covers of his comic books and in the hands of those soldiers who were on the real front lines.

During Weisinger's editorial reign of the Superman family of comic books, science fiction concepts that would take the character to the height of popularity were introduced. These included another Kryptonian survivor, Supergirl, the alternate dimension called the Phantom Zone, the hidden Fortress of Solitude, the shrunken Bottle City of Kandor, the alien villain Brainiac, and multiple colors of kryptonite. Of course these were children's comic books, so it was unlikely that they would overtly address the issues that were beginning to affect the nation's own sense of power and self-identity.

Kent Moves to Television

The second major change of the O'Neil Superman run was the transition of Clark Kent from "mild-mannered reporter" for *The Daily Planet* to broadcast reporter for the Galaxy Broadcasting System. In a nod to the growing age of media conglomeration, O'Neil had GBS owner Morgan Edge purchase *The Planet*. The presentation of the broadcast news media in the story is a mixed bag with cynical suggestions of television news as show business. Yet the immediacy of the television news reporting shown reminds us that it was TV news that brought the realities of America's inner turbulence into the nation's homes.

Since the beginning of the 1960s television had become a larger player in the political and social worlds of the U.S. In 1960 the first televised presidential debate between Kennedy and Nixon foretold of the growing influence of the medium. Three years later, the non-stop coverage of the Kennedy assassination and funeral showed the great importance television would have as an informer and comforter of the American public. Television also played a large part in changing attitudes on great social issues of the decade. Footage of high-pressure hoses and attack dogs being unleashed on unarmed protestors in Birmingham opened the eyes of many towards the justness of the Civil Rights Movement. Vietnam became the first regularly televised war. The medium's leading journalist, Walter Cronkite, turned opinions when he gave his assessment that "...it is increasingly clear to this reporter that the only rational way out then will be to negotiate, not as victors but as an honorable people who lived up to their pledge to defend democracy, and did the best they could."[12] The power of Cronkite and his pronouncement is attested to by President Lyndon Johnson's comment that "If I've lost Cronkite, I've lost the war" and his subsequent decision not to run for re-election.

During the 1960s television journalism came into its own, but Superman's reaction as Clark Kent has an old-fashioned print bias. After Morgan Edge assigns him his first TV assignment, he muses, "This could sort of complicate my life! As a newsman, I was free to switch identities ... nobody could keep close tabs on me! But as a broadcaster, I'll be in full view of millions!"[13]

Kent's distinction between "newsman" and "broadcaster" is made emphatic one panel later as he thinks "It's about time for me to begin my ... er ... showbiz career!"[14] And in *Superman 234* (Feb. 1971) he refers to himself as a "bargain-basement actor."[15] Superman's conservative opinion of the press reaffirms the traditional press' own conservatism during the sixties. As Gaye Tuchman wrote in 1978, "News ... is a social resource whose construction limits an analytic understanding of contemporary life."[16] Due to its standardized constraints and resources, the press reproduces an image of the world that reflects the needs of its ownership. Superman, as an American icon, has many of the same blinders.

Just as Green Lantern's worldview expanded with a little help from Green Arrow in O'Neil's fabled run with artist Neal Adams, Superman slowly displays a similar change in this run. In *Superman #234* (Feb. 1971) the owner of a South Seas island plantation refuses to let his native employees flee when a volcano threatens them. In a display of capitalism at its ugliest he tells Superman "Those people are under contract to work my plantation ... and I aim to enforce those contracts—even if I have to kill a few of the lazy louts!" Superman's law-and-order reaction is to attempt to stop the volcano without stepping on the island, which would be trespassing. After his first attempt fails he thinks, "There must be something I can do—but what ... without breaking the law? Must think fast ... or those innocent people will die—horribly!" A page turn and a panel later, however, Superman concedes to the limitations of truth, justice, and the American way: "I can't let that happen! If worst comes to worst, I'll have to defy Harker—and take the consequences! Because there's a moral law that's above some man-made laws!" Representatives of that moral law soon show up as a United Nations delegation arrives to rescue the islanders and back up Superman's higher morality.[17]

In *Superman #236* (April 1971) the Man of Steel has another valuable insight. In the story's opening Superman and Batman stop a late-night break-in by two anonymous thugs who have apparently cracked open a safe and are making off with a lot of money. Batman notes, "Finally! We've been after this pair for a solid week—." Superman responds, "But we nailed 'em, Batman—thanks to your sharp detective work!"[18] This scene, which would be unsurprising in a 1950s issue of *World's Finest Comics*, reads like an anachronism in the deliberately relevant 1970s. It's one thing for Batman to spend a week tracking down two bank robbers, but why is Superman on hand? The opening of "Planet of the Angels" should make readers question what superheroes, even the most powerful of all, spend their time doing. When not saving the planet from destruction or fighting their arch-enemies they are stopping usually petty crimes. Many stories from the Silver Age begin with foiled bank robberies or jewelry store heists. For this they need super powers?

The question is made even more explicit on the following page. While Batman goes off to sleep, Superman, who doesn't need it, returns to his Fortress of Solitude to continue some experiments. On his way he thinks, "Well, no emergencies tonight! So—how do I occupy the hours between now and dawn?"[19] It's quite the idealized world when Superman has nothing to do between the hours of midnight and six in his local time zone, much less anywhere else in the world. Kurt Busiek attempted a more realistic take on what Superman's life would be like in the first issue of his *Astro City* series in 1995. Busiek's Superman analog, Samaritan, races to situations around the clock, musing at one point "I can't save everybody—people die even while I'm saving lives here—but I can still do what I can. Can't I?" At the story's end, Samaritan notes the amount of time he's had to enjoy the freedom of flying: "Fifty-six seconds. Best day since March."[20]

The Sand Thing

In *1968: The Year That Rocked the World*, Mark Kurlansky writes "The generation that grew up after World War II was so completely different from the World War II generation and the ones before it that the struggle for common ground was constant. They didn't even laugh at the same jokes."[21] The counterculture of young Americans that protested the Vietnam War rejected the entire philosophy of their parents' generation. Their lifestyle, clothing, hair, music, sexual mores, religious beliefs, and drugs of choice all defied adult convention. In America's cities that divergence led to violence, most infamously on the streets of Chicago in August 1968.

Denny O'Neil removed Green Kryptonite as a threat to Superman. He immediately replaced it with a new threat, the Sand Creature that slowly saps the Man of Steel's power over the run of the series. This seems to acknowledge that the main threat to Superman, and by extension the country, was no longer external but internal, since the Sand Creature is shown to be an extension of Superman's inner being. But, as he states, "Although I am woven from your mind, your heart — your very soul — I am my own creature!"[22] Twenty years before the end of the Cold War, while still in the midst of the Vietnam conflict, O'Neil sensed that our greatest vulnerability came from within, and that it was not necessarily the youth of America's counterculture that were the main danger. Speaking of Green Lantern, O'Neil has stated "Green Lantern was, in effect, a cop. An incorruptible cop, to be sure, with noble intentions, but still a cop, a crypto-fascist."[23]

Superman, like Green Lantern and most superheroes, is also a cop, protecting the status quo at virtually any cost. The scandal over recent attempts to rid Superman's oath of "The American Way" and his American citizenship shows the level to which he has been accepted as a government "official." In an era of police violence on the streets of Chicago, the slaughter of innocent villagers in My Lai, and the killing of four students by the National Guard at Kent State the superhero as cop image had to be restrained. In the concluding chapters of his "Sandman Saga" O'Neil briefly returns Superman's full powers with the help of the Eastern mystic I-Ching. Unfortunately, he is also suffering from brain damage, brought on by an assault while powerless. Testing his regained full strength Superman becomes a truly out of control "Super Cop." Spying a speeding car he thinks "No crime is too small for Superman's attention." After an army artillery unit fulfills Superman's request to test their shells on him, he states "Well, next time you want to test an H-Bomb or something, let me know!" When confronted by I-Ching's theory of brain damage he responds "You're just jealous because you're weak ... like everyone else!"[24]

To return Superman to his senses I-Ching surmises he must put him in proximity to the Sand Creature one more time. The creature comes from the Realm of Quarrm, "a state," as I-Ching explains, "of alternate possibilities! A place where neither men nor things exist ... only unformed, shapeless beings!" The explosion that changed all Green Kryptonite to iron also opened a rift between Quarrm and Earth, allowing the formless mist to mingle with Superman's "mental and physical vibrations." The psychic link between them allowed the creature to siphon off Superman's powers when in his proximity.[25]

Though he shares a physical and psychic bond with Superman, the creature makes clear their differences, saying "I am not human! The affairs of mankind mean nothing to me."[26] This severe disconnect between Superman and the creature he had helped create was mirrored in the relationship between the American establishment and members of the counterculture movement. A year earlier, Jerry Rubin, leader of the counterculture Yippie movement, explained the goal of the party:

> Previous revolutions aimed at seizure of the state's highest authority, followed by the takeover of the means of production. The Youth International Revolution will begin with mass breakdown of authority, mass rebellion, total anarchy in every institution in the Western World. Tribes of longhairs, blacks, armed women, workers, peasants and students will take over.[27]

Though among the most radical of the counter-culturalists, the Yippies were not alone in looking for a total overthrow of a society they had no belief or stake in. As Rubin further explained, "The Amerikan [sic] economy has rendered white middle-class youth and black working-class youth useless, because we are not needed to make the economy run."[28]

Theodore Roszak analyzed the generation gap of the 1960s in *The Making of a Counter Culture*. He argues that it is

> ... beyond dispute that the interests of our college-age and adolescent young in the psychology of alienation, oriental mysticism, psychedelic drugs, and communitarian experiments comprise a cultural constellation that radically diverges from values and assumptions that have been in the mainstream of our society at least since the Scientific Revolution of the seventeenth century.[29]

Though they are psychically connected Superman and the creature from Quarrm have no common values. The full strength of one means the non-existence of the other. Similarly much of the sixties counterculture, though born of America, saw the country as a corrupt and evil society that needed to be destroyed. Many adults at the time felt the same way about those in the counterculture.

The climax of O'Neil's "Sandman Saga" in *Superman #242* (Sep. 1971) finds Superman and his new nemesis facing off in final combat. They cannot coexist because, as the Sand Creature explains, "You like your uniqueness! You need being the only one of your kind — a feeling I share!" They battle to a standstill, but in the process they destroy the Earth. In shock Superman cries "For our own selfish ends, we've destroyed — everything!" The destruction is an illusion, however, created by I-Ching to show the pair what could happen should they really battle. The creature capitulates and returns to Quarrm, unwilling to jeopardize the Earth. "I realize I have no right to his body ... or his soul!" he concludes, "There cannot be two Supermen in your world!" For his part Superman rejects I Ching's offer to restore his full powers before the creature returns to Quarrm. "No!" he argues, "I've seen the dangers (of) having too much power ... I am human — I can make mistakes! I don't want — or need — more..."[30]

Potential destruction is here presented as the result of two entities battling for the same space, the same mind, the same soul. In the 1960s that soul belonged to America. In order to stave off that potential, the United States would have to come to the realization, as Superman does, that too much power is not always a good thing. Reliance on brute strength must be replaced by intelligence, and perhaps most importantly, empathy. In the story's last panel Superman stands in silhouette, the city skyline in the distance. The caption reads, "He waits in the gathering darkness, alone ... and none can know his thoughts..."[31]

"... the most powerful being on Earth!"

At the beginning of his saga, on the splash page of *Superman #233*, Denny O'Neil wrote:

> Invulnerability ... strength, speed ... all these things, and many more ... combine to make Superman the most powerful being on Earth! But there is another side to the Man of Steel ... a dark side hidden from both the crowds of admirers and the evil men who hate and fear him![32]

So started the tale designed to make Superman more human. By the saga's end a newly humbled Superman determines that he just might have had too much power and willingly accepts living with less. As in the beginning of his career, Green Kryptonite is no longer needed. Superman is no longer all-powerful. He has conquered his dark side.

After the retirement of Mort Weisinger as *Superman* editor, Denny O'Neil and new editor Julius Schwartz, along with the Man of Steel's finest artist, Curt Swan, promised to change the character from one who, O'Neil stated, had "godlike powers whose activities had become nearly as predictable as Dagwood Bumstead's." They opted to create "a greater similarity between

Superman and his flawed human readers."[33] America needed to do the same, to confront its own power as its greatest potential threat. But did it?

Superman standing in the gathering darkness with his own thoughts is not the last thing we see in *Superman #242*'s main story. Below it is a blurb that reads "Next issue! Another startling story, as Superman meets ... "The Starry-Eyed Siren of Space!" The next issue was not written by Denny O'Neil, who quit the series due to overwork but by Cary Bates, and the new direction of Superman was abandoned before it had begun. Though O'Neil and Schwartz had promised to rid Superman comics of imaginary stories, tales that fell outside of the official continuity of the character and thus had no real impact, "The Sandman Saga" virtually became one. Like another American icon, Coca-Cola, Superman returned to the classic formula when its experiment in change failed.

CHAPTER NOTES

1. Goyer, David S. (w), and Miguel Sepulveda (a). "The Incident." *Action Comics #900* (June 2011). New York: DC Comics.

2. Strasbaugh, John. *Rock 'Til You Drop: The Decline From Rebellion to Nostalgia.* (New York: Verso, 2001).

3. Jones, Gerard, and Will Jacobs. *The Comic Book Heroes.* (Rocklin, CA: Prima Publishing, 1997).

4. O'Neil, Dennis (w), and Neal Adams (a). "No Evil Shall Escape My Sight," *Green Lantern/Green Arrow* 76 (April 1970). New York: DC Comics.

5. Horn, Maurice (ed.). *The World Encyclopedia of Comics.* (New York: Chelsea House Publishers, 1976).

6. O'Neil, Dennis (w), and Curt Swan (a). "Superman Breaks Loose!" *Superman #233* (Jan. 1971). New York: DC Comics.

7. Ibid.

8. Jones, Gerard, and Will Jacobs. *The Comic Book Heroes.* (Rocklin, CA: Prima Publishing, 1997), 150.

9. O'Neil, Dennis (w), and Curt Swan (a). "Superman Breaks Loose!" *Superman #233* (Jan. 1971). New York: DC Comics, 5.

10. Partos, Gabriel. *The World That Came in From the Cold War.* (London: Royal Institute of International Affairs, 1993).

11. Ibid., 10.

12. Kurlansky, Mark. *1968: The Year That Rocked The World.* (New York: Ballantine Books, 2004), 61.

13. O'Neil, Dennis (w), and Curt Swan (a). "Superman Breaks Loose!" *Superman #233* (Jan. 1971). New York: DC Comics.

14. Ibid.

15. O'Neil, Dennis (w), and Curt Swan (a). "How to Tame a Wild Volcano." *Superman #234* (Feb. 1971). New York: DC Comics.

16. Tuchman, Gaye. "News as the Reproduction of the Status Quo: A Summary." In McChesney and Scott (eds.), *Our Unfree Press: 100 Years of Radical Media Criticism.* (New York: The New Press, 2004), 399–404.

17. O'Neil, Dennis (w), and Curt Swan (a). "How to Tame a Wild Volcano." *Superman #234* (Feb. 1971). New York: DC Comics.

18. O'Neil, Dennis (w), and Curt Swan (a). "Planet of Angels." *Superman #236* (April 1971). New York: DC Comics.

19. Ibid.

20. Busiek, Kurt. "In Dreams," in *Kurt Busiek's Astro City* 1 (Aug. 1995). Anaheim: Image Comics.

21. Kurlansky, Mark. *1968: The Year That Rocked The World.* (New York: Ballantine Books, 2004), xix.

22. O'Neil, Denny (w), and Curt Swan (a). "Menace at 1000 Degrees!" *Superman #238* (June 1971). New York: DC Comics, 8.

23. Jones, Gerard, and Will Jacobs. *The Comic Book Heroes.* (Rocklin, CA: Prima Publishing, 1997), 149.

24. O'Neil, Denny (w), and Curt Swan (a). "The Shape of Fear." *Superman #241* (Aug. 1971). New York: DC Comics.

25. Ibid.

26. O'Neil, Denny (w), and Curt Swan (a). "Menace at 1000 Degrees!" *Superman #238* (June 1971). New York: DC Comics, 7.

27. Rubin, Jerry. *Do It! Scenarios of the Revolution.* (New York: Simon & Schuster, 1970).

28. Ibid., 251.

29. Roszak, Theodore. *The Making of a Counter Culture: Reflections on the Technocratic Society and its Youthful Opposition.* (Garden City, New York: Anchor Books, 1969), xii.

30. O'Neil, Denny (w), and Curt Swan (a). "The Ultimate Battle!" *Superman #242* (Sep. 1971). New York: DC Comics.

31. Ibid.

32. O'Neil, Denny (w), and Curt Swan (a). "Superman Breaks Loose." *Superman #233* (Jan. 1971). New York: DC Comics, 1.

33. Jones, Gerard, and Will Jacobs. *The Comic Book Heroes.* (Rocklin, CA: Prima Publishing, 1997), 150.

BIBLIOGRAPHY

Busiek, Kurt. "In Dreams." in *Kurt Busiek's Astro City* 1 (Aug. 1995). Anaheim: Image Comics.

Goyer, David S. (w), and Miguel Sepulveda (a). "The Incident." *Action Comics #900* (June 2011). New York: DC Comics.

Horn, Maurice, ed. *The World Encyclopedia of Comics.* New York: Chelsea House Publishers, 1976.

Jones, Gerard, and Will Jacobs. *The Comic Book Heroes.* Rocklin, CA: Prima Publishing, 1997.

Kurlansky, Mark. *1968: The Year That Rocked the World.* New York: Ballantine Books, 2004.

O'Neil, Dennis (w), and Neal Adams (a). "No Evil Shall Escape My Sight." *Green Lantern/Green Arrow* 76 (April 1970). New York: DC Comics.

O'Neil, Dennis (w), and Curt Swan (a). "How to Tame a Wild Volcano." *Superman #234* (Feb. 1971). New York: DC Comics.

_____. "Menace at 1000 Degrees!" *Superman #238* (June 1971). New York: DC Comics, 8.

_____. "Planet of Angels." *Superman #236* (April 1971). New York: DC Comics.

_____. "The Shape of Fear." *Superman #241* (Aug. 1971). New York: DC Comics.

_____. "Superman Breaks Loose!" *Superman #233* (Jan. 1971). New York: DC Comics.

_____. "The Ultimate Battle!" *Superman #242* (Sep. 1971). New York: DC Comics.

Partos, Gabriel. *The World That Came In from the Cold War.* London: Royal Institute of International Affairs, 1993.

Roszak, Theodore. *The Making of a Counter Culture: Reflections on the Technocratic Society and Its Youthful Opposition*. Garden City, NY: Anchor Books, 1969.

Rubin, Jerry. *Do It! Scenarios of the Revolution*. New York: Simon & Schuster, 1970.

Strasbaugh, John. *Rock 'Til You Drop: The Decline From Rebellion to Nostalgia*. New York: Verso, 2001.

Tuchman, Gaye. "News as the Reproduction of the Status Quo: A Summary." In McChesney and Scott, eds., *Our Unfree Press: 100 Years of Radical Media Criticism*. New York: The New Press, 2004.

"It's Morning Again in America"

John Byrne's Re-Imaging of the Man of Steel

DANIEL J. O'ROURKE AND MORGAN B. O'ROURKE

"Why did we welcome Superman? Because Superman is us and we are Superman."

— *Ray Bradbury (1987)*

The image of a harbor at dawn fills the screen. A tugboat heads out to begin its day. A calm, reassuring voice declares: "It's morning again in America." The scene shifts to people going to work — a businessman heading for a waiting car, a farmer on a tractor, a paperboy delivering the morning news. The narrator tells us "6500 young men and women will be married this afternoon." Images of happy couples and teary-eyed relatives appear before our eyes. "It's morning again in America," the voice reminds us, "and under the leadership of President Ronald Reagan, our country is prouder, stronger, and better." A series of flag-raisings roll by briskly — young people at camp, a firefighter, and a senior citizen at home. All of which begs the narrator to ask: "Why would we ever want to go back to where we were?"[1]

The "Morning in America" campaign commercial is a classic example of epideictic rhetoric. Complicated economic issues such as interest rates, inflation, and consumer confidence are wrapped in images of flags and family celebrations for the sixty-second political advertisement. The strategy of presidential candidate Ronald Reagan was to attack the past records of political opponents, Jimmy Carter in 1980 and Walter Mondale in 1984, by celebrating traditional American values. A political campaign can be viewed as an act of rhetorical renewal. Every four years voters affirm commonly held values by electing the candidate that best embodies those traditions and emotions. A majority of voters affirm or deny the campaign defined by the incumbent candidate or party. In 1984, Ronald Reagan's vision of "Morning in America" was an overwhelming success.

Politics and popular culture may seem to be strange bedfellows, but who could have predicted in the 1950s that the star of the movie "Bedtime for Bonzo" would one day become President of the United States? Superman is a popular culture icon that predates the presidential career of Ronald Reagan by nearly half a century. Unfortunately, sales of Superman comics in the 1980s fell due to changes in the comic book industry and competition from other characters that were perceived as edgier and more reflective of the times. Thus, DC Comics undertook a risky endeavor to re-image Superman as a product for the 1980s. In 1986, John Byrne offered a six-part retelling of the story of "The Man of Steel," which can be analyzed in the context of its era as a form of epideictic rhetoric.

Epideictic Rhetoric

The term "epideictic" has its roots in the classical rhetoric of ancient Greece. Still, its form is so ingrained in Western society that most consumers of popular culture will recognize its application immediately. Commercials and political campaigns invoke this ceremonial form of rhetoric to favorably dispose an audience to a person, idea, or product. Two thousand years ago, Aristotle identified three forms of public speaking in *The Rhetoric*.[2] They were: deliberative (political), forensic (for the courts), and epideictic (ceremonial). In ancient Greece, philosophers valued the persuasive appeals of citizens in politics or the courts. Ceremonial speeches, such as funeral orations, were viewed as little more than idolatry, or as Socrates once put it, "praising Athens to Athenians."[3]

Sophists, the first teachers of public speaking, saw it a different way. They recognized that in "praising Athens to Athenians," a bond was formed between a speaker and the audience. Funeral orations did not just praise the dead; they spoke to the living audience. A speaker might celebrate the bravery of a warrior or the wisdom of a poet as a lesson to the listening community. The message would be clear: Our community values and needs courage and creativity. If you want to be worthy of our praise, you should pursue these noble values. Epideictic or ceremonial rhetoric is a powerful tool in defining or affirming community values. In American history, some of our most important speeches, such as Lincoln's "Gettysburg Address" and Martin Luther King Jr.'s "I Have a Dream," were ceremonial orations.

Ronald Reagan was a master at employing epideictic rhetoric. A trained actor with skilled delivery and impeccable timing, Reagan was at his best in ceremonial occasions. Some of his most memorable addresses were in moments of tragedy, such as the Challenger explosion, or historic moments, such as speaking at the Berlin Wall. The "Morning in America" ad captured the Reagan magic and celebrated American values. The 1970s had been a difficult decade in America. Watergate, Vietnam, the energy crisis, and the Iranian hostage crisis sapped the energy and tested the will of the American people. In popular culture, even Captain America became so despondent in the 1970s that he set aside his shield and patriotic costume to become The Nomad, a Man without a Country.[4] "Morning in America" symbolized Reagan's epideictic call for renewal. The commercial asked: "Why would we ever go back to where we were?" The ceremonial message was clear: Reject the dark nights of the Carter/Mondale 1970s and celebrate the new dawn of the Reagan 1980s. America was "prouder, stronger, and better" and we could see the flags at dawn as a symbol of the Reagan's "New Morning in America."

DC in the 1980s

The political turmoil of the 1970s coincided with significant economic changes in the comic book industry in the same decade. Bradford Wright notes that from 1935 to 1961, the price of a comic book remained constant at ten cents. From 1962 to 1981, however, the price increased by five hundred percent to fifty cents an issue.[5] The costs of production and the market for comic books were changing. Artists and writers sought some royalties for their work and labor incentives such as health care.[6] Direct marketing outlets in the form of specialty comic book stores were replacing the metal racks of comics once pervasive in drug stores and supermarkets. Overall, the market for comic books was shrinking and, for the first time, licensing of characters became more profitable than the publication of comic books.[7] Serious questions were being asked about the viability of the comic book industry as the 1980s began. Nowhere was the concern more palpable than in the offices of Warner Communication, owner of DC comics.

Besides the changing economics of comic book publishing, DC Comics was still reacting to the rise of Marvel Comics. Denny O'Neil, one of DC's chief writers at the time, observed that in that era: "DC was classical, Marvel was romantic. DC was well-made parts, clear art work, a comforting predictability: a Mozart concerto. Marvel was improvised story lines, high energy surprise: a Charlie Parker saxophone solo."[8] It soon became clear that the baby boom generation was partial to jazz and looking for rock n' roll. Wright notes that at the beginning of the 1980s, Marvel was outselling DC two-to-one.[9] Price increases and direct marketing had created a new audience: the twenty-year-old. Gone was the pre-teenager purchasing a funny book for a dime at the local drugstore. In his place stood a twenty-year-old college student with transportation to get to a comic book store and tens of dollars to spend on favorite titles. Former Superman writer and artist Jerry Ordway wrote of the 1980s Superman, "Superman was becoming too 'safe'—which is to say taken for granted."[10] O'Neil went further, writing that the characters of DC comics in the 1980s could be "dull. (S)ometimes deadly dull ... Superman was, alas no exception."[11]

Sales of Superman comics dropped to 80,000 per issue, compared to historic highs of one million copies per month in the 1940s and 1950s.[12] Jenette Kahn, publisher and president of DC, decided that it was time for a "cosmic house cleaning."[13] DC had been employing an editorial trick, creating new alternate universes, for its mainstream characters. O'Neil reports that by the 1980s there were "at least seven separate universes in the DC cosmos."[14] In this way, a writer could offer a dramatic event in the life of Superman on Earth 3 without impacting the traditional narrative of the Man of Tomorrow. Kahn approved the *Crisis on Infinite Earth* series that reduced the story lines to one universe, requiring more consistency across multiple titles. Prior to *Crisis on Infinite Earths* Superman starred in *Superman, Action Comics, World's Finest, The Justice League,* and made guest appearances in *Superman Family. Superman Family* featured ancillary characters of the Superman narrative such as Lois Lane, Jimmy Olsen, and Krypto, the super dog. After *Crisis on Infinite Earths,* this title was cancelled and Superboy and Supergirl were eliminated from the Superman legend. Superman was now the sole survivor of the planet Krypton and more changes awaited the Man of Steel.

Randy Duncan and Michael J. Smith have called the years from 1986 to 1993, "The Era of Ambition." They write: "The three works that engendered the most hope for the future of the comic book all graced the shelves in what might be the medium's greatest year: 1986."[15] DC published two of the three books, *Watchmen* and *The Dark Knight Returns.* The third was *Maus,* the Pulitzer Prize winning graphic novel created by Art Spiegelman. Less attention was paid to a re-imaging of Superman that also appeared that same year.

Watchmen and *The Dark Knight Returns* were gritty, nontraditional stories that questioned the very existence of superheroes and their vigilante brand of justice. These graphic novels pushed the boundaries of comic book stories and appealed to the new, more sophisticated reader of the 1980s. In 1985, John Byrne was hired away from Marvel to address the sagging storyline of Superman. Byrne had successfully reinvigorated such titles as *The Fantastic Four* and *The X-Men.* Under the banner of "The Comics Event of the Century," Bryne offered a six-part, bi-weekly re-imaging of the Superman myth entitled *The Man of Steel*. Byrne declared, "The formula that I have always used is to look back at the book's first year and see what made the magic then — back to basics."[16] So, in the "Era of Ambition," John Byrne began his epideictic campaign to resurrect the Man of Steel.

The Man of Steel

Byrne's vision of the Superman narrative is fundamentally an immigrant story. The writer/artist stated in a 1988 interview that the Man of Steel is the "ultimate American success story — a foreigner who comes to America, and is more successful here than he would be anywhere else."[17] In his six-book series, Byrne celebrates the humanity of Clark Kent and tells the story of how Clark created his alter ego, Superman, and found his place in the world.

In 1938, Cleveland teenagers Jerry Siegel and Joe Shuster hurriedly explained the Kryptonian origin of their hero: Panel one — he was born on Krypton and rocketed to Earth. Panel two — A passing motorist discovers the rocket and takes the infant to an orphanage.[18] No parents or guardians are mentioned on Krypton or Earth. In 1986, Byrne expanded the Kryptonian prologue to eight pages. Readers meet the renowned scientist, Jor-El, and his wife, Lara, the couple whose "seed were mingled in the matrix" to create the young Kal-El. Krypton is a sterile, artificial world whose advanced science has controlled nature for thousands of years. Now the planet is rebelling as a chain reaction in the core is building explosive pressure and creating a radioactive element that has already killed millions of Kryptonians. As the end nears for the planet, Jor-El reveals to Lara his plan to send the infant Kal-El to Earth. Lara is aghast and wonders "what kind of hell" he has chosen for their child. Jor-El assures her that Earth's yellow sun will empower him and "In time, he will become the Supreme Being on that planet, almost a God!" Lara wonders if he will rule the people of Earth. Jor-El simply responds, "Perhaps."

The eruptions begin and Jor-El launches the rocket. Lara laments "never knowing the touch of my child's hand." Surprisingly, the scientist responds in most compassionate terms and touches her face. He explains that he has learned one thing from his study of humans. "I have always loved you."[19]

The first panel on Earth shows a fullback outracing his opponents. The field announcer cheers the player's tenth touchdown of the game and declares: "Smallville High has just never seen a football player like this amazing, all-around champion, young Clark Kent." Clearly, this is not the nebbish alter ego envisioned by Siegel and Shuster. The fans celebrate and cheer but it is clear that Pa Kent has seen something else in the exhibition. The elder Kent insists that Clark skip the post-game celebrations and join him for a talk. After eighteen years, Jonathan finally tells Clark of the rocket ship that he and Martha found nearly two decades ago. An amazing story unfolds about how Clark grew and developed super human strength, x-ray vision, and eventually, the power of flight. The chapter concludes with Clark resolving to use his powers to help others. He vows to do so anonymously.[20]

Seven years have later, Ma Kent has kept a scrapbook of miraculous events listed in the newspaper where catastrophes have been avoided and people saved from certain death. Suddenly, Clark returns home and tells of an event the day before in Metropolis. He rescued an experimental plane and all its passengers, including the lovely reporter, Lois Lane. But when he brought the plane to earth, people swarmed and surrounded him. Clark says despondently, "They all wanted a piece of me, Pa. They all wanted a piece of me."[21]

Clark states, "Obviously, I can't be "On Call" twenty-four hours a day. Even I need time to relax and unwind. To be human for a little while." Clark adapts his personal appearance by borrowing an old pair of glasses from Pa, slicking back his hair, and stooping a bit. Meanwhile Ma Kent has designed a costume — tights, a cape, and boots for a "swashbuckler" look. Clark thanks his mother with a kiss on the forehead and says " ... it's got exactly the symbolic look I wanted." He continues, "So, from now on, whenever there are people who need my very special kind of help, it won't be a job for plain, ordinary Clark Kent ... (He takes flight) ... It'll be a job for Superman."[22]

Byrne has told the origin of Superman from the perspective of the Kent family. Superman is a role created collectively by the family to protect the identity and humanity of Clark Kent. After seven years of searching and serving "the greater good" anonymously, Clark Kent has chosen Metropolis as the place where he will build a life and a home.

In subsequent issues, key characters in the Superman story are introduced and relationships are developed but little new is added the characters of Clark Kent or Superman. Lois Lane, Batman, Lex Luthor, and Bizarro are each highlighted. These chapters are all about relationships. Superman is a hero connected to the people. He finds a job, meets a different kind of superhero, and develops the requisite evil nemesis. Lois Lane slowly becomes more than a co-worker. The immigrant has found success in the big city.

In the final chapter, three years have passed in life of Clark/Superman. He returns to Smallville to visit his family. Clark is discussing his life with his parents and comes to a decision. Clark states: "Superman isn't real. He's just a fancy pair of longjohns that let's me operate in public without losing my private life. And it's that private life that's incomplete without someone like Lois." Later that night, a hologram of Jor-El appears to Clark. The figure touches him and images and stories about the planet Krypton invade Clark's mind. He "awakens" to find himself in a field facing his high school girlfriend, Lana Lang. She helps Clark regain his senses and then the two discuss their last meeting ten years ago. After the big high school football game and the revelation of his origin, Clark went to see Lana to tell her of his decision to serve others. Lana was shocked to learn of Clark's powers and decision. She had hoped that they might be married. It took a long time, she reveals, but she learned "... (Y)ou can never belong to one woman, Clark. You're Superman. And Superman belongs to the world."[23] Needless to say, it is a very confusing evening for Clark/Superman.

To sort things out, Superman flies to the site of the rocket that brought him to Earth. Suddenly, the image of Jor-El reappears and says: "My son ... Be silent. And Learn." Images and histories again invade his mind. Ma and Pa Kent discover Clark kneeling on the ground in pain beside by the glowing figure of Jor-El. Pa grabs a shovel and swings it at Jor-El. The connection is broken and Superman is released from the information download. Superman checks on Pa but then says he must get away and think. Eventually, he lands on a mountaintop, his cape fluttering in the wind and declares: "I may have been conceived out there in the endless depths of space ... But I was born when the rocket opened on Earth, in America. ... It was Krypton that made me Superman ... but it is Earth that makes me Human!!"[24]

The immigrant story is complete. Clark has learned of his origin from his birth father Jor-El. He acknowledges the duality of his existence but chooses to be human and pursue human relationships. The humanity of Clark Kent is real because of the lessons learned from Ma and Pa Kent and his time in Metropolis. Jor-El, Lara, and Krypton are holographic images from a world and existence he never knew.

"Morning in America"

Danny Fingeroth, writes, "[W]hen you think of Superman, you most likely think of the Superman that was in vogue when you were a child. There's been a Superman for every decade since the character was created, as there have been Batmen, Wonder Women, and Spider-Men."[25] Fingeroth's point is that each generation of writers and artists leave a mark on a superhero. Some artists will produce larger, more muscular heroes while writers feature different aspects of a character's personality. In 1986, DC attempted a bold move to revitalize the sales of Superman comics. John Byrne was commissioned to write and draw a retelling of the story of the Man of Steel. The six-part re-imaging of the character was to be followed by a new "Superman" comic, issue number one. The hope was that the new audience of specialty shop comic book readers would begin to collect copies of the inaugural Man of Steel series.

Initially, the plan was successful. Sales jumped from eighty thousand to one million copies for Bryne's origin of the Man of Steel. For the second issue, sales dropped to five hundred thousand copies while subsequent issues in the series remained strong selling more than double the pre–Man of Steel sales.[26] Unfortunately, Byrne decided to return to Marvel after only two years at DC. Jerry Ordway observes that when Byrne departed, "DC was shaken and sales dipped.... It would take a few additional years to 'make Superman cool again.'"[27]

Byrne's strategy was to celebrate the humanity of Clark Kent, the adopted immigrant who became Superman. The immigrant story in America has become politically charged and divisive in the twenty-first century. However, the roots of the epideictic tale are as old as the plaque on the Statue of Liberty, ... Give me your tired, your poor, your huddled masses yearning to breathe free."[28] Byrne's vision of Clark Kent was not that the same as the one created by two Jewish teenagers in the 1930s. The Clark Kent of 1986 is a popular high school athlete, an award winning journalist, and a man every bit the equal of Lois Lane. Byrne's Kent had achieved the goal of Shuster and Siegel: He made it in America and got the girl. Wright believes that this new image fit the America of the 1980s, "Byrne's back-to-basics approach meshed nicely with the politics of Ronald Reagan and the ascendant New Right. ... The Reagan vision appealed to a nostalgic brand of patriotism that recalled basic values that, proponents contended, had united Americans in the first place."[29]

The late actor Christopher Reeve, the face of Superman for a generation of fans, once said: "It's very hard for me to be silly about Superman because I've seen first hand how he actually transforms people's lives. I have seen children dying of brain tumors who wanted as their last request to talk to me, and have gone to their graves with a peace brought on by knowing that their belief in that character is intact. I've seen that Superman really matters."[30] "It's morning again in America, and under the leadership of President Ronald Reagan, our country is prouder, stronger, and better."[31] Only the most die-hard conservatives would confuse Ronald Reagan and Superman, but there was a definite similarity in their messages in the 1980s. John Byrne's six-part series, *The Man of Steel*, celebrated the "successful immigrant" story of Superman as a form of epideictic rhetoric worthy of the decade. Byrne recaptured the imagination of the comic book public as it prepared to celebrate the fiftieth anniversary of the Man of Steel and the second term of President Ronald Reagan. It was "Morning Again in America" and time to celebrate "Truth, Justice, and the American Way."

CHAPTER NOTES

1. "Ronald Reagan TV ad: 'It's Morning Again in America.'" Online posting, Youtube. 6 November 2006.

2. Aristotle. *The Rhetoric.* Trans. W. Rhys Roberts. (New York: The Modern Library, 1954).

3. Ibid., 60.

4. Englehart, Steve (w), and Sal Buscema (a). Collected in *Captain America and The Falcon: Secret Empire.* New York: Marvel Comics, 2005.

5. Wright, Bradford. *Comic Book Nation: The Transformation of Youth Culture.*(Baltimore: Johns Hopkins University Press, 2001), 258.

6. O'Neil, Dennis. "The Man of Steel and Me," *Superman at 50: The Persistence of a Legend.* Ed. Dennis Dooley and Gary Engle. (New York: Collier Books, 1988), 49.

7. Wright, Bradford, 259.

8. O'Neil, Dennis, 49.

9. Wright, Bradford, 251.

10. Ordway, Jerry. "Introduction." *Superman in the Eighties.* (New York: DC Comics, 2006), 8.

11. O'Neil, Dennis, 49.

12. Wright, Lili. "The Man Who Energizes Hulk." The New York Times, 7 May 1989. CN18–19. Print.

13. O'Neil, Dennis, 57.

14. Ibid., 57.

15. Duncan, Randy, and Michael J. Smith. *The Power of Comics: History, Form, and Culture.* (New York: Continuum International Press, 2009).

16. Wright, Lili, CN18–19.

17. Friedrich, Otto, Beth Austin, and Janice C. Simpson. "Show Business: Up, Up, and Awaay!!!" *Time*, 14 March 1988. Online.

18. Siegel, Jerry (a) and Shuster, Joe (a). *The Superman Chronicles: Volume One.* New York: DC Comics, 2006.

19. Byrne, John (w), and (a). "From Out the Green Dawn." *The Man of Steel #1* (Oct. 1986). New York: DC Comics.

20. Ibid.

21. Ibid.

22. Ibid.

23. Byrne, John (w), and (a). "The Haunting." *The Man of Steel #6* (Dec. 1986). New York: DC Comics.

24. Ibid.

25. Fingeroth, Danny. *Superman on the Couch: What Superheroes Tell Us About Ourselves and Our Society.* (New York: Continuum International, 2004), 24.

26. Wright, Lili, CN18–19.

27. Ordway, Jerry. "Post-Crisis." *Superman in the Eighties.* New York: DC Comics, 2006, 105.

28. Lazarus, Emma. "The New Colossus." *The Statue of Liberty and Ellis Island Website.* Online. 14 July 2011.

29. Wright, Bradford, 266.

30. Friedrich, Otto, Beth Austin, and Janice C. Simpson.

31. "Ronald Reagan TV ad: 'It's Morning Again in America.'" Online posting, Youtube. 6 November 2006.

Bibliography

Aristotle. *The Rhetoric.* Trans. W. Rhys Roberts. New York: The Modern Library, 1954.

Byrne, John (w), and (a). "From Out the Green Dawn." *The Man of Steel #1* (Oct. 1986). New York: DC Comics.

_____. "The Haunting." *The Man of Steel #6* (Dec. 1986). New York: DC Comics.

Duncan, Randy, and Michael J. Smith. *The Power of Comics: History, Form, and Culture.* New York: Continuum International Press, 2009.

Englehart, Steve (w), and Sal Buscema (a). Collected in *Captain America and The Falcon: Secret Empire.* New York: Marvel Comics, 2005.

Fingeroth, Danny. *Superman on the Couch: What Superheroes Tell Us About Ourselves and Our Society.* New York: Continuum International, 2004.

Friedrich, Otto, Beth Austin, and Janice C. Simpson. "Show Business: Up, Up, and Awaay!!!" *Time,* 14 March 1988.

Lazarus, Emma. "The New Colossus." *Accessed 14 July 2011,* at http://www.nps.gov/stli/historyculture/index.htm.

O'Neil, Dennis. "The Man of Steel and Me." In Dennis Dooley and Gary Engle, eds., *Superman at 50: The Persistence of a Legend.* New York: Collier Books, 1988.

Ordway, Jerry. *Superman in the Eighties.* New York: DC Comics, 2006

"Ronald Reagan Television ad: 'It's Morning Again in America.'" Accessed 6 November 2006, at http://www.youtube.com/watch?v=EU-IBF8nwSY.

Siegel, Jerry (a) and Shuster, Joe (a). *The Superman Chronicles: Volume One.* New York: DC Comics, 2006.

Wright, Bradford. *Comic Book Nation: The Transformation of Youth Culture.* Baltimore: Johns Hopkins University Press, 2001.

Wright, Lili. "The Man Who Energizes Hulk." *New York Times,* 7 May 1989.

The New "Man of Steel" Is a Quiche-Eating Wimp!

Media Reactions to the Reimagining of Superman in the Reagan Era

JACK TEIWES

By the 1980s, Superman had unquestionably become an American institution, with at least three generations having grown up with the Man of Steel as an indelible figure in the landscape of their popular culture. Even without necessarily having ever read an actual Superman comic, each successive generation had been exposed to the Superman narrative through multimedia incarnations, be it radio and movie serials, the syndicated television show, big and small-screen animation, or, by the turn of the decade, a series of big-budget feature films. Superman was, as one journalist put it, "a multimedia hit before the term existed."[1]

It was this wide-spectrum, intergenerational familiarity with Superman across multiple media which afforded the character a permanent place in the popular consciousness,[2] and yet by the 1980s Superman was not faring well in his parent medium. Despite being one of only a handful of characters to weather the near-extinction of superhero comics in the 1950s and having undergone a resurgence in creative energy during the 1960s, sales of Superman's comics had been in decline for some decades. With all three of Superman's monthly comic books dropping below the sales figures which would ordinarily signal cancellation for any comic starring a less prestigious character,[3] it was decided that something had to be done.[4]

As the cornerstone of a wider strategy to reform the narrative continuity of their superhero properties, DC set about rebuilding the foundations of their ailing flagship hero in the hopes of creating a "new" version of Superman more suited to a 1980's audience. As DC Comics President Jenette Kahn put it, "there was a coat of rust on the man of steel."[5]

125

In doing so, however, DC discovered that in the fervently patriotic climate of Ronald Reagan's America there were those in the mainstream press who took great exception to the alteration of what had come to be regarded as an American icon, and perceptions of masculine identity were to play a key part in this controversy. While the maxi-series *Crisis on Infinite Earths* was the site of the wider reconfiguration of DC's superhero universe,[6] Superman was singled out for a particularly extensive revision of his continuity, taking the opportunity to purge much of his supporting cast and history which had accumulated over the decades to the perceived detriment of the character, making his adventures impenetrable to potential new readers.[7]

In essence, all Superman's previously-published adventures were rendered null and void as his origin story and history could be reinvented with a blank slate that would allow for a new, updated version. This was a radical move on DC's part, as the mastery of diegetic story continuity had by this point become a key preoccupation amongst the subculture of dedicated comic fans,[8] from whose ranks most modern comic writers have sprung.[9] Additionally, it was felt that Superman's powers had gradually ballooned in scope over nearly five decades to the point where the near-omnipotent character was difficult to write and harder to relate to.[10] Finally, there was a concern that the hero had become too preoccupied with his dead homeworld of Krypton,[11] and thus disconnected from humanity.

Identifying this trio of problems led to the mindset at DC that it was audiences' inability to connect with the character for these reasons that had caused Superman's declining sales. Although previously pitched a "fix" by eventual collaborator Marv Wolfman,[12] DC ultimately hired Marvel Comics' superstar writer/artist John Byrne[13] to spearhead the recreation of "a less complicated universe guarded by a more believable hero."[14] To accomplish this transition, DC put Superman's monthly comic books on a three month hiatus during the bi-weekly release of Byrne's six-issue miniseries *The Man of Steel* in 1986, which served to introduce the revised origin of Superman and launch his new status quo.

Byrne's changes were thus all related to a chief motive: making Superman more relatable, more "human." To this end he downscaled Superman's superpowers from the literally godlike to that of a mere demigod,[15] in the hopes readers would be more likely to root for a hero struggling to overcome genuine obstacles and threats.

Yet it was on the issue of Superman's characterization that Byrne's revisions arguably made their greatest deviations from the preceding era. Superman's personal sense of his own humanity despite his alien background was given considerable weight, his adopted parents Jonathan and Martha Kent being depicted as still alive in the present day as a source of love and guidance.

Conversely Krypton and his biological parents Jor-El and Lara were now depicted as far more alien, cold and unappealing than previously utopian portrayals.[16] Superman's Kryptonian heritage was something he no longer pined for, embracing instead his role as an immigrant to Earth.

To reinforce this sense of humanity, Byrne redefined the distinction between the dual personae of Superman and Clark Kent, which traditionally had featured the "mild-mannered" reporter as a highly performative identity, feigning timidity, clumsiness and cowardice as a disguise for his "true" self as Superman. Inspired by George Reeves' far tougher portrayal of Clark Kent[17] in the 1950s television series *The Adventures of Superman* (1952–1958), Byrne now chose to present a more assertive and confident Kent,[18] rationalized by placing far less emphasis on Kent being "an act."

Coupled with this more down to earth approach to Superman's civilian identity, Byrne sought to modernize Clark Kent through the aspirational lens of the 1980s, depicting the character as more "upwardly mobile," a newspaper feature writer, columnist and part-time novelist rather than merely a reporter, with some of the trendy trappings of material success then in the current *zeitgeist*.

While the combination of reducing the hero's superpowers from their previous extremes, simplifying his mythos, de-romanticizing Krypton and creating a more assertive, modernized Clark Kent were all designed to render Superman a more human and approachable figure,[19] it was the announcement of these very details which led to Byrne and DC facing criticism and derision from the mainstream press.

Press Release and Response

In the hopes of garnering a new audience for their rebooted Superman comics from beyond the ranks of dedicated comics readers, DC sought to publicize their new Superman for the 1980s to the mainstream media, announcing the broad strokes of their intended revision more than six months ahead of time in November 1985. Early reports presented short, factual articles without much commentary, noting the comics' poor sales and relaying DC's intentions for a "major overhaul" to include reducing Superman's much-inflated powers and make the hero "like other New Men of the '80s ... open about his feelings."[20]

One 1985 article which was a sign of things to come was a brief yet scathing editorial mocking the idea of Superman receiving a "new image ... for these post–Rambo times." Irritated by the perceived mixed message of the revised Clark Kent, it derided the new version as both "macho [and] open to his feelings, for heaven's sake, a bizarre cross between Frank Furillo and Arnold Schwarzenegger." The piece argued that Kent's traditional persona is integral to the Superman legend, representing an "(e)veryman, decent, vulnerable and ruefully aware that the world does not know the real person behind the facade," a duality that would be notionally ruined by the supposed new "tough guy" portrayal of Kent.[21]

These early salvos aside, the real heat came when DC followed up on these early announcements by publicizing a full outline of their planned revisions in June 1986, the month in which the first issue of *The Man of Steel* was hitting the racks.[22] Many publications, both national and local, reported on the story and while there was a spectrum of different responses, hostile reactions predominated. While articles differed in their objections, there were several recurring themes to their criticisms.

If it ain't broke, don't fix it!

A strong and overarching theme expressed by various commentators was that meddling with Superman was not only unnecessary, but even a form of cultural heresy. "That's akin to painting a mustache on the Statue of Liberty" analogized even one of the more moderate articles.[23]

Several journalists expressed their unwavering support for what they framed as a "traditional" Superman, one stating an unequivocal preference for "the real thing," and offering "(t)o the geniuses at DC Comics as they tamper with a classic, four words of caution: *Remember the New Coke.*"[24] Indeed, more than one journalist writing about the "new" Superman cited the infamous and quickly-reversed failure by The Coca-Cola Company to replace the original formula of their famous beverage with a new flavor in 1985.[25] Although some analyses differ, it was generally believed that the soft-drink company failed to appreciate the beverage's iconic status in American culture and underestimated the backlash, a type of nostalgia-driven rejection of pop cultural change that served as an undercurrent to many of the articles deriding the "new" Superman. Ironically, DC executive vice president Paul Levitz had even specifically stated in one interview that he did not expect a backlash akin to that surrounding New Coke, claiming "We're not changing the formula ... everything that is special about the character is still there and unchanged."[26]

Regardless, many journalists took these alterations by "revisionist writers"[27] to mean quite the opposite. One quoted at length a letter from the public which described the revision of "The beloved, near-sacred origin of Superman" as a horrifying concession to realism in a medium intended for escapism. Claiming that "DC is doing what every tyrannical ... group has done when they take over — they are rewriting history," the enraged writer resolved to buy back issues of the old Superman for posterity, declaring: "After all, I want my children to grow up with the genuine, original outlook on 'Truth, Justice and the American Way.'"[28]

These fools at DC are turning Superman into a wimp!

A common reaction to the reduction of Superman's power levels was to bemoan the change as though the character was being emasculated as a result. The view implicitly suggests that Superman's powers are his defining trait and that any reduction thereof was an insult to the character, and for some, by extension the American values he is perceived to represent. In some articles this included a suggestion that Superman's status in the popular consciousness as a cultural icon supercedes his ownership by DC Comics.

One example condemned "Levitz and his band of mischief makers" for these "outrageous" revisions, decrying that "Truth, justice and the American way are at risk if all these changes are made in Superman comics. That's what I say, and I vote 'no' on everything.... Don't let the Levitz gang do these terrible things to you!"[29]

Although most articles were relatively unconcerned with directing their criticism any more specifically than at DC, a few stuck the boot in to some of the most public and oft-quoted figures involved in the relaunch, mocking John Byrne's credentials, being both English-born and Canadian-raised, "So, obviously he knows all there is to know about a symbol as American as Superman, right?"[30]

Another apparently took exception to Levitz's youth (28 at the time) and presumed education, opining that "Levitz sounds like the sort of bright, young MBA who understands flow charts, market analysis and consumer surveys, in short, everything but human nature."[31]

Perhaps most interesting in terms of the gender discourse surrounding the reboot was another article's quip that Superman's emasculating personality changes were due to DC President Jenette Kahn having a "feminine preoccupation with what characters are thinking and why they act as they do."[32]

Clark Kent has become a quiche-eating yuppie!

Most virulent of all were the objections to the alteration of Clark Kent, although therein lay some of the most drastic exaggerations and misinterpretations of DC and Byrne's intent. The majority of the negative articles fixated on the quote from DC that Kent was to become "upwardly mobile," which in short order became relayed as a "hip upwardly mobile Yuppie"[33] and then extrapolated into the perception that Kent was to be portrayed as an "aggressive Yuppie columnist."[34] This notion was roundly mocked by several of Kent's prospective "fellow" columnists, bemused by the concept of altering Clark Kent's iconic job as a plain old reporter simply for the purposes of depicting him as upwardly mobile.[35] But for most, this was simply code for yuppie, and what was mere skepticism amongst these columnists blossomed into expressions of disdain and strong mockery from many other journalists writing on the story.

"Super Yuppie?"[36] quips one, "Ye gods! ... He's a yuppie!" asserts another,[37] while DC's refutation of the yuppie tag[38] is dismissed in one editorial with the satirical description of this "yuppification" at work: "The "new" Superman will emerge in three months. He's on vacation till then. In the Hamptons. With his ferret."[39] Another opines that these changes will send a lot of older Superman fans packing to a psychiatrist's office "Where they'll find Clark Kent in the waiting room. Reading a copy of GQ."[40]

Confluence

What is fascinating about these common threads in the variety of print media responses is how these three major themes of distress were repeatedly combined to produce a surprisingly consistent view that Superman/Clark Kent was being transformed by meddlesome, overeducated liberals at DC Comics, without a consenting cultural mandate, into an emasculated figure that embodied the most disreputable aspects of 1980s yuppie culture.

Several articles use extended parodic passages describing wholly imagined activities that this "Supersissy" new Clark Kent would engage in, such as eating quiche, displaying fashion-consciousness, fighting world hunger, expressing sensitivity towards women, adopting a vegetarian diet, listening to Vivaldi and watching Casablanca on a VCR, experiencing bouts of impotence, living in a condo and installing a Jacuzzi, espresso-maker and Cuisinart, collecting Lafite Rothschild wines, being domestically abused by Lois Lane, drinking spritzers, attending a therapist, jogging, embracing political liberalism, writing exposés on nuclear waste, splitting the check at sushi bars, attending women's festivals, marching at Greenpeace demonstrations, experimenting with bisexuality, being in touch with his feelings, having the popular appeal of Walter Mondale, and most likely being played by Woody Allen in his next film.[41]

Needless to say, virtually none of these attributes reflect anything said in any of DC's statements to the press, but serve as an extrapolation of the direction it was feared, either genuinely or for laughs, that Superman would be taken. However one correct point from DC that many articles misquoted, either willfully or otherwise, was the idea that Kent would keep a Nautilus machine (an expensive piece of home gym equipment) in his apartment as a means of explaining away his impressive physique which he was no longer at such pains to hide while in his secret identity. The primary response was clearly that the very ownership of a Nautilus machine was an indelible mark of having become one of the hated yuppies. Indeed, the cultural associations attached to this exercise machine seemed to be something of an unexpected point of fixation. Clearly, it was a passing element of Byrne's plan to which an unexpected cultural significance was attributed.

"Why are they doing this to Superman?" bemoaned one journalist, "Gimmie a break! Just when we need symbols of patient, self-assured masculinity, Clark goes the fernbar route. They may as well have turned him into a hairdresser, or an interior decorator."[42]

Yuppies and Reagan's America

While yuppies have never been widely-lauded figures in popular culture, the intensity behind the anti-yuppie sentiment expressed in so many of these articles is somewhat confounding upon reading them a quarter of a century later. The backlash seemingly reflected the sense that a long-cherished popular character such as Superman was being incongruously saddled with the trappings of a distrusted and much-lampooned aspect of 1980s consumerist modernity.

There is a particularly gender-centric issue at the heart of this response, with the notion that yuppies, this new breed of "1980s man," was a gender identity inimical to a traditional conservative view of American masculinity. A mode of masculinity which many of these journalists clearly felt Superman used to, and still should, exemplify.

The frequent references to quiche and the bitingly satirical tone of some of the articles were undoubtedly a reference to the then recent bestseller *Real Men Don't Eat Quiche* by Bruce Feirstein, "a guidebook to all that is truly masculine."[43] Although clearly parodic in its tone and exaggerations, the slim volume provides an illuminating time capsule of the types of behavior and preoccupations that were considered by many as unmanly at the dawn of Reagan's America. Due to its prominence in the popular book's title, being a "quiche-eater" became a topical shorthand for everything that was seen as pretentious and effeminate about yuppies and other sensitive "new men" of the nascent Reagan era.

Of course, "Reagan's America" is itself quite a loaded term, but useful nevertheless in describing the popular culture of an era in which a socially conservative government won two landslide elections, maintained an aggressive foreign policy and restored for many the sense of national pride and patriotic jingoism that had dissipated over the tumultuous upheavals of the previous two decades.

Susan Jeffords' book *Hard Bodies: Hollywood Masculinity in the Reagan Era* discusses at length the rise of blockbuster action movies such as the *Rambo* and *Die Hard* films, and how they were situated within a discourse of masculinity. Jeffords describes Reagan's own political image as self-consciously masculine, drawing on his history as a cowboy actor, and the many aspects of his leadership style being tailored towards portraying himself— and, by extension, America — as strong, decisive, and resolute in the face of all opposition. This self-promoted image was disseminated in intentional contrast to the previous Carter administration, which it retroactively framed as weak, indecisive, and "feminine," presiding over the tail-end of a period of perceived social malaise that had seen American masculinity and national pride notionally in a state of perpetual decline ever since the 1950s, eviscerated by the Vietnam War, and culminating in the perceived inability to take a "strong" stance on the Iranian hostage crisis and the Soviet invasion of Afghanistan.

This downward spiral that the "Reagan Revolution" sought to redress had been reflected through the preceding decade of films that depicted conflicted, often countercultural values, where even its action heroes such as those depicted in films like *Dirty Harry* were, at best, marginalized figures fighting alone against a decaying social order.[44]

Although neither a direct product of Hollywood nor truly within the "Action" genre as constructed by cinema, Superman comics nevertheless existed within the same cultural framework of mainstream action-adventure storytelling. Superman's relaunch was inevitably subject to this newly macho popular culture in the manner of these Hollywood trends that Jeffords discusses.

Indeed, as one report on Superman's comic book revisions puts it: "The Reagan administration ... has brought an insatiable appetite for heroes. Rocky and Rambo fill the cinema screens.... Presidents send in the cavalry hither and yon, and all's right with the world," noting that "(t)hese times should be sweet for Superman, the nonpareil of American strong men," rather than his suffering from low sales and requiring re-evaluation.[45]

It is in this context, then, of a Reaganite *zeitgeist* with a newfound interest in supposedly "traditional" views of masculinity taken to hyperbolic new extremes, that much of the criticism of the announced changes to Superman needs to be understood, as well as the strength of their reactions to his perceived emasculation chiefly through association with yuppie stereotypes of unmasculine pretension and sensitivity. As one disapproving journalist put it:

> Anyone who thinks today's kids hunger for vulnerable, nurturing superheroes, hasn't witnessed two 8-year-olds conquering creation with their Schwartzenegger-musculatured, arsenal-toting Masters-of-the-Universe action figures.[46]

What is perhaps most striking about the tone of disapproval in these articles, ranging from scornful distain to mild hysteria, is the extent to which many of the writers appear to be reacting with a strong amount of knee-jerk assumptions and very little appreciation of the facts. Although the majority of articles were published in July 1986 and many note that the first issue of *The Man of Steel* had already been released, virtually none of the articles involve any kind of textual review of the comic book itself, relying primarily on quotes from Byrne, Levitz, Kahn or other DC sources regarding its content.

There is essentially no direct engagement with the actual material. The only exceptions to this were some instances of quotes from vox-pop interviews with fans and store owners at comic book shops offering varying opinions on the reboot's creative and financial viability, displaying no strong consensus.[47] It was evidently the *phenomenon* of Superman's revision and the potential for controversy therein, rather than the comic itself, that was deemed newsworthy.

To some extent this was perhaps inevitable, as the story was hardly major national news so much as a headline-worthy puff piece, in many cases the fodder of editorials, opinion pieces and columnists. Careful objective journalism was apparently not a high priority, and a few articles were seemingly tongue in cheek.[48]

Indeed, the headline from which this chapter takes its title is that of "Ed Anger's" *Weekly World News* column, a clearly satirical exaggeration of a conservative response to the Superman story, remains nevertheless surprisingly reflective of the sentiments expressed in the majority of negative articles:

> It's bad enough that John Wayne's gone, but now they're steppin' on Superman's cape ... they've changed him into SuperWimp ... a modern, sensitive guy. You know — a spineless wimp who cries to show women that he's one of the gals ... able to burst into tears when his favorite restaurant is out of quiche ... those smarty-pants comic book bozos have changed our "Man of Steel"... It's one thing to update something so it'll sell. But it's another to tamper with American tradition. Superman was the ultimate American. And in these troubled times — with those upstart Libyans and those zappy women's libbers — we need a Superman to look up to.[49]

Anger's article encapsulates many of the concerns regarding the revision, of turning Superman into a wimpy, emasculated yuppie and the implied lack of cultural authority for DC to violate a piece of sacred Americana.

Although many writers cited the flagging sales numbers by way of explanation,[50] few give much credence to DC's stated imperative to revive Superman's circulation and, notably, none whatsoever identify as current comic readers themselves. This is further evident from the number of factual mistakes among the articles, particularly the prevailing assumption that Superman's characteristics had, prior to the relaunch in question, *never* changed and that this assault on the character's status quo was for the first time fundamentally altering a previously sacrosanct formula.[51]

As Byrne himself was keen to point out, this was scarcely the first time Superman's origin, powers or portrayal had been revised, claiming "This is about the fifth time that a 'fix' has been done on the character, but this is the most sweeping."[52] It was also in any case very likely the first time DC had chosen to make so much of a point of doing so as to announce it to the mainstream media.

A particularly intriguing aspect of this is the focus on the supposed emasculation of Kent, given that Byrne's openly stated and oft-quoted goal was quite clearly the opposite, intending to portray a tougher, more assertive Clark with behavior patterned after the unquestionably masculine portrayal by George Reeves. Yet the mere mention of the phrases "upwardly mobile" and "Nautilus machine" were sufficient for many journalists to overlook any changes in Kent's persona as far less significant than the unmanly implications of his change in image or lifestyle.

"He's sensitive, he's caring, he's today's man of mush.... The wimpification of Superman is underway" declared one particularly mocking article, decrying that this new "trendy Superman" would become:

> ... more vulnerable." (Gag me with a chunk of kryptonite!) ... Superman will be more enlightened than Phil Donahue, more sensitive than Alan Alda ... in all likelihood, instead of employing brute force, he'll simply relate to criminals.... Doubtless Clark Quiche will ... jog, play racquet ball, and talk about his need for "personal space." He will join a male consciousness-raising group ... and perhaps become bi-sexual.

To round out his objections to the gender politics, distressed by the prospect of a more equal, "'80s" relationship between Kent and Lois Lane, he snipes "Women's lib conquers comicdom. How depressing." After an extended lampoon imagining "Superwimp" saving endangered species (such as liberal Democrats), beating up slumlords,[53] protesting against South Africa and splitting the dinner check with Lois, the exasperated journalist declares "It is more than I can bear. Henceforth, I shall root for Lex Luthor."[54]

This fixation with lifestyle as a masculine indicator is particularly curious in retrospect, especially if one stops for a moment to consider what Clark Kent was supposedly being changed *from* to become a yuppie. The persona of the rather butch George Reeves notwithstanding, most depictions of Clark Kent were, one would think, quite far from the ideal definition of stoic

Reagan-era masculinity.[55] The traditional pre–*Man of Steel* portrayal of Clark Kent was as a meek, cowardly introvert constantly being bossed around or outright spurned by Lois Lane, hardly the image of a Reaganite macho man.

Why then did so many media responses implicitly contend that the new "yuppie" Clark Kent would be even *less* acceptably masculine than the old "wimpy" version? Perhaps for many the personae of Kent and Superman were on some level lumped together, and many ascribed an assumed model of appropriate masculinity to the perceived "classic" Superman that was thereby inclusive of Kent.

Only a few of the more thoughtful mainstream articles touch on this notion, but their analysis takes a metaphorical bent, viewing Clark Kent as a figure representing children's state of weakness compared to the "true" identity of Superman being one of aspirational adulthood. For example, one columnist identifying as a childhood Superman fan, having dispensed with the predictable jokes about "turning the boy from Smallville into Quicheman" and his desire "to tell this Byrne character [to] Eat Kryptonite!," proceeds to argue a more nuanced case against his perception of the new 'macho' model for Kent:

> The attraction of Superman was that he personified that bundle of inadequacies and insecurities that we call a boy.... Kent was the boy, the reader, and Superman was who the boy could someday be.... They can look at Kent and identify.... Kent is the guy who does not wear his machismo on his sleeve.... He knows that true manliness has nothing to do with aggression or belligerence but, instead, the way you conduct yourself ... the message is a worthy one: being a man takes discipline and self-control.[56]

This takes an interesting view of the gender politics at play, and is rather at odds with the frenzy of anti-yuppie macho angst displayed in other articles, even if it generally agrees with their disapproval of the announced revision. The gender models at play here are also somewhat apart from the wider field of articles, focused less on the binary of "spineless yuppies" and "real men" than on the equally if not more troubling extremes of macho posturing.

While this piece misinterprets and overreacts to the "more assertive" characterization of Clark Kent almost as much as many of the other articles do over the yuppie label, it offers an alternative voice in acknowledging the "wimpy" classic Kent as still being an acceptable male role model, albeit as a somewhat non-diegetic expression of Superman's manly self-restraint.

What conclusions can one draw about the 1986 reboot of Superman and the controversy that ensued in the mainstream print media? There is a temptation to disregard the offended, disdainful response of a group of editorial writers and columnists scattered across America as ill-informed and inconsequential, a soft-target beat-up on a slow news day. Yet this would be both unfair, and short-sighted.

Granted, the controversy was relatively short-lived, its peak of intensity not even outlasting the publication of *The Man of Steel* miniseries, garnering few mentions a mere couple of years later in retrospectives reporting on the character's 50th Anniversary.[57] It was not a major national debate, nor did the backlash have any appreciable effect on the publication of this new reimagined Superman going forward. There was certainly no hurried recall or backdown as with the example of the New Coke raised by some of the mocking journalists.[58]

Indeed, there is little evidence that the mainstream media's attention had any significant creative impact on the future direction of the Superman comics other than perhaps inadvertently publicizing the new comics even more. Even in 1986 the gulf between habitual comic buyers and the disinterested general public was such that the news reports were unlikely to have put off anyone already interested in buying these rebooted titles.

The legacy of Byrne's major revisions to the Superman mythos in *The Man of Steel* and beyond is undeniable, doubling sales[59] and shaping Superman's portrayal in the comics for decades to come, and yet it had little initial impact on the wider American public. It was not until later multimedia incarnations that this modernization of the world's first superhero gained a wider dissemination, most notably in the 1993–1997 television series *Lois and Clark: The New Adventures of Superman* which broadly conformed to Byrne's redefinition of Clark Kent as a relatable, non-performed personality who was more romantically viable to Lois Lane than the unattainable yet humanized Superman.

So what then of this small but intense wave of media disapproval back at the time these changes were first announced? Even though these articles were most definitely not aimed at the comic-buying faithful, they did represent in microcosm a moment in the psyche of Reagan's America where a conservative base was rebelling against change. Change in culture, change in views of acceptable class and gender roles, change in notions of heroic role models. This view of America stood for pride in old-fashioned values, and its cultural icons were not to be meddled with by the dubious hand of revisionism.

While in one sense the evident ignorance and lack of direct engagement with the comics field might seem to diminish the meaningfulness of this media response, in some respects the opposite is true. Similarly radical changes being performed on almost any other character (as in fact *was* happening across DC's product line) certainly did not spark the same level of reaction, if any, in the mainstream press. The notion of changing of Superman, even for those who had not read a comic in decades — if ever — genuinely meant something in the popular consciousness, regardless of whether those commenting upon it did not entirely understand what that meaning might truly be. Inevitably then, these journalists found their own meaning in it. While for DC this was a bold attempt to clean house and garner a new audience by making their character relevant for the 1980s, for many in the press this was a disturbing sign of the times. Superman, they suggested, was not a mere comic book character to be changed at whim to boost sales and reach new audiences, but a patriotic icon of national culture. Thus, drawing very little on the comics of the times, it was this constructed, imagined identity of who and what "the real Superman" was, and what he was presumed to represent in a shared consensus of the popular imagination, that these journalists championed. It was a conglomerate vision of an entirely imagined "classic" or "traditional" Superman which these articles revealed to have gradually assumed a tangible place in American folklore, there on the cusp of the character's 50th Anniversary. As one writer for *Time* magazine put it: "This older image, this Classic Coke, the real Superman, is a figure who somehow manages to embody the best qualities in that nebulous thing known as the American character."[60] While a mocking and irate press may have demonstrated little understanding of the state of Superman comics in 1986, in expressing their revulsion at the notion of change they inadvertently demonstrated just how much the myth of Superman had become an institutionalized touchstone of American popular culture.

CHAPTER NOTES

1. Cobb, Nathan. "Will the New Superman Fly?" *The Boston Globe*, June 13, 1986. 37–38.

2. Goulart, Ron. "Steel Anniversary." *St. Louis Post-Dispatch*, October 29, 1987. 1, 5.

3. One article mentions that Superman's comics were at this time being outsold by relatively obscure Marvel titles such as *Defenders* and *Power Man & Iron Fist*, which were being cancelled due to their sales being deemed too low. Shainblum, Mark, "Time for 'Mild-Mannered Reporter' Kent Is Past." *The Gazette*, December 13, 1985.

4. Comic books starring Superman had fallen to around the 40th rank of DC's titles, and accounted for less than 10% of the company's sales. Moore, Robert, Jr. "New 'Man of Steel' Learning to Bend a Little." *Pittsburgh Press*, June 22, 1986; Chan, Mei-Mei. "A Less Super Superman for the '80s." *USA Today*, May 29, 1986; Cobb, 37–38.

5. Musial, Robert. "Superman, at 50, Gets His Grip Back." *Detroit Free Press*, June 13, 1988. 1B-2B.

6. Wolfman, Marv (w), and George Pérez (a). *Crisis on Infinite Earths #1–12*, (April 1985-March 1986), DC Comics.

7. Van Hise, James. "The Rebirth of Superman." *Comics File Magazine #3* ("Spotlight on Superman: Man of Steel"), 1986. (Canoga Park, CA: Heroes Publishing, Inc), 50–51; Salem, Rob. "Superfan Gives New Superman Thumbs Up." *The Toronto Star*, June 21, 1986. F11.

8. Pustz, Matthew. *Comic Book Culture: Fanboys and True Believers.* (University of Mississippi Press, 1999), 113, 129–130, 132–133, 205.

9. Bongco, Mila. *Reading Comics: Language, culture, and the concept of the superhero in comic books.* (New York: Garland Publishers, 2000), 129; Pustz, 112–113.

10. Belcher, Jerry. "At 48, Superman Has Slowed Down Just a Bit." [Newspaper not

attributed, however writer is credited as a "Times Staff Writer"], June 18, 1986. 3, 23; Mietkiewicz, Henry. "Superman Goes Back to the Drawing Board." *The Toronto Star*, June 21, 1986. F1.

11. As John Byrne put it: "Superman himself didn't even know he was from Krypton until like 1948, but then it became the most *important* thing in his *life!*" Interview from *David Anthony Kraft's Comics Interview #71*, (New York: Fictioneer Books, 1989), 13.

12. Baran, Walter. "New-look Superman Takes Off in Comics." *Star* (presumably *The Star* of Chicago), June 24, 1986. 35.

13. Emery, C. Eugene, Jr. "'Man of Steel' Scrapped and Recycled by Revisionist Publisher to Hype Sales." *Indianapolis Star*, November 2, 1986. 1, 5.

14. Lesie, Michele. "A Tempered Man of Steel for the '80s." *The Plain Dealer* (Cleveland), June 21, 1986.

15. Maeder, Jay (of the *New York Daily News*). "Superman's Image Regresses." *The Lima News* (Ohio), June 16, 1986.

16. Hogan, Pete. "No sleep till Krypton." *Melody Maker*, May 3, 1988, 46; Cohen, Richard. "'New' Superman Eats Quiche, Jogs, and Leaves Boys Without a Hero." *Daily Press* (Newport News, Virginia), June 20, 1986. Article also syndicated under the headlines "If Superman Changes, Boys' Dreams Will Die." *Reno Gazette-Journal*, June 15, 1986, Opinion section 2C, and "Boys Need a 'Real' Superman." *Philadelphia Inquirer* (Pennsylvania), June 15, 1986.

17. Mietkiewicz, F1; Salem, F11.

18. One quote by Byrne that "*Clark Kent is going to be more aggressive — not so squeaky clean... Superman had turned into Mary Worth. We want to try to make him a little more like Dirty Harry*" was widely disseminated via an Associated Press article: Stowell, Linda. "Clark Kent Gains Dirty Harry-style Grit." *Fort Wayne News-Sentinel*, May 16, 1986, 4D. Article also syndicated under the headlines: "DC Comics: New 'Clark' Should 'Make Your Day.'" *Star Magazine* from the *San Antonio Express-News*, May 5, 1986; "Super Redefined[:] New Images for Clark Kent, Lois Lane, Lex Luthor." *Appleton Post-Crescent* (Wisconsin), May 5, 1986; "Modernized[:] Superman Getting New Image." *Beaver County Times* (Pennsylvania), May 5, 1986; "Dirty Superman?" *The Denver Post*, May 5, 1986; Untitled, *The Tri-Valley Herald* (California), May 5, 1986, 2; Untitled, *The Lima News* (Ohio), May 5, 1986.

19. Smith, Marcia. "Now Clark Isn't Such a Wimp." *San Francisco Chronicle*, June 11, 1986. 20, 22.

20. Maeder, Jay. "Slower Than a Speeding Bullet." *New York Daily News*, November 9, 1985; Gates, David. "The Once and Future Superhero." *Newsweek*, November 25, 1985, 6.

21. "Bring on the Kryptonite" (editorial). *The Gazette* (Montreal), December 3, 1985. Note: Frank Furillo was a character from the television series *Hill Street blues* (1981–1987), a police captain who was often depicted sharing his feelings with his wife.

22. Although an exact transcript of the announcement could not be located, there is sufficient overlap in the quotes given by many of the articles reporting on it that much of the substance of DC's statement can be ascertained. The information quoted in the June/July 1986 articles seems to have chiefly derived from a presentation by DC at "Licensing '86," presumably a licensing trade show. Forkan, James P. "It's a bird! It's a plane! But Is It Superman?" [Unclear attribution of newspaper, "AA"], June 16, 1986.

23. Smith, Andy. "Egad! DC Comics Scaling Back Powers of Superman." *Lansing State Journal* (Michigan), August 11, 1986.

24. "It's a Nerd, It's a Pain..." (Unattributed editorial). *The Philadelphia Inquirer*, June 16, 1986. 10-A.

25. Forkan; Smith, Marcia, of the Dallas Times Herald. "Forging a New Life for the Man of Steel," [Unsourced, undated].

26. Rghter [unclear spelling], Larry. "Reinventing Superman: He'll Be Upwardly

Mobile." [Unsourced, but clearly from 1986, most likely June based on close similarity of content to other articles from that month].

27. Dougherty, Dick. "Man of Steel Still Spry for an Old Geezer." *The Times Union* (Rochester, New York), June 10, 1986. 1A–2A.

28. Rogers, Dennis. "Superfan Derides New 'Man of Carbon-Reinforced Plastic.'" *The News and Observer* (North Carolina), July 10, 1986.

29. McWhirter, Nickie. "This New Image Stuff Is Deadlier than Kryptonite." *Detroit Free Press*, June 16, 1986.

30. Nyhan, David. "Superman's New Image." *The Boston Globe*, June 12, 1986. 19.

31. Feder, Don. "Superman Turns Wimpy." *Boston Herald*, June 16, 1986. Article also reprinted under the headline "Out of the Phone Booth Comes Superwimp." *New York Post*, June 18, 1986.

32. Unattributed. "Middle Age Meets Superman." *The Economist*, June 28, 1986.

33. Smith, Andy.

34. Rogers, Dennis.

35. Such as: Greene, Bob. "Great Caesar's ghost! A Superman of [the] '80s." Unsourced, 1986; Ostler, Scott. "This Columnist Would Be a Super Addition to Ranks." *Los Angeles Times*, June 19, 1986; Baker, Russel. "It's a columnist of steel." *Los Angeles Herald Examiner*, June 19, 1986. A15; Goodman, Ellen. "Man of Steel's X-Ray Insights Leap Over Mortal Writers." *The Journal-Gazette* (Fort Wayne, Indiana), June 18, 1896; and MacPherson, Les. "Egads! Superman Gets Macho Image." *Saskatoon Star-Phoenix* (Canada), June 26, 1986; Unattributed. "Dear DC Comics." *Time* (More specific attribution is lacking), June 11, 1986; Gans, Herbert J. (of New York). "A Job for Clark Kent." *Time* (attribution lacking), July 3, 1986.

36. Wolfe, Ron. "Man of Steel's Mid-life Crisis." *The Tulsa Tribune* (Oklahoma), June 20, 1986. 1C, 2C.

37. McWhirter, Nickie.

38. Indeed, Byrne and Levitz were explicitly stating that Clark Kent would *not* be portrayed as a yuppie, to little avail. For example: Maeder, "Superman's Image Regresses"; Rghter, Larry.

39. Unattributed, "Steel Men Don't Eat Quiche." *Daily News* (New York), June 12, 1986. Note: The ferret comment refers to an immediately preceding piece on the same editorial page mocking a recent trend in pet ferret ownership among the "faddish" type of "yupscale human lemmings" with an "appetite for style."

40. Greene. Note: *GQ* is a men's magazine with a focus on fashion and upmarket lifestyles.

41. Variously in Haroldson, Tom. "Superwimp: Flying High 50 Years, a Great Hero Belly-flops"; *Kalamazoo Gazette* (Michigan), June 17, 1987. D1, D2; Nyhan; "It's a Nerd, It's a Pain..." (editorial); Feder; Cohen.

42. Nyhan. Note: "Fern bar" was a slang term for a particular style of plant-decorated American taverns stereotypically frequented by yuppies.

43. Feirstein, Bruce (w), with illustrations by Lee Lorenz. *Real Men Don't Eat Quiche*. 1982. Pocket Books: New York.

44. Jeffords, 2–23.

45. "Middle Age Meets Superman."

46. Feder. Note: *Masters of the Universe*, starring He-Man, was a highly successful action toyline in the 1980s, groundbreaking for its multimedia cross-promotion.

47. Wykes, S.L. "Rebirth of a Legend: It's a Bird! It's a Plane! No, It's Him Again!" *San Jose Mercury News* (California), June [18? Illegible], 1986; Bentley, Rick. "Revamped Superman Comic Book a Hot Seller." *Alexandria Daily Town Talk* (Louisiana), June 25, 1986; Wolfe; Henderson, Tim. "Superman Gets Facelift." *Springfield News-Sun* (Ohio), June 22, 1986. 1A, 4A.

48. One rather bizarre piece cites no true facts whatsoever, presenting an entire article as an apparently po-faced parody of the relaunch of Superman, complete with a fictitious interview with "Joel Smith," would-be creator of the new Superman. "Smith" proceeds to outline ever-more absurd revisions to render Superman more mundane, such as making the hero vulnerable to synthetic fibers instead of Kryptonite, renaming him Jeff Kent, recasting Lex Luthor as his landlord, while Mr. Mxyzptlk as his neighbor is "not a villain exactly, but he is a real asshole." Johnstone, El-Arry. "Man of Steel Revamped: DC Comics Fixes Superman." *USA Today*, undated.

49. Anger, Ed (A *nom de plume* used by multiple writers of the "My America" column. Articles from this period are generally attributed to the creator of the persona, Rafael "Rafe" Klinger). "The New 'Man of Steel' Is a Quiche-Eating Wimp." *Weekly World News*, Undated.

50. This was mentioned in many articles, such as: Maeder; Emery.

51. For example: Smith, Marcia; Baran.

52. See Van Hise; Henderson; Paul Levitz also asserted to the press that this was not the first revision of Superman, in: Rghter.

53. Which is ironic, since this is *exactly* the sort of thing that the socially-conscious, staunchly liberal early Superman did in his pre–1940 comics stories.

54. Feder.

55. At a publicity event celebrating an exhibition on Superman at the Smithsonian Institution, noted feminist Gloria Steinem said of the character: "He's an inspiration to ordinary people — men, especially. Clark Kent went against the traditional idea of masculinity: he was shy and bumbling, and wasn't afraid to appear sensitive, or fall in love. He could be viewed as a wimp, but he was Superman." Unattributed, "Fifty," *The New Yorker*, June 8, 1987. 25–26.

56. Cohen.

57. Such as: Friedrich, Otto. "Up, Up and Awaaay!!!: America's favorite hero turns 50, ever changing but indestructible." *Time*, March 14, 1988. 66–74; Akers, Paul E. "Bring Back the *REAL* Superman." *Washington Post*, December 31, 1988. A19; Pye, Michael. "Many Super Returns." *The Observer* (UK), August 23, 1987. 45.

58. Byrne himself wearily acknowledged having heard countless references to New Coke, yet argued that in many respects his changes were actually bringing Superman back to a classic form more closely resembling his 1938 debut. Van Hise.

59. Pye; Emery.

60. Friedrich.

BIBLIOGRAPHY

Akers, Paul E. "Bring Back the *REAL* Superman." *Washington Post*, December 31, 1988, A19.

Anger, Ed. "The New 'Man of Steel' Is a Quiche-Eating Wimp." *Weekly World News*, undated.

Baker, Russel. "It's a columnist of steel." *Los Angeles Herald Examiner*, June 19, 1986, A15.

Baran, Walter. "New-look Superman Takes Off in Comics." *Star* (presumably *The Star* of Chicago), June 24, 1986, 35.

Belcher, Jerry. "At 48, Superman Has Slowed Down Just a Bit." [Newspaper not attributed, however writer is credited as a "Times Staff Writer"], June 18, 1986, 3, 23

Bentley, Rick. "Revamped Superman Comic Book a Hot Seller." *Alexandria Daily Town Talk* (Louisiana), June 25, 1986.

Bongco, Mila. *Reading Comics: Language, culture, and the concept of the superhero in comic books.* New York: Garland Publishers, 2000.

Chan, Mei-Mei. "A less super Superman for the '80s." *USA Today*, May 29, 1986.

Cobb, Nathan. "Will the New Superman Fly?" *The Boston Globe*, June 13, 1986, 37–38.

Cohen, Richard. "'New' Superman Eats Quiche, Jogs, and Leaves Boys Without a Hero." *Daily Press* (Newport News, Virginia), June 20, 1986.

David Anthony Kraft's Comics Interview #71. New York: Fictioneer Books, 1989.

Dougherty, Dick. "Man of Steel Still Spry For an Old Geezer." *The Times Union* (Rochester, New York), June 10, 1986, 1A–2A.

Emery, C. Eugene, Jr. "'Man of Steel' Scrapped and Recycled by Revisionist Publisher to Hype Sales." *Indianapolis Star*, November 2, 1986, 1, 5.

Feder, Don. "Superman Turns Wimpy." *Boston Herald*, June 16, 1986. Article also reprinted under the headline "Out of the Phone Booth Comes Superwimp." *New York Post*, June 18, 1986.

Feirstein, Bruce, with illustrations by Lee Lorenz. *Real Men Don't Eat Quiche.* 1982. Pocket Books: New York.

Forkan, James P. "It's a Bird! It's a Plane! But Is It Superman?" [Unclear attribution of newspaper, "AA"], June 16, 1986.

Friedrich, Otto. "Up, Up and Awaaay!!!: America's Favorite Hero Turns 50, Ever Changing but Indestructible." *Time*, March 14, 1988, 66–74.

Gans, Herbert J."A Job for Clark Kent." *Time* (attribution lacking), July 3, 1986.

Gates, David. "The Once and Future Superhero." *Newsweek*, November 25, 1985, 6.

Goodman, Ellen. "Man of Steel's X-Ray Insights Leap Over Mortal Writers." *The Journal-Gazette* (Fort Wayne, Indiana), June 18, 1896.

Goulart, Ron. "Steel Anniversary." *St. Louis Post-Dispatch*, October 29, 1987, 1, 5.

Greene, Bob. "Great Caesar's Ghost! A Superman of [the] '80s." Unsourced, 1986.

Haroldson, Tom. "Superwimp: Flying High 50 Years, a Great Hero Belly-flops." *Kalamazoo Gazette* (Michigan), June 17, 1987.

Henderson, Tim. "Superman Gets Facelift." Springfield News-Sun (Ohio), June 22, 1986. 1A, 4A.

Hogan, Pete. "No Sleep till Krypton." *Melody Maker*, May 3, 1988, 46.

Jeffords, Susan. *Hard Bodies: Hollywood Masculinty in the Reagan Era.* 1994. Rutgers University Press: New Brunswick, NJ.

"It's a Nerd, It's a Pain..." (Unattributed editorial). *The Philadelphia Inquirer*, June 16, 1986, 10-A.

Johnstone, El-Arry. "Man of Steel Revamped: DC Comics Fixes Superman." *USA Today*, undated.

Lesie, Michele. "A Tempered Man of Steel for the '80s." *The Plain Dealer* (Cleveland), June 21, 1986.

MacPherson, Les. "Egads! Superman Gets Macho Image." *Saskatoon Star-Phoenix* (Canada), June 26, 1986.

Maeder, Jay. "Slower Than a Speeding Bullet." *New York Daily News*, November 9, 1985.

_____. "Superman's Image Regresses." *The Lima News* (Ohio), June 16, 1986.

McWhirter, Nickie. "This New Image Stuff is Deadlier than Kryptonite." *Detroit Free Press*, June 16, 1986.

Mietkiewicz, Henry. "Superman Goes Back to the Drawing Board." *The Toronto Star*, June 21, 1986, F1.

Moore, Robert, Jr. "New 'Man of Steel' Learning to Bend a Little." *Pittsburgh Press*, June 22, 1986.

Musial, Robert. "Superman, at 50, Gets His Grip Back." *Detroit Free Press*, June 13, 1988, 1B–2B.

Nyhan, David. "Superman's New Image." *The Boston Globe*, June 12, 1986, 19.

Ostler, Scott. "This Columnist Would Be a Super Addition to Ranks." *Los Angeles Times*, June 19, 1986.

Pustz, Matthew. *Comic Book Culture: Fanboys and True Believers*. Jackson: University of Mississippi Press, 1999.

Pye, Michael. "Many Super Returns." *The Observer* (UK), August 23, 1987, 45.

Rghter [unclear spelling], Larry. "Reinventing Superman: He'll Be Upwardly Mobile." [Unsourced, but clearly from 1986, most likely June, based on close similarity of content to other articles from that month].

Rogers, Dennis. "Superfan Derides New 'Man of Carbon-Reinforced Plastic.'" *The News and Observer* (Raleigh, North Carolina), July 10, 1986.

Salem, Rob. "Superfan Gives New Superman Thumbs Up." *The Toronto Star*, June 21, 1986, F11.

Shainblum, Mark. "Time for 'Mild-Mannered Reporter' Kent Is Past." *The Gazette*, December 13, 1985.

Smith, Andy. "Egad! DC Comics Scaling Back Powers of Superman." *Lansing State Journal* (Michigan), August 11, 1986.

Smith, Marcia. "Forging a New Life for the Man of Steel," [Unsourced, undated].

_____. "Now Clark Isn't Such a Wimp." *San Francisco Chronicle*, June 11, 1986, 20, 22.

Stowell, Linda. "Clark Kent Gains Dirty Harry-style Grit." *Fort Wayne News-Sentinel*, May 16, 1986, 4D.

Unattributed. "Dear DC Comics." *Time* (More specific attribution is lacking), June 11, 1986.

Unattributed. "Fifty," *The New Yorker*, June 8, 1987, 25–26.

Unattributed. "Middle Age Meets Superman." *The Economist*, June 28, 1986.

Unattributed. "Steel Men Don't Eat Quiche." *Daily News* (New York), June 12, 1986.

Wolfe, Ron. "Man of Steel's Mid-Life crisis." *The Tulsa Tribune* (Oklahoma), June 20, 1986, 1C, 2C.

Wolfe; Tim. "Superman Gets Facelift." *Springfield News-Sun* (Ohio), June 22, 1986, 1A, 4A.

Wolfman, Marv (w), and George Pérez (a). *Crisis on Infinite Earths #1–12*, (April 1985–March 1986), DC Comics.

Wykes, S.L."Rebirth of a Legend: It's a bird! It's a Plane! No, It's Him Again!" *San Jose Mercury News* (California), June [18? Illegible], 1986

Van Hise, James "The Rebirth of Superman." *Comics File Magazine #3* ("Spotlight on Superman: Man of Steel"), 1986. Canoga Park, CA: Heroes Publishing.

More Human Than (Super) Human

Clark Kent's Smallville and Reagan's America

MICHAEL SMITH

In the mid–80s, DC pried top gun artist/writer John Byrne (*X-Men, Fantastic Four, Alpha Flight*) away from Marvel comics, and gave him free reign to reimagine and reinvigorate the Superman character (and sales) for a contemporary audience. In *The Man of Steel* (July-Sep. 1986) mini-series and then in continuing monthly adventures, Byrne and the other Superman writers made a fundamental shift in the character's identity: Clark Kent isn't just a mask for Superman. He isn't an alter-ego, or an act, or even a playful put-on. Clark Kent is the real person — no, even more, he is *the real hero*, and Superman is "just a fancy pair of longjohns that lets me operate in public."[1] Superman, then, is a *convenience*, a conveyance for Clark Kent's values.

And who is Kent? What are his values? First and foremost, he is the absolutely perfect American son of Ma and Pa Kent, from Smallville, Kansas. And Smallville, itself, is the fulfillment of a particular brand of Reagan-era nostalgia: it is a "town in a bottle," a kind of oasis permanently suspended in an idea of the 1920s and 1930s, a time and place that may never have really existed but which we all somehow acutely remember (even comic book readers too young to have experienced it in the first place). It is a place that, Reagan promised, we could get back to again: a better, simpler, uncomplicated America, with a strong, clear notion of itself and its identity. In those better times, in thousands of places just like Smallville, Americans did not wring their hands, or spend one moment worrying about who we were and what it meant or what was the right thing to do. We just *knew*.

David Foster Wallace, in his essay "The View from Mrs. Thompson's," describes the essence of this quality. The piece begins in the immediate aftermath of 9/11, and focuses on Wallace's initial torturous attempts to somehow find and purchase an American flag, any kind or size of American flag, one that he might put out in front of his house. By the time it occurs to him that he needs one, there has already been a run on flags in all the stores for hundreds of miles around. There are none to be found.[2]

As he hunts for a flag, Wallace is, as he always in his nonfiction, extremely self-conscious. Even as he drives frantically from store to store, finding each one cleaned out, he can't stop wondering about his own need, why he feels he *must* have a flag. Is it just so his house is not the only one on his street — in the entire town, in the whole county — without one? Is it because he doesn't want to draw attention to himself, to have his house seem so conspicuous by a flag's absence? If he *didn't* have a flag, what kind of unintentional message would that send? How would he be perceived? Would it be taken like he was separating himself, making some kind of statement? What statement?

All of this eventually leads Wallace to an uncomfortable question: Is there is anything remotely authentic and/or genuine driving his desire for a flag?

"All those people dead," he writes, "And I'm sent to the edge by a plastic flag."[3]

Most of Wallace's work is concerned with questions having to do with authenticity and genuineness. A lot of it ultimately winds up painting itself into a corner like this: How does a person *register* sincerity? Can you even *attempt* sincerity? And how to do this, today, operating against the accumulated backdrop of irony and cynicism and suspicion driven by all the jaded decades and levels of hyper-aware media and entertainment?

At this point, Wallace backs up and brings us back to earlier in the week, to how he experienced that Tuesday. As a professor, a novelist, he is hyper-educated and hyper-aware, the kind of person who makes a very self-conscious decision *not* to have a television in his house. Catching the news on the radio, he has to run over to a neighbor's — Mrs. Thompson's — to watch. Mrs. Thompson is "exactly the kind of person who in an emergency even if her phone is busy you know you can just come on over."[4] Wallace sits and watches 9/11 unfold in the company of his Bloomington neighbors, "good people" from whom he feels terribly alienated. Here's how he describes them: "These people are not stupid, or ignorant.... What [they] are, or start to seem to me, is innocent. There is what would strike many Americans as a marked, startling lack of cynicism in the room. It does not, for example, occur to anyone here to remark on how it's maybe a little odd that all three network anchors are in shirtsleeves, or to consider the possibility that Dan Rather's hair's being mussed might not be wholly accidental, or that the constant re-running of horrific footage might not be just in case some viewers were only now tuning in and hadn't seen it yet. None of these ladies seem to notice the president's odd little lightless eyes appear to get closer and closer together throughout his taped address, nor that some of his lines sound almost plagiaristically identical to those uttered by Bruce Willis (as a right-wing wacko) in *The Siege* a couple of years back. Nor that at least some of the sheer weirdness of watching the Horror unfold has been how closely various shots and scenes have mirrored the plots of everything from *Die Hard I–III* to *Air Force One*. Nobody's near hip enough to lodge the sick and obvious [post-modern] complaint: We've Seen This Before. Instead, what they mostly do is all sit together and feel really bad."[5]

This, I think, is the place where Wallace begins to put his finger right on something very inchoate, and it's interesting that he can only manage to get to it by coming at it from the side, with this example, for it is indeed very hard to articulate without coming off like either a condescending jerk — or a romantic. But it is this moment that encapsulates the notion (and, one would hope, the reality) of what I will from here on call "Smallvilleness": a baseline of genuineness, made up of the truly decent and innocent (still far from stupid and naive) who operate without self-consciousness, cynicism, or pretense, of people who just *are*, who just *are* American, and they don't really think about it or question it or analyze it or frankly, worry about it too much. They just *know*. If such people actually exist, it does seem like the greatest concentration would be found in the small towns in the Midwest...

Here's what's funny:

Ronald Reagan, an actor, former head of the Screen Actor's guild and governor of California (California, probably the *least* real or genuine place in the country) understood Smallvilleness better than anyone. Certainly, he understood it better than any modern president (perhaps Clinton comes close) — maybe any president, ever. He understood how to appeal directly to Smallvilleness, to touch those who already possessed it, those who had no doubt, who were already "there." More importantly, he could turn it around, expand its reach, and use it to appeal to those who felt its absence inside of themselves most acutely. After the Bay of Pigs and Kennedy and the 1960s, after Woodstock and Vietnam, after Nixon and Watergate, after Carter and the oil embargo and the Iran Hostage crisis, after disillusionment and disco and the 1970s, when there is nothing but confusion about America and its rightful place in the world and, indeed, its very righteousness, Reagan emerges. And Reagan, he *uses* that confusion, that absence, that yearning, promising that he could take us back, get us there again, that if we joined with him, we could get back to that certain land, no questions asked, simple as that.

But how did Reagan come to understand Smallvilleness? Well, he grew up in a series of small, Illinois towns, each one very much like the last: Tampico, Galesburg, Monmouth, Dixon, Tampico again. His father was a shoe salesman, the family moving as he traded jobs from store to store. Reading the letters in which Reagan describes this childhood, one is struck by how consistently he veers away from any suggestion of real difficulty or conflict: the picture he paints is almost uniformly idyllic, and startlingly plain. Even when there is a hint of trouble — as when young Reagan and a friend find his father's shotgun and start playing with it in the attic, unable to get it to fire until Reagan pumps it once and says "Now try it" — it is quickly undercut, glossed over like there's a splotch of self-warming Vaseline thumbed on the lens of memory. (In the case of the shotgun, which produced "a dishpan sized hole in the ceiling," his friend's "two white-faced parents" rush upstairs, push open the door to find the two of us were sitting on the couch studying our Sunday school lessons to beat h--l" — yes, "hell" is actually spelled out H-DASH-DASH-L — "a perfect picture of innocence." At this very moment, the height of conflict — what did the parents *do*? — Reagan cuts it off, saying "Well, I'd better stop there or I'll be doing my whole life story."[6]

Reagan refers to these as "my Huck Finn years," but Huck Finn, with its unreliable narrator, its confused and troubled morality, weird humor, brutality, and occasional bouts of sadism, isn't right at all. (Reagan, I think, is thinking of Huck Finn, imagining Huck Finn, in a Smallvillain way: as the charming story of a rambunctious boy and a raft). The better comparison might be Leo Edwards' series of Jerry Todd books, or "juveniles." Indeed, in his 1965 autobiography *Where's the Rest of Me?*, Reagan says that he had a childhood "much like" Jerry Todd's.[7]

Thomas G. Lee, grandson of Leo Edwards, describes the best-selling Jerry Todd books (there were about a dozen in all) this way: "Jerry is the fictional friend of thousands of boys and girls who read the stories and books written in the 1920's and 1930's by my grandfather Edward Edson Lee who wrote under the pen name of Leo Edwards.... Jerry and his friends lived in Tutter, Illinois, a typical middle-western American small town at the turn of the century. In reality, Tutter was actually based on the village of Utica, Illinois, where [my grandfather] was born in 1884. Utica is about 40 miles from Tampico, Reagan's birthplace.[8] ... Lee concludes: "[My grandfather's] stories were always based on real people and real locations. He captured in his books a particular enduring quality about growing up in America, a quality found in the philosophy of Ronald Reagan."[9]

The 1920s and 1930s is a period which became permanently fixed for Reagan, frozen in a bottle, serving as kind of touchstone or baseline for his understanding of what being an American was all about. In his letters, Reagan paints a picture of an innocent and straight-forward time, relentlessly cheery and wholly divorced from the existent reality of what must have been his family's financial struggles and the Great Depression. You may remember that one of the more frequent criticisms of Reagan, particularly in the latter half of his presidency (and long before any suspicions of his having Alzheimer's were publicly confirmed), was about how he was "losing touch with reality," and that by the day, he was growing ever more forgetful and confused. More than this, even, was the suggestion that he had lost not only his grasp of the chronology of events, but the essential reality of those events. That is, he got confused about whether he had *actually* served in combat in World War II (he hadn't) or had only *played* someone in a movie who had been a soldier in World War II. The frequency with which Reagan revisited the story of George Gipp, and how often he did so in a weird sort of first person which seemed to make no real distinction between the movie character and himself, led more than one commentator to suggest that maybe he had come to actually believe that he actually *was* or really *had* been George Gipp in *Knute Rockne: All-American*, somehow suspended in time, urging his teammates to win just one for the Gipper.

But the suggestion, here, is that for Reagan, there's really no point in making these kinds of postmodern distinctions — between real and pretend, or in thinking about how the pretend comes not just to reflect but to influence the real. These are distinctions that David Foster Wallace, for one, can't help himself from drawing, as he sits there on Mrs. Thompson's couch and contemplates how much Bush reminds him of Bruce Willis. For Reagan, those sorts of distinctions not only ceased to matter, but in point of fact, *they never really mattered at all.*

It's true that, before he was a politician, Reagan was an actor. But if you stop and think about it, there's really not such a much of a difference between those two jobs. And Reagan was an actor/politician who *believed* the role. He believed in Smallville.

It is Reagan's insistent Smallvillness that is most reflected in Byrne's revision of Superman. It is why it is not just the entire history of the character's amazingly complicated dual identity that gets simplified — the character is now just Clark, Superman is Clark in longjohns — it is his very Otherness, his status as an orphan, as alien, as Kal-El, the Last Son of Krypton, that gets eliminated or rather, elided in Byrne's revision. Krypton, as far as Clark is concerned, is nothing more than the doomed planet where he "may have been conceived." Given access to its entire history through a strange holographic mind-projection, Clark quickly dismisses that knowledge as "ultimately meaningless," since he was "born on earth, when the rocket opened." Memories of Krypton transmitted to him by the ghosts of his biological parents are "curious mementos of a life that might have been."[9]

This (re)conception is continually explored in all three of the monthly Superman books that hit the reset button after *Man of Steel*. In *Superman #2* (Feb. 1987), the villainous multi-gazillionaire Lex Luthor confronts the very essence of Smallvilleness, and is totally, if subtly, defeated by it. He is completely undone, actually, without even knowing it, and without Clark/Superman himself having to so much as lift a finger. It is Clark's character and values alone — his impossible genuineness and authenticity — that do the heavy lifting for him, that protect him.

Noticing over coffee one morning that nearly every Superman scoop in *The Daily Planet* appears to be written by Clark Kent, Luthor decides to explore the "mysterious connection" between the two. He puts his best analysts, his best computer people, and his best criminal henchmen on the case. Combing all available news footage of Superman's deeds, they discover that Lana Lang (Clark's first love) seems always to be on the scene, a face in the crowd, a witness to all Superman's rescues and battles. When Lex's henchmen break into Ma and Pa Kent's house, they find an unusual scrapbook offering further clues. Lex's people combine these discoveries with all the available physical data they've managed to gather on Superman and all the material they've accumulated on Clark Kent (including his complete educational records and medical history, which reveal he "has never missed a day of school or work due to illness"), and stick it into a gigantic computer for "cross referencing." The computer clicks, whirls, and spits out: "Clark Kent is Superman."[10]

Lex's chief computer technician is thrilled: "Oh my goodness! That would never have occurred to me! And yet ... given the body of evidence ... it's so logical! So flawlessly logical!" Luthor, however, absolutely refuses to believe it. "Logical? Is it? To a machine, perhaps. Yes.... A soulless machine might make that deduction. But not Lex Luthor! I know better! I know that no man with the power of Superman would ever pretend to be a mere human! Such power is to be constantly exploited! Such power is to be used!!"[11] Here, it is Luthor's very cynicism about human nature, his inability to recognize genuineness, to conceive of an absence of ulterior motive, that prevents him from seeing — from accepting — a very obvious reality. A scientist who leveraged his genius into the largest, and most corrupt, corporate empire on the planet, Luthor is the polar opposite of Smallvillness. He is the kind of guy who hires Lois Lane's sister, gives her cancer, and then develops a once-a-month treatment just to maintain some kind of ongoing contact with Lois.[12] He is the kind of guy that starts a "Youth Intervention Program" to alleviate the city's gang problem, uses it as a recruitment and training ground for his private criminal army, and then writes the whole thing off in taxes.[13] It is his belief in the hidden, darkest corners of the human heart that blinds him to the fact of Superman's secret identity.

It is only the *second* issue of the new Superman monthly comic, and Superman has been indisputably revealed to Luthor as Clark Kent, and yet ... his secret couldn't be *more* safe. Later, after rescuing Lana, Clark says of his parents: "Everything I am, I owe to them. They gave me the guidance, the moral courage, to use my powers wisely. They taught me to love this world, to love humankind so much, that when I discovered my true, alien origin, it didn't matter. Ma and Pa taught me how to be human."[14] *Human?* One can almost hear Luthor's snorting (or gagging) at that. For Luthor, the ability to be so straight-forward and plainly sincere, to simply be the same on the inside as on the outside — indeed, to have *no* inside and outside, to have no real separation between the two, and to just ... *be a good person?* This plainly has nothing at all to do with being human. Not possible.

This matter of somehow reconciling Superman's impossibly authentic goodness with his humanity is a recurrent theme — one might even call it the primary concern — in all three of the ongoing Superman monthlies that picked up after the revision in *Man of Steel*. In *The Adventures of Superman #427* (April 1987), for example, Superman takes it upon himself to "disarm" the Middle Eastern nation of Qurac after a terrorist attack in downtown Metropolis. Even as he decimates the Quraci air forces, readers are told that this "violates his sensibilities" and that, while "He has the strength to rule this world ... he has the wisdom to not even consider it. He has the power to make things in his image, but not the ego to succumb to such selfish whims."[15] While he turns his attention to smashing a battery of tanks, Clark ruminates: "I've always hesitated before using my powers to affect the course of life on Earth. I can't let myself act like some god even if some people think I may be one. But if I were around in World War II, I would have had to confront Hitler, or I'd be shirking my responsibility. I may have special powers, but I'm still only a man."[16]

Clark's actions and his phrase "still only a man" presents something of an impossible contradiction at this point (and not just because he is busy tying a tank barrel into a knot at the time). If most of us tend toward the cynical, and think naturally along the similar lines as Lex Luthor, we might presume that Clark's humanity would lead him to shirk his responsibility, not lead him *to* it. But Clark insists, again and again, here and elsewhere that he is "just a man," as if that is his saving grace. For Clark never refers to or thinks of himself *as* "Kryptonian" or "from Krypton." Yes, his Kryptonion's physiology happens to give him unbelievable power, but it is — somehow — his humanity, the Smallvillness installed by Ma and Pa Kent, that prevents him from taking unfair advantage of his powers.

The Adventures of Superman #427 (April 1987), in particular, is preoccupied with exploring these contradictions, although mostly, it ends up running in place. As it turns out, members of some sort of long trapped or exiled alien race called "The Circle" happen to live in the sewers under Qurac. Prana, some kind of cat-man-lizard dressed in robes and a turban, telepathically enters Clark's mind, thinking Clark might be a long lost savior who has finally returned to deliver them. Prana's clumsy probing triggers a series of dream sequences. First, a projection of Clark as an infant meets versions of his Kryptonian parents, who suggest that he should use his power to rule: "How else should he use his abilities, but to show the barbarians how wrong they are and how right he is?" Baby-Clark rejects this, arguing: "I'm not a god — I'm not going to rule. They're people, just like we are. People — even better than we! ... I've got more to learn from them than they can from all of Krypton's so-called progress." When his biological mother scolds him, insisting that he is superior "and not even human," besides, baby screams "No! I'm human! I'm a man! I'm not some heartless beast! I care!" Asked *why* he cares so much, he answers "Because we all must help each other!"[17]

It's not much of an answer, really, but the dream sequences continue. Clark is confronted by a group of his enemies, among them Lex Luthor. Luthor says "For a long time, Superman, I've questioned your altruism. Nobody could be that unselfishly good, without an ulterior motive!" The kryptonite-powered Metallo adds "Yeah, crud — what is it? What's your *real* game?" They attack, trying to force the answer from him, to beat him until they can discover his "real plan," and he responds again: "I don't want anything ... anything but to help." Luthor, of course, refuses to believe it: "Nobody with your power would use it for anything other than furthering their own ends! Nobody is that unselfish! Nobody is that insane!" Again, Superman says "I've told you the truth! I want to ... help! That's all I want!"[18]

There is a kind of bottoming out in this answer. Really, Clark's motivations aren't complex, although that doesn't make them any less impenetrable, to Luthor or, indeed, to the rest of us. Smallvilleness is like that. It is like a thermodynamic miracle — it defies analysis or explanation, it just is.

Strangely, in the dream, Clark insists his authenticity *isn't* a miracle, isn't special or unique: "There are millions like me, Luthor.... Why do you assume everyone is as twisted as you? Are you so far gone you can't see honesty in any form?"[19] This is a great question, actually, especially if we stop to recall the reason for the 1980's revision of Superman in the first place: to streamline and update the character for a contemporary audience in order to reinvigorate sales. "Updating the character" is another way of saying: modernize his appeal. Make him more believable, more relatable.

More human.

The core problem faced by John Byrne, Marv Wolfman and the other Superman writers was that the one inescapable fact of Superman's identity —

the one thing which could never be revised or altered or updated, or else Superman was no longer Superman — was the very thing that made him hard for a modern audience to connect with: his incredibly unrealistic, altruistic, thermodynamic levels of decency and authenticity. His Smallvilleness. It wasn't believable. It wasn't relatable. And it sure wasn't human.

Their solution to the problem was to pretend this really wasn't a problem at all, and to perform a little authorial sleight of hand. First, have Clark disavow his "cold" alien origins whenever possible. Then, suggest that the more unaccountably decent he seemed, the more truly *human* he was. Meanwhile, by constantly raising the question of Clark's motivations (and placing those questions most often in the mouth of the chief villain), the texts consistently maneuver the reader into a difficult rhetorical position. For, when Clark says "There are millions like me," and "Are you so far gone you can't see honesty in any form?" he is asking Luthor, yes, but he is also asking the audience: Why isn't being good for goodness sake good enough? Isn't that what being human really is? Isn't that really the only reason why we're here — to *help* each other? Why shouldn't that be *acceptable* to you? What's wrong with you that you don't buy it?

The reader is then in a very self-conscious place, of the sort familiar to David Foster Wallace in "The View from Mrs. Thompson's": "Why can't I relate? Why can't I understand how some people can be so decent and sincere, so easily and naturally? Why should this seem so ... *phenomenal* to me? What kind of a louse does that make me, if I don't *get* it? Why can't I just be a good person?"

The suggestion in the texts is that — inspired by Superman's example of what being human really means — you can. It is actually pretty simple, as long as you don't think about it *too* much. In *The Adventures of Superman #433* (Oct. 1987), for example, Jimmy Olsen intervenes when an armed street gang tries to robs his corner market. Single-handedly, he knocks out one member and fires his gun to scare off the other three. He then engages one gang member in an extended motorcycle chase, leaping from one bike to the back of another like Indiana Jones. Reflecting on these events, and his motivations, Jimmy decides "I sometimes can't believe how anyone could be as perfect as he [Superman] is.... Perfect, and caring.... He makes me want to be just like him. Oh, not with his powers — that's for strange visitors from other planets, I guess — but with the heart, with my deeds. I think when you know greatness can be achieved, you aspire to it."[20]

Still, if we take a step back and just look at what takes place in the three continuing series *Superman*, *Action Comics*, and *The Adventures of Superman* in the late 1980s, we'll see that one particular kind of plot device is deployed time and again, and its near omnipresence suggests that many questions having to do with authenticity and identity are still very much being worked out. Indeed, once your attention is drawn to the recurrence of possession, mistaken identity, mind control, amnesia, disguises, body switching, imposters (robotic, mystical, alien), mind-transference and what-have-you, it's impossible to ignore. In *Action Comics #584* (Jan. 1987), for example, a crippled scientist constructs a machine and contrives to take over Superman's body and run wild in Metropolis.[21] Meanwhile, in *Superman #3* (March 1987), Superman finds himself transported to the evil planet of Apokolips, where he first disguises himself as a street urchin, then falls into an inter-planetary firepit which causes him to forget his identity completely.[22] That story continues in *The Adventures of Superman #426* (March 1987), where he emerges as a champion — "the Savior" — for the planet's tyrannized populace.[23] In *Action Comics #586* (Feb. 1987), we learn that this identity is itself a fake, and that actually an amnesiac Superman was recruited by the evil Darkseid, and so has been *pretending* to be a hero all along, the better to gather the scattered resistance together and lead it into a trap.[24]

Shifts in identity continue in all the series. In *Superman #4* (April 1987), a rampaging, schizophrenic killer named Bloodsport is revealed to have confused or fused his own identity with that of his younger brother, a crippled Vietnam veteran who adopted Bloodsport's name and fought in his stead when Bloodsport dodged the draft.[25] Superman disguises himself as a mob enforcer to get information in *The Adventures of Superman #428* (May 1987).[26] He fights a mummy that actually turns out to be a robot housing the souls of an ancient alien race who then take control of Lois Lane's body in *Superman #5–6* (May-June 1987).[27] He fights an orange giantess who he *thinks* is Lois Lane transformed by the effects of radiation in *Superman #7* (July 1987),[28] then fights a younger version of *himself*— or, rather, Superboy, who is an "alternate timeline" version of himself— in *Action Comics #591* (Aug. 1987).[29] He fights a man with a weather machine who believes he's become an Olympian God in *The Adventures of Superman #431* (Aug. 1987).[30] The Joker uses a Superman robot in *Superman #9* (Sep. 1987)[31] and Mr. Mxyzptlk, a creature from the Fifth Dimension, takes on the form of the handsome Ben DeRoy the better to seduce Lois Lane in *Superman #11* (Nov. 1987).[32] Sleez, a creepy outcast from Apokolips, uses mind-control to force Superman and Big Barda to make (or *almost* make) a porn movie in *Action Comics #592–593*.[33] A terrorized and seemingly innocent young southern girl is revealed to be a vampire in *Action Comics Annual #1* (1987),[34] the hero Booster Gold attacks Superman and turns out to be a robot in *Action Comics #594* (Nov. 1987),[35]and Clark's college girlfriend turns out to be secretly a mermaid in *Superman #12* (Dec. 1987).[36]

Maybe this constant need for identity switching and indirection and misdirection is simply the narrative result of featuring a hero so powerful (even after the reduction in Superman's might that was part of the *Man of Steel* revision) that very little can present a direct or physical challenge. But it is also tempting to suggest that this constant instability is revealing of an undercurrent of uneasiness and insecurity about American identity in the Reagan Era. For even as Reagan spoke with absolute conviction, with total seeming genuineness, about America as "the shining city upon the hill," and even as he relied, as the Superman texts relied, on the idea of Smallvilleness as the foundation for his brand of Americanism, it must have been hard, after all, to forget that he was an actor from California. Reagan's Americanism, then, is like Clark's Smallvilleness: strongest when it comes easily and you don't stop to think too much about it. It is only the cynical who ask: what is genuine and what is an act? Is this real, or are we all just pretending this is real?

CHAPTER NOTES

1. Byrne, John (w, a). "The Haunting." *The Man of Steel #6* (Sep. 1986). New York: DC Comics, 4.

2. Wallace, David F. "The View from Mrs. Thompson's." *Consider the Lobster.* (New York: Little Brown, 2007), 128–140.

3. Ibid., 131.

4. Ibid., 135.

5. Ibid., 140.

6. Reagan, Ronald. "Reagan: A Life in Letters." Eds. Kiron K. Skinner, Annelise Anderson, and Martin Anderson. (New York: Simon & Schuster, 2003), 5–6.

7. Lee, Tom. "Ronald Reagan, the President who Grew Up Like Jerry Todd." *Leo Edwards*, 24 July 2010. Web. 20 June 2011. <http://mysite.ncnetwork.net/res116wrb/Leo Site/history/articles/reagan_dad.html>.

8. Ibid.

9. Byrne, 21–22.

10. Byrne, John (w, a). "The Secret Revealed." *Superman #2* (Feb. 1987). New York: DC Comics, 21.

11. Byrne, 22.

12. Wolfman, Marv (w), and Jerry Ordway (a). "Man O' War." *The Adventures of Superman #424* (Jan. 1987). New York: DC Comics.

13. Wolfman, Marv (w), and Jerry Ordway (a). "Gangwar Part One: From the Streets to the Streets." *The Adventures of Superman #432* (Sep. 1987). New York: DC Comics, 7–9.

14. Byrne, 19.

15. Wolfman, Marv (w), and Jerry Ordway (a). "Mind Games." *The Adventures of Superman #427* (April 1987). New York: DC Comics, 1.

16. Ibid., 2.

17. Ibid., 8–10.

18. Ibid., 12–13.

19. Ibid., 14.

20. Wolfman, Marv (w), and Jerry Ordway (a). "Gang War Part Two: A Tragedy in Five Acts." *The Adventures of Superman #433* (Oct. 1987). New York: DC Comics, 4.

21. Byrne, John (w, a). "Squatter." *Action Comics #584* (Jan. 1987). New York: DC Comics.

22. Byrne, John (w, a). "Legends from the Darkside." *Superman #3* (March 1987). New York: DC Comics.

23. Wolfman, Marv (w), and Jerry Ordway (a). "From the Dregs." *The Adventures of Superman #426* (March 1987). New York: DC Comics.

24. Byrne, John (w, a). "The Champion." *Action Comics #586* (Feb. 1987). New York: DC Comics.

25. Byrne, John (w, a). "Bloodsport." *Superman #4* (April 1987). New York: DC Comics.

26. Wolfman, Marv (w), and Jerry Ordway (a). "Personal Best." *The Adventures of Superman #428* (May 1987). New York: DC Comics.

27. Byrne, John (w, a). "The Mummy Strikes" and "The Last Five Hundred." *Superman #5–6* (May-June 1987). New York: DC Comics.

28. Byrne, John (w, a). "Rampage!" *Superman #7* (July 1987). New York: DC Comics.

29. Byrne, John (w, a). "Past Imperfect." *Action Comics #591* (Aug. 1987). New York: DC Comics.

30. Wolfman, Marv (w), and Erik Larson (a). "They Call Him — Doctor Stratos." *The Adventures of Superman #431* (Aug. 1987). New York: DC Comics.

31. Byrne, John (w, a). "To Laugh and Die in Metropolis." *Superman #9* (Sep. 1987). New York: DC Comics.

32. Byrne, John (w, a). "The Name Game." *Superman #11* (Nov. 1987). New York: DC Comics.

33. Byrne, John (w, a). "A Walk on the Darkside" and "The Suicide Snare." *Action Comics #592–593* (Sep.-Oct. 1987). New York: DC Comics.

34. Byrne, John (w), and Art Adams (a). "Skeeter."*Action Comics Annual #594* (1987). New York: DC Comics.

35. Byrne, John. (w, a). "All That Glisters." *Action Comics #594* (Nov. 1987). New York: DC Comics.

36. Byrne, John. (w, a). "Lost Love." *Superman #12* (Dec. 1987). New York: DC Comics.

BIBLIOGRAPHY

Byrne, John (w, a). "All That Glisters." *Action Comics #594* (Nov. 1987). New York: DC Comics.

_____. "Bloodsport." *Superman #4* (April 1987). New York: DC Comics.

_____. "From the Dregs." *The Adventures of Superman #426* (March 1987). New York: DC Comics.

_____. "The Haunting." *The Man of Steel #6* (Sep. 1986). New York: DC Comics, 4.

_____. "Legends from the Darkside." *Superman #3* (March 1987). New York: DC Comics.

_____. "To Laugh and Die in Metropolis." *Superman #9* (Sep. 1987). New York: DC Comics.

_____. The Last Five Hundred." *Superman #5* (May 1987) . New York: DC Comics.

_____. "Lost Love." *Superman #12* (Dec. 1987). New York: DC Comics.

_____. "The Mummy Strikes."*Superman #6* (June 1987). New York: DC Comics.

_____. "The Name Game." *Superman #11* (Nov. 1987). New York: DC Comics.

_____. "Past Imperfect." *Action Comics #591* (Aug. 1987). New York: DC Comics.

_____. "Rampage!" *Superman #7* (July 1987). New York: DC Comics.

_____. "The Secret Revealed." *Superman #2* (Feb. 1987). New York: DC Comics, 21.

_____. "Squatter." *Action Comics #584* (Jan. 1987). New York: DC Comics.

_____. "The Suicide Snare." *Action Comics #593* (Oct. 1987). New York: DC Comics.

_____. "A Walk on the Darkside" *Action Comics #592* (Sep. 1987). New York: DC Comics.

Byrne, John (w), and Art Adams (a). "Skeeter."*Action Comics Annual #594* (1987). New York: DC Comics.

Lee, Tom. "Ronald Reagan, the President Who Grew Up Like Jerry Todd." Accessed 24 July 2010 at http://mysite.ncnetwork.net/res116wrb/LeoSite/history/articles/reagan_dad.html.

Reagan, Ronald. "Reagan: A Life in Letters." Kiron K. Skinner, Annelise Anderson, and Martin Anderson, eds. New York: Simon & Schuster, 2003.

Wallace, David F. "The View from Mrs. Thompson's." In *Consider the Lobster*. New York: Little Brown, 2007.

Wolfman, Marv (w), and Erik Larson (a). "They Call Him — Doctor Stratos." *The Adventures of Superman #431* (Aug. 1987). New York: DC Comics.

Wolfman, Marv (w), and Jerry Ordway (a). "From the Dregs." *The Adventures of Superman #426* (March 1987). New York: DC Comics.

_____. "Gangwar Part One: From the Streets to the Streets." *The Adventures of Superman #432* (Sep. 1987). New York: DC Comics, 7–9.

_____. "Gang War Part Two: A Tragedy in Five Acts." *The Adventures of Superman #433* (Oct. 1987). New York: DC Comics, 4.

_____. "Man O' War." *The Adventures of Superman #424* (Jan. 1987). New York: DC Comics.

_____. "Mind Games." *The Adventures of Superman #427* (April 1987). New York: DC Comics.

_____. "Personal Best." *The Adventures of Superman #428* (May 1987). New York: DC Comics.

The "Triangle Era" of Superman

Continuity, Marketing, and Grand Narratives in the 1990s

MATTHEW J. SMITH

I blame Stan Lee. Even if he wasn't responsible for creating the idea of close relationships between different comic book series,[1] he certainly did a lot to make it a staple of the modern superhero genre. In the early 1960s Lee wrote the characters from one of his burgeoning Marvel Comics series into another, famously guest-starring the Fantastic Four in the first issue of *Amazing Spider-Man*, for instance. Then one hero's foe would confront another, and soon it became apparent that entire line existed in one inter-related fictional world. If a contradiction between stories arose, Lee, who was both editor and principal writer, didn't always try to explain the inconsistencies himself but instead invited the readers to offer up explanations, awarding them "No Prize" recognition for their creativity. Through both his storytelling and playful interaction with the reader, Lee made embracing the complexities of a superhero "universe" enjoyable and entertaining, and for devoted fans of the superhero genre the expectation that interrelationships would — and should — be a part of the genre was irrevocably entrenched. Hence a "Marvel Universe," an "Ultimate Universe," not to mention a "DC Universe" of course, and so on and so on have become as much an integral part of the superhero genre as superpowers or secret identities.

Consequently, continuity must be studied if superheroes are to be understood. Continuity is the quality of inter-relatedness among stories, and although Marvel may have first formulated its modern expectations, no where was it better exemplified — or better executed — than in DC Comics' Superman titles of the late 1980s and throughout the 1990s, the "triangle era" of the character's never-ending battle.

Beginning with *Superman #51* (Jan. 1991),[2] the three monthly titles featuring the Man of Steel (*Superman*, *Adventures of Superman*, and *Action*

Comics) formalized their inter-relatedness with a trade dressing that would continue to appear for more than a decade, ending in January 2002. On that initial cover and each subsequent issue of the line for the next eleven years, the publication year and sequence number of the issue within the Superman family of comics would appear in a triangle (and later the S-shield itself), marking each issue's relationship to all of the others in the line and reinforcing the strict inter-connectedness among the stories that they told working with one another. This sequence number was independent of the actual issue number, and revealed the order the stories were progressing in the larger family of Superman titles, and not the individual series.

Of course, the economic advantage of tight continuity is obvious to any reader who has ever bought a comic book with a "cross-over" between two popular characters or, as was the case in the Superman line, a continuation of a story from one title to another. Faithful readers find themselves obligated to purchase multiple comic books to enjoy the complete story. Decades of sales data confirms what Stan Lee surmised years before: continuity sells comic books. The success of the triangle era as a particular marketing exercise is reflected in the best-selling "The Death of Superman" storyline, in the increased number of Superman titles at this time (with the addition of the monthly *Superman: The Man of Steel* in July 1991 and the quarterly, *Superman: The Man of Tomorrow* a new Superman comic book was for sale every week of the year), and the impact that the technique had on its competitors, who felt pressure to tighten their own continuity among titles (e.g., Spider-Man line's "The Clone Saga") or adopt a similar trade dress (a Bat-signal numbering titles in the Batman line).

But while the economic impact of continuity is worth considering, what's more complex is contemplating issues of artistry in such an environment. Claims of artistry may seem extreme to those who believe that monthly comics produced for the masses cannot be very good. After all, they are made in an assembly-line like fashion where tasks are parceled out to different contributors (rather than the results of an individual auteur's vision) and they often pander to the lowest common denominator in their quest for the largest possible audience. But to dismiss the mass production of an inter-related line of comics as typical industrial dribble overlooks what the so-called "Super-team" of creators was able to accomplish working within these conditions during the "triangle era."

Editorial Guidance

Key to maintaining such tight continuity among a variety of monthly titles is coordinating the disparate creative teams who are working on them.

For the Superman line, such a sustained effort went far beyond the linking of titles into a storyline lasting a few issues or even a few months. The original editor behind the highly coordinated effort, Mike Carlin, directed creative input on an expansive story that helped place Superman titles at the top of many fan's pull lists each week at a competitive time when comics were enjoying their best sales in decades. Shortly after DC Comics' high-profile reboot of Superman by writer-artist John Byrne in 1986, Carlin came on board in April 1987 to assist Andy Helfer with editing the Superman line. By October 1987, Carlin had taken over the line from Helfer entirely. Carlin then enjoyed a considerable tenure as editor of the Superman line, wrapping his run with January 1996's titles (concluding "The Trial of Superman!" storyline),[3] and was succeeded briefly by K.C. Carlson before Joey Cavalieri took the helm from September 1996 until November 1999. Though his two immediate successors continued to observe strict continuity among the titles, it was Carlin who instituted both the "triangle era" and the distinctive storytelling initiative that was to last for more than a decade.

When Carlin had come on board the Superman line, it consisted of three monthly titles, all of which were loosely connected within the same broader continuity but each of which had a distinct identity. Fan favorite John Byrne was writing and drawing both *Superman* and *Action Comics*, but he used *Action* as a team-up book pairing Superman with different guest stars each month. The line's third title, *The Adventures of Superman*, was written by Marv Wolfman and penciled by Jerry Ordway, and events there infrequently led directly to or from events in Byrne's books. The titles did coalesce a little more when Wolfman left and Byrne took over scripting chores on all three titles, but the intricate coordination that was to come still hadn't gelled. At about that time DC decided to turn *Action Comics* into a weekly anthology, reducing Superman's role in the title to just a two-page spread and leaving the Superman line with essentially just two monthly titles. After Byrne left in late 1988, Ordway stepped up to also write *Adventures* and Roger Stern came on board to write *Superman*. Gradually, the storylines began to exhibit tighter and tighter continuity.

Following DC's company-wide crossover event, *Invasion!*, in early 1989, Ordway and Stern crafted a storyline, "Superman in Exile," that would crossover between their respective titles over the next six months, including a two-part guest stint by an up and coming talent, Dan Jurgens, who would later go on to be an integral contributor to the Superman line. At the same time as that extended story arc reached its conclusion, the experiment that was *Action Comics Weekly* came to an end and a reinstated monthly *Action Comics* was reincorporated into the line. Superman was back to appearing in three monthly titles by July 1989. But something was different now, the stories—

most especially the subplots — became increasingly interwoven among the different titles.

The tight continuity would become even more apparent in major story arcs that cut across the titles with each featuring trade dresses on the covers that helped to connect the chapters visually as part of a series. The six-part "The Day of the Krypton Man" (March-April 1990), the three-part "Dark Knight over Metropolis" (June 1990), the three-part "Soul Search" (Aug.-September 1990), and the four-part "Krisis of Krimson Kryptonite" (Nov.-December 1990)[4] all demonstrated increasing emphasis on interlocking the three titles in the line. After the triangle dress became a regular feature in January 1991, the first major story arc to follow was the seven-part "Time and Time Again!" (March-May 1991), a story that cast a time-lost Superman hopping from prehistory to the far-flung future issue-by-issue in a quest to return to his own era. The approach was working so well that DC quickly added a fourth monthly title to the line, *Superman: The Man of Steel* that July. The four Superman titles that month each had pages contributed by the four different creative teams, marking these as the most ambitious cross-coordination attempted by Carlin and his team yet. By the time the next major arc, the eight-part "Panic in the Sky!" (Feb.-Apr. 1992) was published, the so-called "Super-Team" had its collaborative formula down pat. Each creative team told a chapter in what had truly evolved into a never-ending battle. Week-by-week, year-in-and-year-out the now seamless saga of Superman rolled on, each weekly episode woven into a larger storytelling tapestry under Carlin's watchful eye. Remarkably, the formula worked so well that even when the creative teams decided to kill their golden goose, the titles rolled right on.

The Triumph of Continuity in the Death and Life of Superman

"The Death of Superman" is remembered as one of the seminal events in modern comics history.[5] While attention from the popular press helped fuel the sales, the story itself was also quite deftly managed over a period of issues. DC boldly claims that it is "The Best-Selling Graphic Novel of All Time!" atop the trade paperback that collects the story. With several million copies in print, it is undoubtedly one of the most widely circulated comic book stories of modern times.[6] Despite its impressive sales, nationally prominent retailer Chuck Rozanski says that the stunt burst the bubble for speculators trying to cash in on comics as commodities and subsequently sent the comic book industry into a financial downturn, driving away readers and closing comic book specialty stores across the country.[7] Love it or hate, there is no denying that the "Death of Superman" had an impact on the industry and that it represented Carlin's team's most prominent attempt at interconnected continuity among its titles.

In fact, while Superman may have died in *Superman #75* (Jan. 1993),[8] the "Doomsday" storyline (as it was referenced in the initial spate of serialized comics) ran for the course of six issues over a period of a month and a half over four titles. The follow-up story, "Funeral for a Friend," then covered the aftermath of Superman's death in the next two months, or eight issues, all without the participation of the series star. Instead, the strong supporting cast that Carlin's team had been nurturing stepped forward. In detail we get to see what Superman's death means to the lives of people like Lois Lane, Lex Luthor, Supergirl, his colleagues in the Justice League, and the citizens of Metropolis. In an unprecedented effort to tease readers, then, DC did not publish a single one of the regular Superman titles in the next three months, offering instead a select few tribute specials (e.g., *The Legacy of Superman*, March 1993). At the time, advance solicitations for upcoming comic books came out three months in advance, and in a canny move to cement its reputation as having done the deed, DC manipulated the impression that it had indeed killed off its most iconic character and canceled all of his top-selling titles.

But, that, of course, was not going to be the case for long. After the three-month hiatus, the storyline picked up with the arrival of four replacement Supermen in *The Adventures of Superman #500* (June 1993).[9] The four stand-in supermen then each claimed one of the four Superman titles and the subsequent "Reign of the Supermen" storyline would run the next four and a half months of increasingly interconnected continuity, along the way providing for the return of the original Man of Steel himself (in *Superman: The Man of Steel #25* (Sep. 1993).[10]

What "Funeral for a Friend" and "Reign of the Supermen" made clear about the Super-Team's approach was that they were not only writing a saga about an inspiring character whose banner appeared on each issue's cover, but telling stories that involved a powerful cast of recurring characters. The Super-Team's ensemble cast often regularly provided both outright challenges for the Man of Steel to confront (such as when Cat Grant's son, Adam is murdered by the Toyman, prompting Superman to track down the killer) but also engaging subplots that could be sustained across multiple months and brought to fruition in their own time (e.g., Jimmy Olsen loses his job at the Daily Planet and must find gainful employment, eventually landing a job as a television reporter). In addition to stalwarts like Lois, Jimmy, and Perry White, the introduction of characters like Catherine Grant (an entertainment reporter for the Planet), Jose Delgado (also a competing vigilante in Metropolis known as Gangbuster), Bibbo Bibbowski (owner of the Ace of Clubs bar), Professor Emil Hamilton (an eccentric inventor who becomes Superman's scientific advisor), Ron Troupe (a young reporter on the Planet staff), among many additional recurring characters helped develop the series in terms of its complexity. These characters did not simply guest in a single issue and were gone once the challenge of the week was thwarted; instead, their lives became intimately entwined with Superman's and his alter ego, Clark Kent.

While Carlin was certainly directing the Super-Team effort, credit also has to go to the creative individuals who participated in the development process, many of them with impressive long-term runs on their series. "I have fifteen or sixteen people working simultaneously on Superman," Carlin noted. "I want a real creative collaboration, and I want Superman to be the star."[11] While Superman may have indeed been the top draw, members of the Super-Team were also scoring recognition among readers for both their creativity and endurance. Among the most enduring participants were Jon Bogdanove, Jackson Guice, Tom Grummett, Stuart Immonen, Dan Jurgens, Karl Kesel, David Michelinie, Jerry Ordway, Louise Simonson, and Roger Stern. Ordway's longevity was particularly impressive, having signed on for the Superman relaunch in 1987 as artist for *The Adventures of Superman* but continuing on as a storyteller in the line until 1999, outlasting a succession of colleagues to hold one of the most lasting tenures as a chronicler of the Man of Steel in modern times.

Twilight of the Super-Team

Carlin's Super-Team approach would continue on for the rest of the decade, well after his own tenure as series editor came to an end in 1996. Carlin himself went on to become executive editor of DC Comics, and his formula was followed by his successors (perhaps at Carlin's direction, as he was now the boss). Though none of the subsequent storylines would garner the attention (or sales) of "The Death of Superman," the fact that the effort to sustain the formula for such a time was a testimony to its favor among editorial and creative staff and the readers. While multi-part arcs such as "The Death of Clark Kent" and "The Trial of Superman" were expansive, they did not garner nearly as much attention, as if anything else could. In one notable attempt that began in April 1997, then group editor Joey Cavalieri orchestrated a year-long story arc that saw Superman's powers transformed into a range of electro-magnetic abilities and his costume substituted with a new blue and white, lightning-embossed uniform. By the time that storyline had finished in May 1996, "Superman-Blue" had split into a second being, "Superman-

Red,"[12] before the status quo was restored. Likewise, the last major attempt to tie the multiple titles together so tightly, the "King of the World" storyline that ran from January to June 1999 ended only after many complications and nearly two dozen individual comic books could tell the tale.

Clearly, such an approach to continuity can be a double-edged sword, both encouraging fans to pay for their weekly fix of the saga but also warding off would-be readers who are not already immersed in the richly intertwining plots and subplots. At the height of the "triangle era," to take up collecting one Superman title, it was essentially necessary to commit to all four or five titles in order to capture details of the more protracted storytelling aspects. Such a financial commitment could have been beyond many would-be readers. Perhaps this explains why the next Superman group editor, Eddie Berganza, moved away from such tight continuity when he took the reigns in December 1999. Berganza allowed each title's creative team to take the character along their distinctive storylines with looser connections across the line. Although the group of titles would periodically feature cross-title continuity (see, for example, the twelve-part crossover, "Our Worlds at War" in August-October 2001), Berganza encouraged the four[13] Superman titles to develop and maintain separate storylines. Although Berganza retained the "triangle" cover feature until January 2002, it had atrophied into a mere indication of what order the comics had been released that year and came to have increasingly little to do with the inter-relations of the titles themselves.

While it lasted, though, the impact of the "triangle era" was felt across the comic book industry, and the reverberations were felt both by Superman's colleagues and competitors. At DC, editor Denny O'Neil found himself orchestrating a nineteen-part cross-over between *Batman* and *Detective Comics* in 1993. "Knightfall" chronicled the defeat of Batman at the hands of a new foe, Bane, and the selection of a successor to assume the mantle of the Caped Crusader. A subsequent storyline, "Knightquest," which chronicled Bruce Wayne's return was even more complex, crossing over among six different titles in the Batman line bringing in *Batman: Shadow of the Bat* and *Legends of the Dark Knight* as well as the *Robin* and *Catwoman* series into the mix this time around. Though O'Neil was less disciplined than the Super-Team in keeping the continuity tight on every title thereafter, special cross-over events like 1996's "Contagion" would bring the titles working into concert with one another periodically. By decade's end, the year-long "No Man's Land" storyline had all four titles carrying the story forward week-to-week.

Of course if imitation is the sincerest form of flattery, than to see one's competitors mimic one's strategy is high praise indeed. Thus, when the Spider-man line began to transition to the formula established by the Super-Team, Carlin's approach received external verification. Marvel first experimented with the tactic with the fourteen-part "Maximum Carnage" storyline in the spring of 1993. A year later editor Danny Fingeroth oversaw a four-part cross-over story, "Pursuit," that ran one chapter through each of the four Spider-titles of the time,[14] and that October the entire line began to coalesce week-to-week as the creative team began to develop the infamous "Spider-Clone" saga. For the next two years, each one of the four monthly Spider-man titles led from one to another in chronicling the return of the spider-clone, Ben Reilly. Though Marvel opted not to include a triangle-like feature to show the connection, distinct trade-dress on each storyline — along with blurbs inside each issue directing readers to the next chapter — helped to coordinate readers' reading and corresponding spending habits. Other franchises, including DC's Justice League of America, and Legion of Super-Heroes and Marvel's Punisher and Midnight Sons lines, all worked with the formula for varying periods. Though all would ultimately shift away from the approach by the turn of the new millennium, in the 1990s franchise titles followed the Super-Team's lead in marketing comics through similar intensive pitches.

Lessons from the Line

Beyond its impact on the industry lies consideration of the message that the "triangle era" told. To my reading, it reflected a larger narrative that America was telling itself in the late eighties and on through to the nineties. With the gradual decline and eventual dissolution of the Soviet Union in 1991, the United States had effectively won the Cold War. As the world's sole remaining super-power, Americans could feel confident that the greater narrative that had guided them through that protracted struggle had been justified. As the "triangle era" progressed through the nineties, America also gradually transitioned from a recession into an era of economic prosperity. The expansive Superman narrative that ran parallel to this period seemed well matched in its euphoria for large, All-American stories of triumph.

It was fitting then, that the "triangle era" of Superman would come begin to phase out even as America's grander narrative was itself becoming increasing contested. At the turn of the new century America became a house divided. A contentious presidential election between Republican candidate Governor George W. Bush and Democratic candidate Vice President Al Gore indicated that American unity was sharply divided politically. Later, the terrorist attacks of September 11, 2001 indicated American security vulnerabilities. While these events may have steeled American's resolve to secure its borders, resulting in the massive restructuring of Homeland Security, the implication of the unprovoked attack was that we were living in a much more complicated world than we had been aware of before. Chief among those complications came a begrudging recognition that the world was full of fragmented, often competing narratives rather than one grand super-narrative guiding all of the world's people.

Though successive editors would continue to sponsor occasional cross-over events among the titles in the Superman line, the series would not enjoy the integrity of storytelling that had characterized the "triangle era" again. In addition, even the number of regularly published Superman titles would not match the oftentimes weekly output of the period. In one curious instance of ignominy from 2009–2010, editor Matt Idelson replaced Superman in *Action Comics* with fellow Kryptonians Nightwing and Flamebird in the lead role and supplanted Superman's appearance in his own eponymous title with Mon-El of the Legion of Super-Heroes. Superman found himself exiled in the pages of a single comic book, *Superman: The World of New Krypton* (May 2009-April 2010). How the mighty had fallen! At the conclusion of that maxi-series, Superman found his way back to his own title but his spot in *Action* had been co-opted by his archenemy, Lex Luthor! Thusly, for the better part of two years (May 2009-May 2011), Superman was reduced to starring in one monthly title. Just a decade before, he had been the headliner in four monthly series. When the Last Son of Krypton finally reclaimed the lead in *Action*, the story line pursued a different path than that being chronicled in *Superman*. But by then the "triangle era" and its creative and financial successes were long forgotten.

By the time DC prepared its "DCnU" re-launch in the summer of 2011, plans called for two ongoing Superman titles, one set in the past and one in the present, chronicling two different eras for the Man of Steel. Clearly, DC had no plans to return to the tighter continuity of the "triangle era" any time soon. Indeed, almost all of the publisher's franchise books, including Batman and the Justice League now shy away from the formula, though occasional crossovers continue to appear, as they did even before the triangle era. However, lest one think a good idea like this is now fallow, one need look no further than the Marvelous competition to see variations of the formula at work. In fact in 2008, Marvel canceled two other spider-titles and began to publish *Amazing Spider-Man* three times a month. The "Brand New Day" approach was characterized by rotating creative teams, each turning in story arcs of several issues before ceding the title over to the next crew and rotating back a few months later. That's not quite what Carlin and his Super-Team had done, carefully choreographing storylines, creative input, and market considerations issue-by-issue. But the comics marketplace — and indeed the world — were different places by then. And I can't blame Stan Lee for that.

CHAPTER NOTES

1. Arguably, *All-Star Comics #3*, which assembled the Justice Society of America for the first time, started this trend way back in 1940.

2. Ordway, Jerry (w, a), "Mister Z." *Superman #51* (Jan. 1991). New York: DC Comics.

3. Carlin received a curious homage upon his departure. His very first issue of *Superman #4* (April 1987) had featured a John Byrne cover of the male Bloodsport shattering the Superman logo with a powerful gun blast; Carlson's first issue editing the line without Carlin featured an homage by Kieron Dwyer of a female Bloodsport imitator, Demolitia, shattering the *Superman in Action Comics* logo (Feb. 1996) in similar fashion.

4. A fifth part of the story, identifiable with the same trade dress but labeled "Part Two/A," was featured in *Starman #28* (Nov. 1990), which was also being written by then *Action Comics* scribe Roger Stern.

5. As documented in numerous histories of modern comics, including Bradford W. Wright, *Comic Book Nation: The Transformation of Youth Culture in America* (Baltimore: Johns Hopkins University Press, 2001).

6. Marvel Comics' *X-Men #1* (Oct. 1991) holds the record for a single issue. Its five variant covers managed to sell eight million copies.

7. Rozanski, Chuck. "'Death of Superman' Promotion of 1992." *Tales from the Database*. June 2004. Web.

8. Jurgens, Dan (w, a). "Doomsday!" *Superman #75* (Jan. 1993). New York: DC Comics.

9. Ordway, Jerry (w), and Tom Grummet (a). "Life and Death." *The Adventures of Superman #500* (June 1993). New York: DC Comics.

10. Simonson, Louise (w), and Jon Bogdanove (a). "The Return!" *Superman: The Man of Steel #25* (Sep. 1993). New York: DC Comics.

11. Les Daniels, *Superman: The Complete History* (San Francisco: Chronicle Books, 1998), 161.

12. The premise of duplicate Supermen (one red, one blue) came from an imaginary story, "The Amazing Story of Superman-Red and Superman-Blue" in *Superman #162* (July 1963) Leo Dorfman (w) and Curt Swan (a).

13. *Superman: The Man of Steel* ended its run with issue 134 in March 2003.

14. Those titles were the venerable *Amazing Spider-Man* and its surrogates: *Spectacular Spider-Man, Web of Spider-Man,* and *Spider-Man.*

BIBLIOGRAPHY

Daniels, Les. *Superman: The Complete History.* San Francisco: Chronicle Books, 1998.

Jurgens, Dan (w),(a). "Doomsday!" *Superman #75* (Jan. 1993). New York: DC Comics.

Ordway, Jerry (w, a). "Mister Z." *Superman #51* (Jan. 1991). New York: DC Comics.

Ordway, Jerry (w), and Tom Grummet (a). "Life and Death." *The Adventures of Superman #500* (June 1993). New York: DC Comics.

Rozanski, Chuck. "'Death of Superman' Promotion of 1992." *Tales from the Database.* Accessed June 2004 at http://www.milehighcomics.com/tales/cbg127.html.

Simonson, Louise (w), and Jon Bogdanove (a). "The Return!" *Superman: The Man of Steel #25* (Sep. 1993). New York: DC Comics.

Wright, Bradford. *Comic Book Nation: The Transformation of Youth Culture in America.* Baltimore: Johns Hopkins University Press, 2001.

Searching for Meaning in
"The Death of Superman"

Joseph J. Darowski

"The Death of Superman."

A simple, direct title for a comic book storyline. Perhaps lacking nuance, but it is certainly attention grabbing. And DC Comics certainly garnered attention for their 1992 storyline centering on the Man of Steel's demise at the hands of a villain known only as Doomsday. The storyline is one of the highest selling in the history of comics, but despite that commercial success it remains to this day a very controversial event.

In the early 1990s the comic book industry was experiencing a significant economic boom. Successful media adaptations such as the *Batman* films and the *X-Men* cartoon series had introduced superheroes to new customers, the rise of the direct market comic book store meant that older fans with disposable income spent more money on their hobby, and, perhaps most significantly, the increase in the value of back issues spurred the idea that comic books were sound financial investments. This last factor, which was based on a faulty premise, created a speculator's market. Customers would buy multiple copies of comic books they believed would be significant and preserve them in mint condition with the plan to sell them for a tidy profit at a later date.[1]

Publishers encouraged this speculator boom through special event comics, gimmicky covers with holographs or chrome, and special limited edition issues. New publishers, such as Image Comics, made an impact in the industry by highlighting artistic renderings of impossibly muscled men and improbably curvaceous women instead of clear storytelling. As Chris Ryall and Scott Tipton explain, "Storytelling and character development took a back seat to flashy covers.... The core audience that was invested in the characters felt increasingly unimportant as it watched hopeful investors fill comic shops to buy multiple copies as investments...."[2] While these types of comic books sold extremely well in the short term, in the long term they had a negative impact on the industry. Most of the publishers were perceived to be emphasizing flash over substance by producing a large number of comics that sold well but had weak narratives. Eventually, the traditional fans of comic books became tired of the gimmicks and the speculators realized their "investments" were actually diminishing in value because so many people were collecting and preserving them. Many members of both groups ceased to buy comic books and the near-simultaneous loss of many traditional fans and the new speculators crippled the industry for a number of years.

Because DC Comics's marketing and handling of the event, "The Death of Superman" has often been criticized as one of the excesses comic book publishers indulged in during the boom of the 1990s. When the mainstream media picked up on the story, many casual fans of Superman, often who were only familiar with the character through media adaptations, purchased copies because of the apparent significance of the event. Investors bought multiple copies in the hopes of the issue increasing in value exponentially. Many of the stories in the mainstream media reported the event as though this would be a permanent end to Superman. Traditional comic book fans in all likelihood anticipated a resurrection for the character, as that is a common trope of superhero comic book storytelling, but many of them still purchased the issue with Superman's death, *Superman #75* (Jan. 1993).[3]

By any reckoning "The Death of Superman" was one of the best-selling storylines of all time, with the issue featuring Superman's death "at the hands of the Image-inspired muscle-bound monster named Doomsday" far better than any other issue of Superman.[4] Copies of Superman comic books had been selling approximately a hundred thousand copies, and the death issue was reported to have sold in excess of six million copies.[5] But was it merely one of the attention-grabbing and sales-inducing stunts publishers engaged in during the early 1990s?

Some certainly believe so. Entrepeneur.com named "The Death of Superman" one of the Top 10 Successful Marketing Stunts of all time.[6] Christopher Knowles refers to the story as a "cynical ... publicity stunt," giving the story very little creative credit.[7] Chuck Rozanski, operator of one of the largest comic book retailers in the world, goes so far as to call "The Death of Superman," "the greatest catastrophe to strike the world of comics since the Kefauver Senate hearings[8] of 1955." Rozanski also argued that: "...the 'Death of Superman' promotion inadvertently exposed to the general public (many of whom ignorantly bought into the prevailing delusion that all comics were collectibles that infinitely rose in value) the 'Ponzi Scheme' reality of the market for recent back issue comics."[9]

If the question this essay was seeking to answer was simply "Was "The Death of Superman" one of the event comics common in the industry in the early 1990s?" the answer would be yes and the essay would be done. However, because the question is "Was "The Death of Superman" simply an event comic which was all flash and no substance?" the answer may take a little longer to explain. There was undeniably a corporately generated hype around the event. But because hindsight has painted a picture in which the producer of the comic got greedy and the purchaser of the comic was naive, the story itself has not generally been critically analyzed. Most discussion of "The Death of Superman" revolves around the hype, the hysteria, and news around the story, not the story itself. However, the story is a product of the early post–Cold War period in American history, as the country sought to reestablish its identity in the wake of the Soviet Union's collapse. Despite being, on one level, a promotional stunt mandated by larger corporate concerns, "The Death of Superman" remains a product of its times, revealing several of the pressing fears, concerns, and hopes of the time period. As Bradford Wright argued, the story stands as a "powerful metaphor for American culture ... in the post–Cold War era."[10]

The Storyline

The origins of "The Death of Superman" actually begin with the wedding of Clark Kent and Lois Lane. The comic book writers in charge of Superman comic books had a year's worth of stories planned out which was to end with the marriage of Clark and Lois. However, due to the new television series *Lois and Clark: The New Adventures of Superman* on ABC television, Warner Bros., the corporate owners of DC Comics, mandated that the marriage in the comic books be put on hold for a year so that it could coincide with the planned marriage of the two characters on the television show. Suddenly, a year's worth of stories needed to be created, while the planned storylines were put on hold.[11]

In frustration, one of the writers is said to have called out in a creative meeting, "Let's just kill 'im!" as a means of preventing Superman from marrying Lois for one year. The idea actually took hold. Obviously, the plan would be for Superman to return and marry Lois, but in the meantime they could tell an event story about Superman's death and resurrection.[12]

"The Death of Superman" begins when Doomsday tears its way out of the bowels of the earth. No explanation is offered as to what the creature is, where it comes from, or what its origins are. Doomsday tears a path of destruction across the United States, damaging property, killing any living creature in its path, and easily defeating various superheroes who attempt to stand in his way. Superman arrives on the scene and barely slows Doomsday's progress. As the battle reaches Metropolis Superman uses all of his force as he and Doomsday trade blows. Finally, Superman and Doomsday simultaneously strike each other with such powerful blows that both drop dead in the streets of Metropolis.[13]

Following "The Death of Superman" DC Comics published a brief storyline called "Funeral for a Friend," which was then followed by a storyline called "Reign of the Supermen." Shortly after Superman's funeral it is discovered that his body has disappeared from his tomb. Soon four new Supermen appear, each wearing Superman's S-shield. The new Supermen include an armored hero called the Man of Steel or simply Steel, a young version of Superman called Superboy, a cyborg who has the same appearance as Superman with robotic parts in the portions of his body which were most injured in the battle with Doomsday called the The Man of Tomorrow or the Cyborg Superman, and a visored Kryptonian who also looks just like Superman called the Last Son of Krypton.[14]

The readers come to learn that Steel is really John Henry Irons, a weapons engineer whose life was saved by Superman a few days before the Doomsday attack. During Doomsday's rampage in Metropolis, Irons attempted to attack Doomsday to help repay Superman for saving his life, but Irons was buried in rubble. Upon crawling out of the rubble, Irons builds an armored suit and fights crime to honor Superman's mission and sacrifice.[15]

Superboy is revealed to be clone of Superman which Lex Luthor was creating using Superman's blood. However, the clone escaped from the lab before being aged to full adulthood and before Luthor was able to implant mental commands which would have allowed him to control him. The clone asks to be called Superman, but is often referred to by other characters as Superboy due to his teenaged appearance.[16]

Because Superman's body is missing, audiences were supposed to wonder if the Cyborg Superman or the Last Son of Krypton were the real Kal-El returned from the dead. Both characters were hinted at to be the real Superman. The Cyborg Superman allows himself to be tested by a scientist who had been studying Superman's physiology, who declares his body to be genetically identical to Superman's, though the Cyborg Superman claims to have "blurry" memories when Lois Lane confronts him with facts she knows about Superman, such as his secret identity. The Last Son of Krypton has all of Superman's knowledge, telling Lois Lane he knows who she is and what her relationship was with Clark Kent and Superman. However, he has none of Clark Kent's humanity. Though he still patrols Metropolis stopping crime, he is brutal in how he deals with criminals, killing some and maiming others. To keep readers in suspense about whether or not Superman has actually returned, less is revealed to readers about the origins of these two characters than was shown about Steel and Superboy.[17]

Eventually, at the conclusion of "Reign of the Supermen" the Cyborg

Superman is revealed to be Hank Henshaw, a man who years before had developed the ability to live within machinery after his body disintegrated following an accident with cosmic rays. Henshaw transferred his consciousness into Kal-El's birthing matrix, the ship which brought Superman from Krypton to Earth, and traveled the universe. However, he eventually became insane and blamed Superman for his wife's death and for his bodiless fate. Upon learning of Superman's death, Henshaw planned to use the memory of Superman to help lead an alien invasion of Earth and forever tarnish Superman's legacy. Henshaw uses the birthing matrix to grow a body with Kryptonian biology, but with mechanical parts to house his consciousness. He uses the public's trust that he is Superman to help facilitate an alien invasion.[18]

Readers also find out that The Last Son of Krypton is an alien being called the Eradicator who, despite what his name implies, has the sole purpose of preserving all remaining Kryptonian life. The Eradicator took Superman's body from his grave and placed it in a regeneration matrix in The Fortress of Solitude, trying to revive Superman. Through a convoluted process, the Eradicator creates a body identical to Superman's, believes himself to be Superman for a time, and fights crime in Superman's name though without the small town upbringing which kept Superman from crossing moral lines when fighting for truth and justice.[19]

In the end, the true Superman, none of the four replacement Supermen, returns (with a mullet, an unfortunate stylistic sign of the times from when the story was published), and defeats the Cyborg Superman. In this last battle The Last Son of Krypton sacrifices himself to save the original Superman while Steel and Superboy fight beside the original Superman and then continue on as superheroes.

The Death of Superman and America's Identity Crisis

Since his inception Superman has been emblematic of America, and part of America's own pseudo-mythological tradition. Daniel J. Boorstin argues that the creation of American mythologies is unique in world history for various reasons:

> Two crucial distinctions [...] mark the American making of a popular legendary hero. First, there was a fantastic chronological abridgement: from elusive oral legend to printed form required here a few years rather than centuries. Legends hastened into print before they could be purified of vulgarities and localisms. Second, the earliest printed versions were in a distinctly American form; they were not in literature but in "subliterature"-writings on popular and vulgar subjects, belly-laugh humor, slapstick and tall tales, adventures for the simple-minded. Crockett was not written down in any American counterpart of the *Historia Regum Britanniae* or in any *Morte d'Arthur*....[20]

Comic books are a continuation of this unique "subliterature" developed in America, and Superman's narrative can be see as an extension of early tall tales. America's popular culture began with tales of frontiersmen in dime novels, then progressed to cowboys, then private detectives, then pulp crime fighters. Comic book superheroes are simply another stage in this evolution of Boorstin's "popular legendary hero," and Superman was the first comic book superhero.

In his essay, "A Flag with a Human Face," Gary Engle calls Superman *the* great American hero and goes on to explain:

> Among the Davy Crocketts and Paul Bunyans and Mike Finks and Pecos Bills and all the rest [...] only Superman achieves truly mythic stature, interweaving a pattern of beliefs, literary conventions and cultural traditions of the American people more powerfully and more accessibly than any other cultural symbol of the 20th century, perhaps of any period of our history.[21]

Superman embodies many aspects of the American literary traditions, from immigrants' tales to frontier heroes, and is often treated as representative of America itself.

"The Death of Superman," and the subsequent rise of four replacement Supermen, came along at a historical period when America was having its own identity crisis. For decades, the country and its citizens had been defined as much as not-the-Soviet-Union or not-Communists as The United States of America or Americans. Political, social, economic, and personal identities were linked to the Cold War and America's position as one of two superpowers in the world.

The collapse of the Soviet Union, which was officially declared to be dissolved in December of 1991, and the end of the Cold War significantly altered the world stage and America's place on it. "The Death of Superman" and "Reign of the Supermen" were published in 1992 and 1993, during this period of redefinition of national identity. America's place on the world stage, and the role it should take on a global scale, were in question.

There was another significant change occurring in the America at this time: the dawn of the information age as technology was revolutionized and began to alter the everyday life Americans. Not only was technology expediting communication, transportation, and work in general, and it was simultaneously shrinking in size. Technology that once would have stayed at home or the office began to be carried with us everywhere. Technology became more pervasive, even invasive, in everyday life.

Two of the replacement Supermen can be read as representative of America's undefined position in the world, and also fears about what America would become as the dominant superpower without The Soviet Union to keep it in check. The other two replacement Supermen are associated with hopes and fears of the technological revolution. In both instances one of the two character embodies the hopeful possibilities while the other characters is associated with the fears and concerns of a changing society.

Superboy and the Last Son of Krypton: America's Role After the Cold War

Superboy was a new character with superpowers who is uncertain of how to best use them and what role he is meant to take in the world. He was a teenager, an age of transition and uncertainty. America, a very young country when compared to established countries such as China, India, or the European powers, suddenly found itself the lone "superpower" in the world. Like Superboy, the country had phenomenal power, but there was inexperience in the new role it found itself in. Superboy had the powers of Superman, but not the experience or maturity to use them without help and guidance. Superboy was a teenager who insisted on being called Superman, not because of his maturity, but because he felt he deserved respect by virtue of the situation he found himself in. At the conclusion of the Cold War, there was uncertainty in how America would act on the world stage.

Other nations had centuries of experience, good and bad, to draw on as they navigated the world stage in varying positions of influence. America was at best an adolescent nation wielding unparalleled power on the world stage. How would this young country react to having military, technological, and economic strength? These concerns are not only seen in the actions of the brash young Superboy, but in the Last Son of Krypton.

The fears about how America would act now that it had lost its greatest check can be seen in the Last Son of Krypton. The Last Son of Krypton had Superman's powers, but not his small town values. He still had an ethical or moral center, he was not out committing crimes or promoting anarchy, but his methods were brutal. The enforcement of his morals on others caused more harm than good. The Last Son of Krypton always acted "for the greater good" and in the name of "doing the right thing," but his methods were unreasonable. America, in its new position, had enormous influence, but how would that influence be handled? America had engaged in controversial wars in Vietnam and Korea, in the name of the greater good, but now would have an easier time of imposing its will on the world if it so chose. The Last Son of Krypton was representative of the identity America some feared America could have taken in the world at that time, a policeman with the power to enforce order, but without outside factors constraining that power.

America is the only nation to have used the nuclear bomb but the most significant inhibitor to America's subsequent use of the bomb had just been removed by the collapse of the Soviet Union. Would America choose to police the world in the same manner the Last Son of Krypton used Superman's powers? A newspaper article headlined "U.S. Goal: Only 1 Superpower" from March of 1992 discusses papers from the Pentagon that define "a world in which there is one dominant military power whose leaders 'must maintain the mechanisms for deterring potential competitors from even aspiring to a larger regional or global role.'"[22] Such rhetoric could be seen as America flexing its young muscles on the world stage, and it was unclear where such actions would lead. Societal uncertainty about America's future role in the world played out on the pages of superhero comic books.

Steel and the Cyborg Superman: Technology and America's Changing Lifestyle

At the same time that America was adapting to a new world stage, the technological revolution was changing daily life for most Americans. As consistently happens with new technologies, it was impossible to predict how it would evolve. At the same time that technology was seen as a benefit, there were concerns about it dehumanizing individuals and interpersonal relationships. In 1990 Lewis Mumford, a sociologist who had "implored people to place a higher value on human feelings than on dehumanizing technology," died and many newspapers carried stories discussing his views, publicizing his concerns anew in a technologically evolving world.[23] Today concerns are raised about texting, IMing, Facebook, online gaming, and online relationships. How "real" are these technological interactions? Is the skill of interacting cordially face-to-face being lost by the rising generation?

Similar concerns were being raised in the early 1990s. Personal computers had been available since the late 1970s, but in 1989 the concept of the World Wide Web was introduced, and changed people's interactions with and through technology forever. The Cyborg Superman can be read as a representation of the concerns about how technology could affect people's lives, specifically, the fear of the dehumanizing affect of technology. The Cyborg Superman, as finally revealed, embodies these fears literally, as the character's consciousness can no longer be housed in a biological body. Henshaw can only exist in machinery, and that existence has led to a devaluation of human life. These fears and concerns about technology are classic themes of science fiction, and are explored in everything from Isaac Asimov short stories to blockbuster films such as *The Matrix*. However, due a greater penetration of technology into the everyday lives of Americans in the early 1990s than what had been seen in previous years these themes may have resonated more at that time.

Not only was technology entering the homes through computers, much as radios and televisions had in previous generations, it was becoming attached to our very movements. Pagers, cell phones, laptop computers, all represented a change towards mobile technology which, in essence, became a part of us. Wherever we went, our technology was now able to follow. Even while recognizing the convenience of technology, concerns were voiced about its encroachment into all aspects of our lives. In 1992 Phil Robinson, the director of the computer-based heist film *Sneakers*, expressed a warning about technology, "Our lives are being shaped by rapidly changing times. I don't believe we're at all prepared to catch up with the technology that's leaping ahead of us."[24] While Robinson was promoting a film about our evolving interaction of technology, business, and crime, his concerns mirrored many voiced at the time.

Conversely, Steel is representative of the hopes that technology will aid humanity, that it will be a tool for good. In the hands of John Henry Irons, technology saves lives and increases an individual's ability to do good in the world.

A key distinction between Cyborg Superman and Steel, both of whom are technologically based, is that in one instance technology is encroaching on biology, and in the other the two are kept separate. In the Cyborg Superman, technology has gone too far and entered realms it should not, realms that are perceived as dangerous and unnatural, while with Steel the natural order is maintained. The biological John Henry Irons can remove technology and operate as a purely biological being, while the Cyborg Superman can only shed his biological parts to functions solely as a machine. In fact, in the climactic battle Irons must shed his technological suit to gain a tactical advantage over the Cyborg Superman, while the Cyborg Superman is defeated after his consciousness fully enters a massive, alien machine. It is John Henry Irons's biology and humanity which allows him to escape the villainous technology-driven Cyborg Superman.

"The Reign of the Supermen" ends on a very positive and even hopeful note. The true Superman, with his immigrant heritage and small town values, returns and vanquishes the villain who has let technology eliminate his humanity. The alien Last Son of Krypton learns that he has abused his power, and in a moment of self-realization sacrifices himself so that the true Superman can survive. Steel survives, not because of his technology, but because of his human spirit and drive. And Superboy, the young superhero who is learning his role in the world also survives, and is given the chance to mature and become a hero in his own right. Thus, in the end, the symbolic representations of America's fears are laid to rest, and the moral, honest, and strong America rises again. Technology can be a tool to aid us, adolescence is a time for learning, and great power can be used responsibly. "The Death of Superman" acknowledges the societal fears that existed as America moved into a new global environment and grappled with rapidly evolving technologies, but embraces a hopeful future.

CHAPTER NOTES

1. The high value of early comic books is directly related to the fact that nobody was buying and saving them. The very act of speculators preserving comics to increase their value limited the likelihood of high demand for those products at a later date. Many of the comics that were purchased at this time as investments are worth less than their original cover price.

2. Ryall, Chris, and Scott Tipton. *Comic Books 101: The History, Methods and Madness.* (Cincinatti: Impact Books, 2009), 45–46.

3. Jurgens, Dan (w), (a). "Doomsday!" *Superman Vol. 2 #75* (Jan. 1993). New York: DC Comics.

4. Duncan, Randy, and Matthew J. Smith. *The Power of Comics: History, Form, and Culture.* (New York: Continuum Press, 2009), 76.

5. DeHaven, Tom. *Our Hero: Superman on Earth.* (New Haven, CT: Yale University Press), 13.

6. "Top 10 Successful Marketing Stunts of All Time," Entrepeneur.com. Online. 4 April 2009.

7. Knowles, Christopher. *Our Gods Wear Spandex: The Secret History of Comic Book Superheroes.* (San Francisco: Weiser Books, 2007), 123.

8. At the height of a public panic about comic books corrupting youth the Senate held hearings to determine if comic books caused juvenile delinquency.

9. Rozanski, Chuck. "'Death of Superman' Promotion of 1992," milehighcomics.com.

10. Wright, Bradford W. *Comic Book Nation: The Transformation of Youth Culture in America.* (Baltimore: Johns Hopkins University Press, 2001) 283.

11. Cronin, Brian. *Was Superman a Spy? and Other Comic Book Legends Revealed!* (New York: Plume Books, 2009), 20.

12. "Requiem and Rebirth: Superman Lives!" (supplementary material on DVD release of *Superman: Doomsday*). DVD. Warner Bros., 2007.

13. Jurgens, Dan (w), and (a), Jerry Ordway (w), Louise Simonson (w), Roger Stern (w), Tom Bogdanove (a), Tom Grumett (a), and Jackson Guice (a). *The Death of Superman.* Ed. Bob Kahan, New York: DC Comics, 1993.

14. Jurgens, Dan (w), and (a), Karl Kessel (w), Louise Simonson (w), Roger Stern (w), Gerard Jones (w), Tom Grumett (a), Jackson Guice (a), John Bogdanove (a), and Mark Bright (a). *The Return of Superman.* Ed. Bob Kahan, New York: DC Comics, 1993.

15. Ibid.

16. Ibid.

17. Ibid.

18. Ibid.

19. Ibid.

20. Boorstin, Daniel J. *The Americans: The National Experience.* (USA: History Book Club, 2002), 328.

21. Eagan, Patrick L. "A Flag with a Human Face," *Superman at Fifty: The Persistence of a Legend.* Eds. Dennis Dooley and Gary Engle. (Cleveland: Octavia Press, 1987), 88–95.

22. Tyler, Patrick E. "U.S. Goal: Only 1 Superpower." New York Times News Service, 9 Mar. 1992. Online.

23. "Cities Critic Mumford Dies at 94." The Milwaukee Journal, 28 Jan. 1990. Online.

24. Straus, Bob. "*Sneakers'* Ensemble Cast Thrives on Diversity." Los Angeles Daily News, 11 Sep. 1992. Online.

BIBLIOGRAPHY

Boorstin, Daniel J. *The Americans: The National Experience.* U.S.A.: History Book Club, 2002.

"Cities Critic Mumford Dies at 94." *The Milwaukee Journal,* 28 Jan. 1990. Accessed at http://news.google.com/newspapers?nid=1499&dat=19900128&id=UmcaAAAAIBAJ&s jid=BywEAAAAIBAJ&pg=6197,2976646.

Cronin, Brian. *Was Superman a Spy? and Other Comic Book Legends Revealed!* New York: Plume Books, 2009.

DeHaven, Tom. *Our Hero: Superman on Earth.* New Haven, CT: Yale University Press.

Duncan, Randy, and Matthew J. Smith. *The Power of Comics: History, Form, and Culture.* New York: Continuum Press, 2009.

Eagan, Patrick L. "A Flag with a Human Face." In Dennis Dooley and Gary Engle, eds., *Superman at Fifty: The Persistence of a Legend.* Cleveland: Octavia Press, 1987.

Jurgens, Dan (w, a). "Doomsday!" *Superman Vol. 2 #75* (Jan. 1993). New York: DC Comics.

Jurgens, Dan (w), and (a), Karl Kessel (w), Louise Simonson (w), Roger Stern (w), Gerard Jones (w), Tom Grumett (a), Jackson Guice (a), John Bogdanove (a), and Mark Bright (a). *The Return of Superman.* Ed. Bob Kahan, New York: DC Comics, 1993.

Jurgens, Dan (w, a), Jerry Ordway (w), Louise Simonson (w), Roger Stern (w), Tom Bogdanove (a), Tom Grumett (a), and Jackson Guice (a). *The Death of Superman.* Ed. Bob Kahan, New York: DC Comics, 1993.

Knowles, Christopher. *Our Gods Wear Spandex: The Secret History of Comic Book Superheroes.* San Francisco: Weiser Books, 2007.

"Requiem and Rebirth: Superman Lives!" (supplementary material on DVD release of *Superman: Doomsday*). DVD. Warner Bros., 2007.

Rozanski, Chuck. "'Death of Superman' Promotion of 1992." Accessed June 2004 at http://www.milehighcomics.com/tales/cbg127.html.

Ryall, Chris, and Scott Tipton. *Comic Books 101: The History, Methods and Madness.* Cincinatti: Impact Books, 2009.

Straus, Bob. "*Sneakers'* Ensemble Cast Thrives on Diversity." *Los Angeles Daily News,* 11 Sep. 1992. Accessed at *http://news.google.com/newspapers?nid=1454&dat=19920911&id=s-pOAAAAIBAJ&sjid=sBQEAAAAIBAJ&pg=4993,4191181.*

"Top 10 Successful Marketing Stunts of All Time." Accessed at *http://www.entrepreneur.com/slideshow/163762#6.*

Tyler, Patrick E. "U.S. Goal: Only 1 Superpower." *Pittsburgh Post Gazette,* 9 Mar. 1992. Accessed at *http://news.google.com/newspapers?nid=1129&dat=19920309&id=xttRAAAAI BAJ&sjid=yW4DAAAAIBAJ&pg=5021,1993774.*

Wright, Bradford W. *Comic Book Nation: The Transformation of Youth Culture in America.* Baltimore: Johns Hopkins University Press, 2001.

Death, Bereavement, and the Superhero Funeral

JOSÉ ALANIZ

We did eight issues of Superman's funeral, where he was literally a dead body, and we thought that was the most daring part of the whole plan. There was a strong analogy for how we felt, which was that Superman was being taken for granted. We wanted to remind people that some of the values that Superman stands for are still important.

— *Mike Carlin*[1]

Superman died on November 18, 1992. America paid attention.

The event, picked up by news outlets throughout the country and beyond, reported the end of an era; after 54 years, the DC comics hero with the forelock, garbed in red, yellow and blue, who fought for nothing less than "truth, justice and the American way," had perished as befits what one commentator called a "secular American messiah"[2]: fallen gloriously in battle, saving his hometown Metropolis from a monstrous menace.

Though of course, like many superheroes before and since, Superman did not *die,* he "died." Six months later, he came back to a grateful world and notably apathetic press — setting off a pattern of reportage which has continued with the recent "deaths" and returns of Batman/Bruce Wayne and Captain America/Steve Rogers.

But the 1992–1993 "Death of Superman" storyline, whatever its level of penetration into American mainstream consciousness, has definitively emerged in fan discourses of the last 20 years as a touchstone for everything gone wrong in the superhero comics industry of the 1990s, with its obsessive focus on speculator-driven, media-stoking "mega-events"; lack of respect for beloved decades-old characters and long-devoted fans who bristle at seeing their icons tarnished; and crass commercialism leading to a mid-decade comics collectibles bubble and crash.[3] The storyline's title thus acquired a double meaning: the "death" of the character Superman as well as — goes the argument — the demise of a pre–'90s model of superhero comics production that privileged nostalgic reverence over short-term profit.

More than that: the "Death of Superman" story arc stands accused of trivializing death, through a cheap dramatic gimmick with no real repercussions, since publisher DC and its parent company Time Warner would never seriously consider eliminating one of their best-known corporate emblems, with its merchandising, TV and movie revenue stream.[4] Quite the opposite: the storyline temporarily revived a comics series that had found itself in a serious sales decline since the end of the Christopher Reeve films. And to better capitalize on the collectibles mania, DC sold the issue in various formats, including a Direct Market Memorial Collector's Edition, which featured the comic book in a black polybag with the "S" logo dripping blood (others featured a tombstone façade with the engraving "Herein Lies Earth's Greatest Hero"), containing a commemorative card, poster, stamp, *Daily Planet* death edition/obituary and black armband.[5]

Despite its reputation as a gimmick, as the best-known example of superhero mortality and its repercussions in the genre, the "Death of Superman" arc serves as a valuable case study in, among other things, how a supposedly death-averse society like late 20th century America addresses the end of life and bereavement through its popular culture. Indeed, the storyline offers a compelling snapshot of American attitudes to grief and the "celebrity funeral" at the dawn of the 1990s, a period when those attitudes — due in part to the Death Awareness and Death with Dignity movements; the AIDS epidemic and reassessments of the Vietnam conflict — were in flux. "If human social life is an attempt to construct a refuge of meaning and purpose against the meaningless chaos that is nature," wrote Clive Seale, "then study of the human approach to death and bereavement affords an unusually clear opportunity to perceive some of the most fundamental aspects of these constructions."[6]

Death, Representation and Body Politics

The study of death in the humanities, as social phenomenon and ideological construct, has exploded in the last 30 years.[7] This attention is owing to various cultural changes in post-war American life, particularly since the 1960s. Death in this period evolved — from a subject little-discussed and treated as impolite (even likened to pornography)[8] to a more accepted part of the social fabric.

In this evolution, two figures stand out: the muck-raking journalist Jessica Mitford, whose jeremiad against the funeral industry, *The American Way of Death,* appeared in 1963, and the Swiss-trained psychiatrist Elizabeth

Kübler-Ross, for her pioneering Death and Dying seminars at the University of Colorado Medical School, in which terminal patients were invited to answer questions on their experiences, fears and disappointments with their care. Their complaints — insensitive doctors; feelings of abandonment; taboos on speaking about death — started a national conversation after Kübler-Ross published her findings in the landmark *On Death and Dying* (1969). In addition, the modern, technologically-based legal criterion of "brain death" came to replace millennia of thought and custom on the border between the living and the dead, a process begun by a 1967 Harvard Medical School committee convened to study artificial life support.[9]

A vogue for the subject spread throughout the 1970s, spurred by books such as the thanatologist Ernest Becker's *The Denial of Death* (1973), which depicted death-terror in a psychoanalytic frame, as a fundamental human drive, and, more controversially, Derek Humphry's *Jean's Way: A Love Story* (1978), which advocated assisted suicide. Discussions of euthanasia and Right-to-Die cases proliferated, including that of Karen Ann Quinlan, a young woman in a vegetative state whose family succeeded in convincing the New Jersey Supreme Court to permit them to remove her from a ventilator, and Nancy Cruzan, who had lain in a coma since 1983, and was allowed to die in 1990 after the U.S. Supreme Court ruled constitutional the withdrawal of her feeding tube, as argued by her parents. Both cases proved influential in the development of advance directives laws, including living wills, culminating in the Patient Self-Determination Act of 1991.[10] In short, by the time the "Death of Superman" storyline saw print, America had been engaged for at least three decades in an at times acrimonious conversation on death and dying.

Throughout the "Death of Superman" storyline Superman's body appears precisely as an object to be "appropriated," whether physically by Lex Luthor and rogue U.S. government agents, or symbolically, be it by a mourning nation or commemorative funeral merchandise hawkers. It is, after all, in the deaths of our most revered figures that we see an intensification of the effect that Elizabeth Bronfen (referencing Maurice Blanchot) ascribes to the power of the dead human body as a polyvalent signifier disruptive of the social status quo:

> [T]he corpse initially marks a moment of total destabilization of categories like position, site and reference ... the cadaver is not in its place, not here and yet it is not elsewhere. A stability of categories must again be recuperated, namely in the act of representation, so that we move from the experience of decomposition to composition, from the dying body/corpse to a representation and narration of the dying body/corpse.[11]

Furthermore, as Bronfen and Sarah Goodwin write in *Death and Representation,* the corpse is a (warped) mirror upon which culture views its own desired reflection: corpse as tragedy, corpse as tranquility, corpse as indictment, corpse as national rebirth. In this sense,

> Every representation of death is a misrepresentation. Thus the analysis of it must show not only how it claims to represent death, but also what else it in fact represents, however suppressed: assertion of alternative power, self-referential metaphor, aggression against individuals or groups, formation of group identities or ideologies, and so forth. Whether as state or as event, death cannot be represented. Attempts at representation therefore seek to appropriate that resistant power.[12]

The anthropologist Katherine Verdery, in *The Political Lives of Dead Bodies,* reads the corpse in much the same way, with an emphasis on its ideological uses:

> Remains are concrete, but protean.... Different people can invoke corpses as symbols, thinking those corpses mean the same thing to all present, whereas in fact they may mean different things to each. All that is shared is everyone's *recognition* of this dead person as somehow important. In other words, what gives a dead body symbolic effectiveness in politics is precisely its ambiguity, its capacity to evoke a variety of understandings.[13]

Simply put, the sheer unknowability of death and the material nature of its evidence (the corpse), combined with its stark terror for a society inured to optimism and the "good life," necessitates a robust sociocultural response to contain death's destabilizing power. These responses are open to being shaped by various political actors and for various ideological aims. Who represents death, narrativizes it or tells its story, can direct a culture's strong emotional recoiling from death.[14]

Moreover, the famous deceased — such as America's first and greatest superhero — bear an outsize weight in how they affect the "national narrative." As Verdery argues, they "come with a curriculum vitae" which, through proper handling, can itself serve to authorize particular values and de-legitimize others — with, of course, no resistance from the dead person: "Words can be put into their mouths — often quite ambiguous words — or their own actual words can be ambiguated by quoting them out of context. It is thus easier to rewrite history with dead people than with other kinds of symbols that are speechless."[15]

Who speaks for Superman, in that liminal space between his death and resurrection? In service to which values is his long, much-lauded "curriculum vitae" conscripted? What aspects of early-90s culture are thrown into relief by the spectacle of his funeral? Such questions of death, representation and nationhood inform the reading that unfurls below — as does A. David Lewis' observation that "America — notorious in thanatological literature for its unwillingness and or inability to accept mortality — is the birthplace of the superhero."[16]

The Deaths of Superman

Perhaps the best essay on Superman, Umberto Eco's 1962 "The Myth of Superman," is in some sense an elaborate explanation for why he cannot die, yet remains haunted by death: caught between a mythological and a romantic mode of serial narrative, Eco maintains, the superhero acts, but in acting "consumes himself," "takes a step toward death"—yet, "Superman cannot consume himself, since a myth is 'inconsumable'"[17] or timeless. As a result, Superman's writers concocted various ways around that paradox, including an "extremely hazy" relationship to time and the Imaginary Tales, in which such "consumption" constraints do not apply.[18] Another way scholars have framed the question of Superman's "immortality" is through the trope of human perfectibility; Douglas Wolk, for example, calls him "a perfect person," though "[t]he catch is that he's not actually human."[19] Richard Reynolds calls Superman a "man-god."[20] This of course signals religious, especially Christological associations, as argued by, among others, Koosed and Schumm: not unlike Jesus, they contend, "Superman always gets back up, his body heals from injury almost instantaneously, and even death is only temporary."[21] Daniels compares him to Moses and Jesus, "sent from above to redeem the world."[22] Thus, in 1992, the seemingly real prospect of the Man of Steel fallen and, so to speak, not rising on the third day, seized the imagination.

Funeral for a Friend

Dispersed over some 30 issues of continuity in various Superman and non–Superman publications, the "Death and Return of Superman" story arc (as it came to be called) dealt with an apocalyptic villain dubbed Doomsday, who carves a path of destruction across the country. In *Superman #75* (Jan. 1993), through a series of single-panel splash pages, this landmark issue depicts an exhausted and battered Man of Steel sacrificing himself to finally deliver the knock-out punch; hero and villain collapse together among the rubble. Caught up in a weeping Lois Lane's arms (an allusion to Michelangelo's *Pietà*), Superman breathes out his last words: "Doomsday ... is he ... is he ..."[23]

While the death seemed a standard (if unusually prolonged) heroic sacrifice, what unfolded over the next eight issues of various *Superman* titles, in an arc called "Funeral for a Friend," proved a radical departure from the generic norm. Superman the person recedes, replaced by an inert object — his corpse — wrangled over, poked, manipulated and ultimately interred (and almost immediately stolen). The impact of his unimaginable death on his friends, family and enemies takes center stage: his fiancée Lois weeps inconsolably, but insists on working through her sorrow at the *Daily Planet;* photographer Jimmy Olsen agonizes over the sale of a career-making scoop, his picture of Superman's final collapse; the corporate magnate Lex Luthor publicly praises the Man of Steel and finances his memorial, but secretly seethes at having been robbed of his just vengeance ("Try as I might, I couldn't *kill* Superman, but sure as *hell*.... I'm going to *bury* him")[24]; Superman's adoptive parents, Ma and Pa Kent, mourn helplessly in Kansas as their son's body receives a lavish state funeral in faraway Metropolis. "We lost a son," utters a heartsick Jonathan Kent, "but the world lost a *hero* ... and they're gonna bury that hero with *full honors*."[25]

As that quote announces, a major theme woven through these episodes is the authenticity of private grief (Lane, the Kents, Lana Lang, Bibbo Bibbowski) contrasted with the cynicism and theatricality of public mourning (Luthor, the merchandise hawker, Agent Westfield). Page design underscores that distinction at several points. The Luthor and Kent dialogue cited above appears on facing pages, with Metropolis depicted in sunny tones, while the Kent home interior appears in shadow (its inhabitants' dejected faces never clearly seen). Most starkly, the page depicting Superman's actual interment, as Wonder Woman and Green Lantern slide the stony lid over his sarcophagus, the panels bordered by the faces of mourners,[26] confronts its opposite: the Kents alone, sorrowfully burying some mementos of the deceased in the field where they first found him as an infant.[27] Crucially, Lois, the link between public and private grief, appears among the above-mentioned border portraits (evocative of 19th century funeral cards), though she actually is not at the funeral; disgusted by the ceremony, she at that moment is telephoning the Kents.

Lois' there/not there depiction as regards her public lamentations attests to the ways societal rules of "proper mourning" shape — but are also resisted by — private grief, amounting to a blurring of the two. The British sociologist Tony Walter has critiqued what he considers the too-neat formulation of grief as private, "natural" emotional expression over loss and mourning as public "cultural" expression over loss, arguing that culture affects, polices and determines "private" grief to no less a degree than it does public mourning. It is a process not without a degree of oppression: "[M]any ... mourning rituals seem designed more to assist the dead and the power structure of society than the bereaved individual," he notes.[28]

In contrast, "Funeral for a Friend," with its insistent juxtaposition of the extravagant burial ceremony "with *full honors*" and Superman's loved ones in isolation, inventing their own private rituals of commemoration, seeks to maintain a private (authentic)/public (inauthentic) dichotomy for the reaction to loss.[29] "We'll say goodbye to our son in *our* way..." Jonathan says.[30]

In the rigid moral hierarchy of "Funeral for a Friend," two unavoidable aspects of modern American life come in for considerable abuse: the media and the public. The former comes off as coarse and mendacious: a broadcast news anchor, mere hours after the death, declares, "... So I *guess* that *Superman* wasn't so *super* after all!"[31] This prompts José Delgado, a.k.a. the superhero Gangbuster, to toss his helmet through the TV screen. More than once, the Kents switch off their set, infuriated and saddened at the sensationalistic coverage; "They just want a *piece* of him," sighs Martha Kent.[32] At least one of Olsen's co-workers compliments him on his photo, telling an embarrassed Jimmy, "Lighten up, guy. It's gonna make you *famous*. After this, you can write your *own ticket*."[33] Intriguingly, this distrust and indignation over the media belies how everyone in the story (as well as ourselves, the readers) absolute rely on it for news.[34] At the end of the climactic Superman/Doomsday battle (*Superman #75*), our hero's fall itself appears reflected in Jimmy's camera lens, while Lois' embrace of her doomed lover after the fall is seen on the Kent's television screen before being depicted "in the flesh." The ubiquity of television, a year after CNN's ratings triumph with its First Persian Gulf War coverage, is reflected here through such tensions.

But "the people" also misbehave. The main theme of "Funeral for a Friend," in fact, is that American public styles of mourning fall far short of the propriety required to register such a momentous passing; America has forgotten how to grieve with grace. "Where's the *dignity*?" Martha Kent exclaims, watching the televised funeral deteriorate into a "circus."[35] The unruly masses turn into a mob requiring superhero crowd control; in the aftermath of Superman's demise, innumerable frauds step forward to claim some link to him, including a "Mrs. Superman" who purportedly lived with him in secret in a New York penthouse[36]; others declare themselves his tailor, business manager, etc.[37]; and the aforementioned funeral merchandise salesman peddles his wares at the ceremony — though a confrontation with Bibbo reveals he is just a family man out of work, who needs to make a buck.[38]

Everyone, in short, seeks to profit from, reinterpret or otherwise appropriate Superman's body, to make it "speak" for them. Institutions — the press, the corporation, the government — as well as the man on the street seem engaged only to compete over, regulate and, if possible, exploit the reality of death. The people, it must be said, come out looking the best in the end: along with the frauds and cynics, anonymous crowds leave tokens of affection, such as cards, photographs and flowers, at Superman's monument; Jimmy calls it "a very solemn place."[39] This sort of spontaneous public tribute had become especially pronounced at the Vietnam War Memorial in Washington, D.C. (dedicated in 1982), where by 1993 visitors had left up to 250,000 objects commemorating their loved ones.[40] It should come as no surprise, then, that the Doomsday victim Mitch declares the crowd's impromptu shrine at Superman's monument, "Just like the Vietnam Memorial."[41]

The Best and the Brightest or the 500

"Death universally calls into question the order upon which most societies are based," write Michael Leming and George Dickinson. "As a marginal experience to everyday life, death not only disrupts normal patterns of interaction, but also challenges the meaningfulness of life."[42] The deaths of public figures whom most of us have never met in person nonetheless have the potential, through our mediated reality, to touch more lives.[43] But whether anonymous or famous, death is experienced as a trauma in a community; this is what the poet and undertaker Thomas Lynch means when he writes that it is the living "to whom death happens, if it really happens to anyone.... Theirs is the pain and the pleasure of memory."[44]

Over a century of anthropological observation has construed mourning as a painful liminal period, encumbered with social obligations. Writing in 1909, Arnold van Gennep described it as a rite of passage that for a time sets the survivors off from the rest of the socius: "During mourning, the living mourners and the deceased constitute a special group, situated between the world of the living and the world of the dead."[45] At the same time, age-old structures assist in the labor of mourning and reintegration with the world. As Robert Jay Lifton and Eric Olson discern, "Societies and social institutions — when people believe in them — are able to aid in mastering death anxiety by generating shared images of continuity beyond the life of each single person."[46]

A crucial role here is played by the tales a people tells itself. As Tom Lutz puts it, "Making a narrative out of the competing emotions of grief makes therapeutic sense — it is a way for people to name, give shape to, and help manipulate their own experience."[47] Lutz is writing of personal grief narratives, but clearly popular cultural productions like "The Death of Superman" function similarly (if perhaps modestly) to help us grapple with such overwhelming questions as death, mourning, and carrying on in the face of loss. When the scope of death encompasses an entire country, as in the death of a sitting president, the work of culture, its deployment of nostalgia and national symbols for healing (and, it need be said, social control) become of critical concern.

As Kitch elaborates when discussing media coverage of "large-impact" deaths:

> Such stories take on mythic qualities when they allow discussion of cultural ideals, when the real "story" is that of ... the passing of an era, the punishment of greed

and evil, the triumph of the underdog, the loyalty and sacrifice of patriots, or the loss of American innocence but resilience of American spirit.[48]

The foregoing, I believe, goes far to explain why a reader of "Funeral for a Friend" — particularly the burial issue, "Funeral Day" — might wonder why Superman's coffin is carried by horse and carriage rather than a hearse (or, for that matter, Green Lantern's power ring) and why the entire funeral sequence looks so "nostalgic."

Superman #75 appeared in stores almost exactly 29 years after November 25, 1963, when the assassinated President John F. Kennedy was laid to rest at Arlington National Cemetery in Washington, D.C., in a state ceremony. Clues abound that that ceremony served as the basis for the look of Superman's own funeral: the carriage (though Kennedy's body was borne by a gun carriage, not the coach depicted in the story); the closed casket with an American flag draped over it[49]; the eternal flame; even the massed crowds and park setting for the monument recall photographs and newsreel footage of that day.[50] A further hint occurs after the funeral, when Lois places her engagement ring in her slain lover's coffin (197) — recalling the same gesture made by Jacqueline Kennedy with her wedding band.[51] The Kennedy funeral, like Superman's, even spawned a collectibles craze; for example, Time-Life, Inc. still enjoyed brisk sales of commemorative photographs, reprints of memorial editions of *Life* magazine, and other wares 25 years after the event.[52]

Why Kennedy? Part of the reason must be the extraordinary impact of that particular national tragedy, as well as the way it was covered. As the historian Gary Laderman explains:

> The dramatic impact of the funeral and the outpouring of grief and sorrow across the country was unparalleled in U.S. history. Although there are obvious grounds for comparison with Lincoln's assassination and funeral ceremonies, the presence of the media at the ceremonies, and the mediated presence of Kennedy's dead body in the lives of millions of television viewers, created an instantaneous sense of common suffering on a scale never seen before.[53]

But a deeper answer lies more specifically in the way Americans (certainly in 1992, and much more so today) consume national tragedies as media events, which by the nature of their presentation take on familiarly "mythic" grand themes of "American resilience" and the "American spirit." In other words, the big news stories carry a strong sense of déjà vu, an "I've seen this movie before" quality, as described by Kitch:

> When the significance of a news event lies in past events (especially events the news media has covered), the storyline of current news is threaded into an existing tapestry. In its coverage, memory is simultaneously invoked and constructed.... The "story" — whether it is the death of a celebrity, a political sex scandal, a World

Series victory, soldiers' departure for war, or even a terrorist attack — is one we at least partly already "know."[54]

This national repetition compulsion, cultivated by the press, entered its modern phase with the Kennedy funeral — whose pattern we follow to the present day. As Zelizer argues, news correspondents do far more than simply report the facts, particularly at times of national upheaval: "[T]he media's coverage of Kennedy's funeral made them into *masters of ceremonies* who were celebrated for their active part in healing the nation."[55]

The writers and artists of "The Death of Superman" integrated, perhaps unconsciously, these enduring tropes, conventions and clichés dating back to the Kennedy funeral to lend the proceedings a tone of solemnity, gravitas and nostalgia. In doing this, they throw into relief the assumptions, expectations and blind spots of American culture's engagement with death and bereavement in the early 1990s.

The consumption of national deaths as packaged, digestible units (a process of which "The Death of Superman" is a fictional, pop culture example), relates to art historian Erika Doss' analysis of national sites of mourning erected since the Vietnam War Memorial, such as the Oklahoma City National Memorial (1999), built to commemorate the 168 victims of Timothy McVeigh and Terry Nichols' terrorist bombing of the Alfred P. Murrah building on April 19, 1995. For Doss, these modern monuments shed light on the "complicated narratives and processes that surround ... public commemorations of tragic and traumatic events, of events that Americans have generally refused to consider critically in terms of cause and sociopolitical consequence."[56] Her thesis holds that, in these monuments, "memory overwhelms history" by "encourag[ing] forgiving and forgetting, rather than the urgency of facing the cause of bereavement"; they are "largely anaesthetic because the historical and political context of why these deaths occurred has been effaced."[57]

Depoliticized memory overwhelms history, too, in "Funeral for a Friend": the Big Death eclipses, for the most part, the little deaths. Doomsday's human victims, which number at least 500, receive scant attention, save for a reference in President Clinton's speech and some rebuilding done by the superheroes. No public outcry follows the near-leveling of Metropolis, or great swathes of America, by the monster. No questioning of superheroes' right to operate outside the law, or their ineffectuality, colors the proceedings.

It would, of course, be misguided to require the "Death of Superman" to address questions it was never intended, nor all that keen, to answer. The storyline depicts the memorialization of a hero, tragically fallen, with all the attendant pathos — naturalizing what Doss terms the effacement of political context through powerful emotions, dramatic force, in short, the anaesthetic of storytelling.

All the same, "The Death of Superman" is a cathartic work, venturing deeper into taboo territory few mainstream continuity series will ever hazard — and uncovering valuable insights into grief, superheroic paradox and the visual culture of national trauma in 1990s America.

It serves, among other things, as a colorful reminder of Sigmund Freud's 1915 formulation on the psychological advantages of art for the human confrontation with death:

> [We] seek in the world of fiction, in literature and in the theatre compensation for what has been lost in life. There we still find people who know how to die.... In the realm of fiction we find the plurality of lives which we need. We die with the hero with whom we have identified ourselves; yet we survive him, and are ready to die with another hero.[58]

Or, as it happens, with the same one, resurrected.

CHAPTER NOTES

1. Daniels, Les. *Superman: The Complete History : The Life and Times of the Man of Steel in Color.* (New York: DC Comics, 1998), 168. Mike Carlin served as an editor on the *Superman* titles at the time of the "Death of Superman" story arc.

2. Daniels, Les, 19.

3. Writing in 2011, the blogger Avi Green summed up the hard feelings with which many in the fan community now regard the storyline: "[I]t's been nearly two decades since that farce, and nobody's going to pay diddly for the story today; it's utterly worthless and just clutters the bargain bins. But more alarming is the kind of attitude cultivated at the time — to care more about monetary than entertainment value." Green, Avi. "When Superman 'Died' in 1992, Some Bought It for Profit, Not Because They Cared About the Story." *The Four-Color Media Monitor.* January 27, 2011.

4. For more on the commercial untenability of superhero death in a mainstream publishing context, see Alaniz, José. "Death and the Superhero: The Silver Age and Beyond." *International Journal of Comic Art,* Vol. 8, No. 1 (Spring/Summer), 2006: 234–248. and Duffy, William. "Sing, Muse, of the Immortal Hero: Using Epic to Understand Comic Books." *International Journal of Comic Art,* Vol. 8, No. 1 (Spring/Summer), 2006: 258–270. As the latter succinctly put it: "The same economic and narratological factors that forced [Superman] to be killed also mandated that he be revived" (260).

5. De Haven, Tom. *Our Hero: Superman on Earth.* (New Haven, Conn.: Yale University Press, 2010), 11.

6. Seale, Clive. *Constructing Death: The Sociology of Dying and Bereavement,* (Cambridge UP, 1998), 11.

7. Some important works that address death as a cultural phenomenon, published in the last 30 years, include Ariès, Philippe. *The Hour of Our Death.* (New York: Knopf, 1981); Irina Paperno, Irina. *Suicide As a Cultural Institution in Dostoyevsky's Russia.* (Ithaca, New York: Cornell UP, 1997); and Gilbert, Sandra M. *Death's Door: Modern Dying and the Ways We Grieve.* (New York: W.W. Norton, 2006).

8. The British sociologist Geoffrey Gorer's important 1955 essay, "The Pornography of Death" argued that most modern people considered death's natural processes "morbid and unhealthy" to ponder, much less bring up in conversation. Gorer, Geoffrey. *Death, Grief, and Mourning.* (Garden City, N.Y: Doubleday, 1965), 196. His thesis has been challenged by, among others, Tony Walter.

9. For a discussion of the brain death concepts and the debates they launched, see

Greenberg, Gary. "As Good as Dead: Is There Really Such a Thing as Brain Death?" *The New Yorker*, August 13, 2001, pp. 36–41; Zucker, Arthur. "Rights and the Dying." *Dying: Facing the Facts*. Hannelore Waas and Robert A. Neimeyer, eds. (Washington, D.C.: Taylor & Francis, 1995) 385–403; and Singer, Peter. *The Essential Singer: Writings on an Ethical Life*. (New York: Ecco Press, 2000), 171–176.

10. For a useful summary of these cases and laws, see Webb, Marilyn. *The Good Death: The New American Search to Reshape the End of Life*. (New York: Bantam Books, 1997).

11. Bronfen, Elisabeth. *Over Her Dead Body: Death, Femininity, and the Aesthetic*. (New York: Routledge, 1992), 52.

12. Goodwin, Sarah M. K. W, and Elisabeth Bronfen. *Death and Representation*. (Baltimore: Johns Hopkins University Press, 1993), 20.

13. Verdery, Katherine. *The Political Lives of Dead Bodies: Reburial and Postsocialist Change*. (New York: Columbia University Press, 1999), 28–29 (emphasis in original).

14. See, for example, the recent controversy over whether the media would/should be allowed to publish photographs of coffins of American war dead returning from the Iraq and Afghanistan theaters, and Taylor, John. *Body Horror: Photojournalism, Catastrophe and War*. (Manchester: Manchester University Press, 1998).

15. Verdery, 29.

16. Lewis, A. David. "Ever-Ending Battle: Introduction." *International Journal of Comic Art*, Vo;. 8, No. 1 (Spring/Summer) 2006: 163–173.

17. Eco, Umberto. "The Myth of Superman." *Arguing Comics*. Jeet Heer and Kent Worcester, eds. (Jackson, Miss: University of Mississippi Press, 2005), 150.

18. Eco wrote at a time before continuity had become a standard element of American superhero comics.

19. Wolk, Douglas. *Reading Comics: How Graphic Novels Work and What They Mean*. (Cambridge, MA: Da Capo Press, 2007), 97.

20. Reynolds, Richard. *Super Heroes: A Modern Mythology*. (London: B.T. Batsford, 1992), 12.

21. Koosed, Jennifer L., and Schumm, Darla. "From Superman to Super-Jesus: Constructions of Masculinity and Disability on the Silver Screen." *Disability Studies Quarterly*, Vol. 29, No. 2 (Spring, 2009).

22. Daniels, Les, 19. For more on Superman as a Jesus figure, see Kozlovic, Anton K. "Superman As Christ-Figure: the American Pop Culture Movie Messiah." *Journal of Religion and Film*. 6.1 (2002).

23. Ordway, Jerry (w), and Grummett, Tom (a). "Death of a Legend." *Adventures of Superman #498* (Jan. 1993). New York: DC Comics. All page numbers for the "Funeral for a Friend" storyline come from the trade paperback collection *World Without a Superman*, London: Titan Books, 1993.

24. Ibid., 58, emphasis in original. Original story: Simonson, Louise (w), and Bogdanove, Jon (a). "Funeral Day." *Superman: Man of Steel #20* (Feb. 1993). New York: DC Comics.

25. Ibid., pg. 59, emphasis in original.

26. Ibid., pg. 77.

27. Ibid., pg. 76.

28. Walter, Tony. *On Bereavement: The Culture of Grief*. (Buckingham: Open University Press, 1999), 29.

29. In one sentimentalized scene, Lois returns to the apartment she had shared with Clark Kent/Superman; tall, thin panels, many dominated by black, underscore her sorrow. Captions, figuring her thoughts, read: "Don't cry, Lois" and "I'm alone. So terribly lonely ..." (85). Inside she discovers the Kents, come to Metropolis to join her (they embrace on the next page, made up mostly of more conventional square panels): a private community of grief. Their rectangular "reunion" panel bears the same thick black border as the covers

(86). Original story: Jurgens, Dan (w, a). "Metropolis Mailbag II." *Superman #76* (Feb. 1993). New York: DC Comics.

30. Ibid., 73, emphasis in original. Original story: *Superman: Man of Steel #20.*

31. Ibid., 13, emphasis in original. Original story: *Adventures of Superman #498.*

32. Ibid., 73, emphasis in original. Original story: *Superman: Man of Steel #20.*

33. Ibid., 59, emphasis in original. Original story: *Superman: Man of Steel #20.* This episode recalls the opening of Leo Tolstoy's novella *The Death of Ivan Ilyich* (1886), the first modern depiction of death, in which the eponymous character (now dead) is mentioned to his office co-workers, prompting them each to think of how the new vacancy will advance their careers. Tolstoy, Leo, Richard Pevear, and Larissa Volokhonsky. *The Death of Ivan Ilyich and Other Stories.* (New York: Alfred A. Knopf, 2009).

34. A major theme of Brooke Gladstone and Josh Neufeld's comics manifesto on the media: Gladstone, Brooke, Josh Neufeld, Randy Jones, and Susann Jones. *The Influencing Machine: Brooke Gladstone on the Media.* (New York: W.W. Norton, 2011).

35. *World Without a Superman,* (London: Titan Books, 1993), 73, emphasis in original. Original story: *Superman: Man of Steel #20.*

36. Ibid., 83. Original story: *Superman #76.*

37. Ibid., 84. Lois calls these people "morbid leeches" (ibid., pg. 83).

38. Ibid., 69.

39. Ibid., 96. Original story: *Superman #76.*

40. Doss, Erika. "Death, Art and Memory in the Public Sphere: the Visual and Material Culture of Grief in Contemporary America." *Mortality.* 7.1 (2002): 63–82, pg. 66. They received still more prominent media attention in the wake of the 1995 Oklahoma City bombing and the 1999 Columbine school shootings. As Doss notes, "The images, artifacts and rituals of these visibly public death-shrines ... framed issues of memory, tribute and collectivity in contemporary America; their visual and performative dimensions clearly embodied a vast collaboration of mourners and media" (69).

41. *World Without a Superman,* (London: Titan Books, 1993), 97. Original story: *Superman #76.*

42. Leming, Michael R., and Dickinson, George E. "The American Ways of Death." *The Unknown Country: Death in Australia, Britain, and the Usa.* Kathy Charmaz, Glennys Howarth and Allan Kellehear, eds. (New York: St. Martin's Press, 1997), 172.

43. For a detailed discussion of television and the press' influence on mourning practices, see Walter, Tony, Jane Littlewood, and Michael Pickering. "Death in the News: the Public Invigilation of Private Emotion." *Sociology,* Vol. 29, No. 4 (1995): 579–596.

44. Lynch, Thomas. *The Undertaking: Life Studies from the Dismal Trade.* (New York: W.W. Norton, 1997), 7.

45. Van Gennep, Arnold. "The Rites of Passage." *Death, Mourning, and Burial: A Cross-Cultural Reader.* Antonius C. G. M. Robben, ed. (Malden, MA: Blackwell Pub, 2004), 214.

46. Lifton, Robert Jay, and Olson, Eric. "Symbolic Immortality." *Death, Mourning, and Burial: A Cross-Cultural Reader.* Antonius C. G. M. Robben, ed. (Malden, MA: Blackwell Pub, 2004), 39.

47. Lutz, Tom. *Crying: The Natural and Cultural History of Tears.* (New York: W.W. Norton, 1999), 222.

48. Kitch, 305.

49. Strictly speaking, Superman had not earned a flag on his coffin, having served neither in government nor the military.

50. The scene before the Children's Aid Society (66) recalls the famous photograph of "John-John" (the three-year-old John F. Kennedy, Jr.), though none of the kids salutes the passing coffin.

51. Laderman, xxxiii.
52. Zelizer, Barbie. *Covering the Body: The Kennedy Assassination, the Media, and the Shaping of Collective Memory.* (Chicago: University of Chicago Press, 1992), 166.
53. Laderman, xxxi. To cite another connection between these two national heroes, in 1964 DC published the story "Superman's Mission for President Kennedy" (*Superman #170*, July, 1964) which had previously been slated for publication but withdrawn due to the assassination. The story appeared at the personal request of President Lyndon B. Johnson. See Waid, Mark, Jerry Siegel, and Joe Shuster. *Superman in the Sixties.* (New York: DC Comics, 1999) 180.
54. Kitch, 304.
55. Zelizer, 37, my emphasis.
56. Doss, 66.
57. Ibid., 78.
58. Freud, Sigmund. "Thoughts for the Times on War and Death." *Standard Edition of the Complete Psychological Works of Sigmund Freud,* ed. James Strachey, (London: Hogarth Press, 1957) 291.

BIBLIOGRAPHY

Alaniz, José. "Death and the Superhero: The Silver Age and Beyond." *International Journal of Comic Art,* 8. 1 (Spring/Summer), 2006: 234–248.
Ariès, Philippe. *The Hour of Our Death.* New York: Knopf, 1981.
Bronfen, Elisabeth. *Over Her Dead Body: Death, Femininity, and the Aesthetic.* New York: Routledge, 1992.
Daniels, Les. *Superman: The Complete History.* New York: DC Comics, 1998.
De Haven, Tom. *Our Hero: Superman on Earth.* New Haven, CT.: Yale University Press, 2010), 11.
Doss, Erika. "Death, Art and Memory in the Public Sphere: the Visual and Material Culture of Grief in Contemporary America." *Mortality,* 7:1 (2002): 63–82
Duffy, William. "Sing, Muse, of the Immortal Hero: Using Epic to Understand Comic Books." *International Journal of Comic Art,* 8:1 (Spring/Summer), 2006: 258–270.
Eco, Umberto. "The Myth of Superman." In Jeet Heer and Kent Worcester, eds., *Arguing Comics.* Jackson: University of Mississippi Press, 2005.
Freud, Sigmund. "Thoughts for the Times on War and Death." *Standard Edition of the Complete Psychological Works of Sigmund Freud,* ed. James Strachey. London: Hogarth Press, 19571.
Gilbert, Sandra M. *Death's Door: Modern Dying and the Ways We Grieve.* New York: W.W. Norton, 2006.
Goodwin, Sarah M. K. W, and Elisabeth Bronfen. *Death and Representation.* Baltimore: Johns Hopkins University Press, 1993.
Gorer, Geoffrey. *Death, Grief, and Mourning.* Garden City, NY: Doubleday, 1965.
Green, Avi. "When Superman 'Died' in 1992, Some Bought It for Profit, Not Because They Cared About the Story." *The Four-Color Media Monitor.* January 27, 2011.
Greenberg, Gary. "As Good as Dead: Is There Really Such a Thing as Brain Death?" *The New Yorker,* August 13, 2001, 36–41.
Jurgens, Dan (w),(a). "Metropolis Mailbag II." *Superman #76* (Feb. 1993). New York: DC Comics.
Kitch, Carolyn. "A Death in the American Family: Myth, Memory and National Values in the Media Mourning of John F. Kennedy, Jr." *Journalism and Mass Communications Quarterly,* Vol. 79, No. 2 (Summer, 2002): 294–309.
Koosed, Jennifer L., and Schumm, Darla. "From Superman to Super-Jesus: Constructions

of Masculinity and Disability on the Silver Screen." *Disability Studies Quarterly*, 29:2 (Spring, 2009).

Kozlovic, Anton K. "Superman as Christ-Figure: The American Pop Culture Movie Messiah." *Journal of Religion and Film*, 6:1 (2002).

Leming, Michael R. and Dickinson, George E. "The American Ways of Death." In Kathy Charmaz, Glenys Howarth and Allan Kellehear, eds., *The Unknown Country: Death in Australia, Britain, and the U.S.A.*. New York: St. Martin's Press, 1997.

Lewis, A. David. "Ever-Ending Battle: Introduction." *International Journal of Comic Art*, 8:1 (Spring/Summer) 2006: 163–173.

Lutz, Tom. *Crying: The Natural and Cultural History of Tears*. New York: W.W. Norton, 1999.

Lynch, Thomas. *The Undertaking: Life Studies from the Dismal Trade*. New York: W.W. Norton, 1997.

Ordway, Jerry (w), and Tom Grummett (a). "Death of a Legend." *Adventures of Superman #498* (Jan. 1993). New York: DC Comics.

Paperno, Irina. *Suicide As a Cultural Institution in Dostoyevsky's Russia*. Ithaca, New York: Cornell University Press, 1997.

Reynolds, Richard. *Super Heroes: A Modern Mythology*. London: B.T. Batsford, 1992.

Seale, Clive. *Constructing Death: The Sociology of Dying and Bereavement*. Ne York: Cambridge University Press, 1998.

Singer, Peter. *The Essential Singer: Writings on an Ethical Life*. New York: Ecco Press, 2000.

Taylor, John. *Body Horror: Photojournalism, Catastrophe and War*. Manchester: Manchester University Press, 1998.

Tolstoy, Leo, Richard Pevear, and Larissa Volokhonsky. *The Death of Ivan Ilyich and Other Stories*. New York: Alfred A. Knopf, 2009.

Verdery, Katherine. *The Political Lives of Dead Bodies: Reburial and Postsocialist Change*. New York: Columbia University Press, 1999.

Walter, Tony. *On Bereavement: The Culture of Grief*. Buckingham: Open University Press, 1999.

Walter, Tony, Jane Littlewood, and Michael Pickering. "Death in the News: the Public Invigilation of Private Emotion." *Sociology*, 29:4 (1995): 579–596.

Webb, Marilyn. *The Good Death: The New American Search to Reshape the End of Life*. New York: Bantam Books, 1997.

Wolk, Douglas. *Reading Comics: How Graphic Novels Work and What They Mean*. Cambridge, MA: Da Capo Press, 2007.

Zelizer, Barbie. *Covering the Body: The Kennedy Assassination, the Media, and the Shaping of Collective Memory*. Chicago: University of Chicago Press, 1992.

Zucker, Arthur. "Rights and the Dying." In Hannelore Waas and Robert A. Neimeyer, eds., *Dying: Facing the Facts*. Washington, D.C.: Taylor & Francis, 1995.

Superman and the Corruption of Power

STEFAN BUCHENBERGER

A question often asked about Superman is, "Why he has never been corrupted by his own immense power?" His somewhat one-dimensional character as a universal do-gooder, or as a kind of "boy scout," prevents him from using his powers in such a way that, while perhaps helping millions of people, would also make them totally dependent on him, and invest him with a god-like persona. And that would only be the best case scenario, one that does not take into account the notion of Superman using his powers to rule the earth by force. The strong moral values — the proverbial "truth, justice and the American way" — that he became imbued with as he was being raised by his adoptive parents Jonathan and Martha Kent, a farmer's couple from the American heartland, have always prevented him from abusing his powers.

But what would happen if Superman were to lose his moral compass and be corrupted by his own power? The potential for such a crisis to develop has been addressed in numerous Superman comics, as for example in "Must there be a Superman?" which was originally published in *Superman #247* (Jan. 1972),[1] where Superman has to realize that he cannot interfere with humans too much but must still "help those who need it," a moral dilemma he is faced with quite often. If Superman were actually to morally fail, how would this reflect on the American society whose values he so clearly represents?

Three recent graphic novels explore alternate scenarios in which Superman is corrupted by his own powers. In *JLA: Earth 2*, written by Grant Morrison and drawn by Frank Quitely, Superman and the Justice League of America (JLA) are faced with a mirror universe and their own evil counterparts, where Ultraman, Superman's evil reverse image, and the Crime Syndicate rule by fear and corruption.[2] In *The Dark Knight Strikes Again*, written and drawn by Frank Miller, a future version of Superman has become the lackey of his arch enemies Lex Luthor and Brainiac, who rule the USA through a virtual president and by blackmailing the Man of Steel, threatening him with the extinction of the last survivors of the Kryptonian race. For all his power, Superman is forced by his own weakness into aiding his enemies.[3] In *Superman: Red Son*, written by Mark Millar with art by Dave Johnson and Kilian Pluncket, an alternate universe story in which the Kryptonian rocket carrying Superman lands in Soviet Russia and Superman becomes the leader of a Soviet Union that is the only superpower left on earth. Superman's believes he is only using his power for the greater good while he is, in reality, oppressing everyone on Earth.[4]

By putting Superman in new and imaginative contexts that confront him with complex moral dilemmas, these three graphic novels ask fundamental questions about the use and the abuse of power, and the dangers of totalitarian systems created by such abuses. Many of the same flaws depicted in these alternative versions of Superman have been perceived by some in the United States as it has used its influence and military on the world stage.

JLA: Earth 2: Total Corruption

The universe of Earth 2 exists parallel to the DC Comics' mainstream universe. It is an antimatter mirror universe, with a corrupted version of Superman who calls himself Ultraman. The first Ultraman appeared in 1964 as a villain of Earth 3, but he was killed together with his entire parallel universe in the *Crisis on Infinite Earths* mega crossover event in 1985.[5] In the antimatter universe of Earth 2 Alexander Luthor is the only hero, and the mirror version of the JLA that rules his world, is made up of villains that are transpositions of the original heroes of Earth 1. When Luthor escapes from Earth 2 to Earth 1 he seeks out the Justice League of America, who accompany him back to the anti–matter universe to bring down the Crime Syndicate. Trapping the villains in their fortress on the moon, the heroes begin to clean up crime and corruption, not realizing that all their efforts are in vain in an antimatter universe where evil is the normal way of existence. That is also why the villains who escape to the positive matter universe are unable to succeed in a universe where good triumphs on a regular basis. However, the whole switch of heroes and villains is part of a bigger plan: the alien computer-being Brainiac tries to destroy both positive matter and antimatter universes, an act that will provide him with limitless energy to evolve into a godlike being. Brainiac is defeated when the Crime Syndicate returns to the antimatter universe and both worlds revert to their status quo.

In Superman's universe evil cannot win. In the end, no matter how heavy the losses, good always triumphs over evil. However, in the antimatter universe of Earth 2 evil always triumphs, and since the idea of the heroes always triumphing over the villains makes perfect sense in comic books but not in the real world, one might ask whether the corrupted earth of Ultraman is not the real world after all, or at least closer to reality.

The political implications are obvious but the ways in which they are inserted into the text are subtle. Instead of telling a simple story about Superman and the Justice League beating their evil counterparts Morrison has the heroes acknowledge that they cannot win on the home turf of their mirror-image adversaries. The JLA defeat Brainiac, who threatens to destroy both worlds, but they cannot change the antimatter earth. Just like the villains who travel to the positive matter universe, who hatch one deluded plan to conquer the world after another, all bound to fail, Alexander Luthor's idea of changing the culture of his antimatter earth is likewise the idea of a deluded mind.

Superman's mirror image Ultraman represents his society in all its infamy. More powerful than any other living being, he is interested only in absolute rule which he reluctantly shares with the other members of the Crime Syndicate. He watches from the orbiting station of the Crime Syndicate, killing whoever criticizes him openly. However, it is the nonhuman Brainiac who tries to destroy both worlds while Superman and his counterpart keep their respective societies functioning. Even the ruthless Ultraman, who was human before he became a super villain, has a limit in terms of the scope of his crimes, which Brainiac does not.

However, inasmuch as the antimatter earth's dominant power is a corrupt American society, ruled by corrupt politicians and crime bosses according to rules set up by the Crime Syndicate, Ultraman represents American society's evil as much as Superman stands for its good.

The Dark Knight Strikes Again: Corruption Due to Weakness

While this is a story about Batman, the antagonism between him and Superman is one of its central themes. *The Dark Knight Strikes Again* is also a scathing satire of American media, politics, and society as a whole at the beginning of the 21st century, and it is within that context that it tries to answer the question, "What would Superman do in such a corrupted country?" The resurrection of Superman from depression is actually the major character development in *The Dark Knight Strikes Again*.

The United States of *The Dark Knight Strikes Again* is a police state in which the Bill of Rights has been revoked and the president is a computer generated image; but as one citizen puts it: "Who cares if the president doesn't exist? He's a great American!"[6] Batman decides once again, after he first came back from retirement in *The Dark Knight Returns* (1986), to fight against a corrupt system and, in the process, against Superman. Batman starts by liberating his old Justice League comrades Ray Palmer (Atom), and Barry Allen (Flash).

Superman has basically given up the fight, "and come to terms with the way things are."[7] His archenemies, Lex Luthor and Brainiac, destroyed his Fortress of Solitude and now hold the shrunken Kryptonian bottle city of Kandor hostage. When Superman confronts Batman he gets soundly thrashed, leaving him at an all time low, helpless against his blackmailers and powerless to get his former friends to listen. "We're beaten. Crushed. We're a joke. We're worse than a joke. We run about stopping this disaster and that — quietly, secretly — and do nothing about the evil that rules the world."[8]

Even stronger than his fear of the destruction of Kandor is Superman's desire to protect his daughter Lara, whose mother is Wonder Woman, from also being enslaved by Luthor. Totally demoralized, he is about to give up when Wonder Woman rouses him from his depression.

When Superman's friends Captain Marvel, Perry White, James Olson and Lois Lane all perish in a fierce battle with one of Brainiac's robots, Superman acknowledges the disparity between his possession of god-like powers on the one hand, and on the other the minimal effect his presence has on the real problems of the world.[9]

Superman finally decides to fight back, rejecting what his adoptive human parents taught him: "I am not human. And I am no man's servant. I am no man's slave. I will not be ruled by the laws of men. I am no man. I am Superman."[10] Only by breaking his self-imposed moral code can he succeed against real evil. In *The Dark Knight Strikes Again* Superman obeys human laws which leave him powerless against the machinations of a corrupt government. Only when he decides to go beyond these laws can he effect real change, which is in effect Miller's answer to the question asked in the introduction. Superman could be more than just an emergency helper if only he chose to ignore human laws but doing so would also start him on the slippery road towards tyranny, a fact he that acknowledges himself.

Superman: Red Son: *Corruption Due to Good Intentions*

Superman, the first-person narrator of *Red Son*, begins his story during the Cold War in the 1950s, when news of his existence starts a new stage in the global arms race. To counter the Soviets the American government instructs the smartest man alive, Lex Luthor, to destroy him. Meanwhile, Superman, reluctantly, becomes the leader of the Soviet Union after Stalin's death when he realizes the plight of the common Soviet people.

In the 1970s, Luthor continues to try to destroy Superman as the world comes increasingly under communist rule. Together with Brainiac, he shrinks the city of Stalingrad. The Russian Batman, whose parents were shot by the KGB, tries unsuccessfully to imprison Superman and kills himself before being captured.

In 2001 the world has become completely communist with the exception of the USA, where Luthor has become president and has turned the previously war-torn country into a success story, which provokes Superman to begin an all out attack on the USA. However, on the brink of victory Luthor makes Superman realize that his actions have been morally unjustifiable, and Brainiac is revealed as the real power behind Superman's attempt at global domination. Before he can kill Superman, Luthor destroys Brainiac while Superman seemingly sacrifices himself to save the earth. Luthor then starts building a true utopia which, led by his descendants, lasts a billion years while Superman watches in secret. When earth is about to be destroyed by its exploding red sun, Luthor's descendant Jor-L sends his infant son Kal-L back in time, where he will have super powers.[11] His time-traveling space vessel lands in the Ukraine in 1938 with the story starting all over again.

Although Millar's text was already finished before the second Iraq War, it has been interpreted as an allegory about the results of American interference in other countries' affairs. Millar himself sees his work as a reaction to the end of the Cold War, and a comment upon the dangers inherent in the existence of a sole superpower.[12] Superman's corruption by his own power symbolizes this danger, as Red Son provides another answer to the question concerning what would happen, were his power not to be restricted by core human values, if the icon of American power were to lose his moral compass.

The Legend Lives On

These three alternate versions of Superman operate against a different background than the usual DC Comics' universe, and in all three scenarios Superman fails to a certain extent: Ultraman, for all his power has no moral values; in The Dark Knight Strikes Again Superman is portrayed as weak, and in Red Son Superman has been manipulated into thinking his tyranny is for the greater good. But the scenarios in which these developments occur always leave him with an escape, so that the legend of Superman survives, together with the hope for an American society that lives up to its ideals, dreams and hopes, a confirmation of Superman's character as it was originally created by Jerry Siegel and Joe Shuster. Ultraman is not Superman, and like every super villain he too is regularly defeated by the "good" Superman. In *The Dark Knight Strikes Again* Batman makes Superman realize that, no matter what, he has to fight against his oppressors. In *Red Son* Brainiac is revealed as the real power behind Superman's attempt at world domination, and in the end Superman seemingly sacrifices himself for earth, never interfering with humanity again.

The Dark Knight Strikes Again is the most radical of the three texts, with its future version of Superman as the weakest of all three. In contrast to the mirror-image Superman, who is just plain evil and the alternate reality communist Superman, who is idealistic while being manipulated both by the system he grows up in and by Brainiac, in *The Dark Knight Strikes Again* Superman's future self is being blackmailed into subservience. Superman's realization that he shall not be bound by human rules enables him to fight back, and leads him to say to his daughter, " what exactly shall we do with our planet, Lara?," which makes one wonder whether he will continue to protect earth or whether he will use his powers to rule it.[13]

However, in order to be true to his role in the in the DC Comics universe as the protector of humankind, and in the real world as an icon of American popular culture, Superman has to adhere to his basic moral code. Superman can neither be god nor devil without ceasing to be himself. Underlying all three texts are core American values, such as individual freedom and equal rights for all human beings. Though these values are threatened by undemocratic, oppressive regimes they all triumph in the end, emphasizing their central importance to American society. For all the controversy and uncertainty facing American society at the beginning of the 21st century, the ideals embodied in the traditional character of Superman are extolled, even in the three texts introduced here, providing hope for the future.[14]

CHAPTER NOTES

1. Maggin, Elliot S. (w), and Curt Swan (a). "Must There Be a Superman?" *Superman #247* (Jan. 1972). New York: DC Comics.

2. Morrison, Grant (w), and Frank Quitely (a), 2000. *JLA: EARTH 2*, New York: DC Comics.

3. Miller, Frank (w/a) and Lynn Varley (a), Nov. 2001–Jul. 2002. *The Dark Knight Strikes Again*. New York: DC Comics.

4. Millar Mark (w), Dave Johnson (a) and Kilian Plunkett (a), Jun. 2003–Aug. 2003. *Superman: Red Son*. New York: DC Comics.

5. Conroy, Mike. *500 Comicbook Villains*. (London: Collins & Brown, 2004), 190–191.

6. Miller, Frank (w/a) and Lynn Varley (a), *The Dark Knight Strikes Again #2* (2002). New York: DC Comics, 47.

7. Miller, Frank (w/a) and Lynn Varley (a), *The Dark Knight Strikes Again #1* (Nov. 2001). New York: DC Comics, 51.

8. Miller, Frank (w/a) and Lynn Varley (a), *The Dark Knight Strikes Again #2* (2002). New York: DC Comics, 22.

9. Miller, Frank (w/a) and Lynn Varley (a), *The Dark Knight Strikes Again #3* (July 2002). New York: DC Comics, 12, 13, 18, 19.

10. Ibid., 49.

11. Both names, written slightly differently as Jor-El and Kal-El, are, of course, the original Kryptonian names of Superman and his father.

12. Millar, Mark: *Red Son*, 2003. *http://superman.nu/a/ges/redson*.

13. Miller, Frank (w/a) and Lynn Varley (a), *The Dark Knight Strikes Again #3* (July 2002). New York: DC Comics, 75.

14. For additional information about the works discussed, please see: Boztas, Senay, "Superman declares war on America." The Sunday Times, April 27, 2003. *http://www.times online.co.uk/tol/news/uk/scotland/article869790.ece* (accessed June 3rd, 2011); Sanderson, Peter: "Comics in Context *#30*; Knight after Knight," posted February 13, 2004: *http:// comics.ign.com/articles/595/595592p1.html* (accessed April 25th, 2011); Gravett, Paul. *GRAPHIC NOVELS: Everything You Need to Know.* (New York: Collins Design, 2005); Kannenberg, Gene, Jr. *500 Essential Graphic Novels.* (New York: Collins Design, 2008); Morris, Tom, and Matt Morris (eds.) *Superman and Philosophy.* (Chicago, IL: Open Court, 2005); Wright, Bradford W. *Comic Book Nation. The Transformation of Youth Culture in America.* (Baltimore & London: Johns Hopkins University Press, 2001).

BIBLIOGRAPHY

Boztas, Senay. "Superman Declares War on America." *The Sunday Times*, April 27, 2003.

Conroy, Mike. *500 Comicbook Villains.* London: Collins & Brown, 2004.

Gravett, Paul. *GRAPHIC NOVELS: Everything You Need to Know.* New York: Collins Design, 2005.

Kannenberg, Gene Jr. *500 Essential Graphic Novels.* New York: Collins Design, 2008.

Maggin, Elliot S. (w), and Curt Swan (a). "Must There Be a Superman?" *Superman #247* (Jan. 1972). New York: DC Comics.

Millar, Mark (w), Dave Johnson (a) and Kilian Plunkett (a). *Superman: Red Son* (June 2003–Aug. 2003). New York: DC Comics.

Miller, Frank (w/a) and Lynn Varley (a). *The Dark Knight Strikes Again #1* (Nov. 2001). New York: DC Comics.

_____. *The Dark Knight Strikes Again #2* (2002). New York: DC Comics.

_____. *The Dark Knight Strikes Again #3* (July 2002). New York: DC Comics

Morris, Tom, and Matt Morris (eds.) *Superman and Philosophy.* Chicago: Open Court, 2005.

Morrison, Grant (w), and Frank Quitely (a). *JLA: EARTH 2* (2000). New York: DC Comics.

Sanderson, Peter: "Comics in Context #30; Knight after Knight," posted February 13, 2004. Accessed at comics.ign.com/articles/595/595592p1.html.

Wright, Bradford W. *Comic Book Nation. The Transformation of Youth Culture in America.* Baltimore: Johns Hopkins University Press, 2001.

This Isn't Your Grandfather's Comic Book Universe

The Return of the Golden Age Superman

Jeffrey K. Johnson

Two of Superman's most important traits are his ability to change over time and his ability to always serve as a symbol of American values. While these two qualities would at first seem to be diametrically opposed to each other, their relationship is one of the keys to Superman's significance as a revered American mythological icon. Since 1938, the Man of Steel has been able to transforms his outlook and character in order to meet American society's needs while retaining his ethical and inspirational values. These transformations have not always been smooth and simple, but they have allowed Superman to remain relevant to a contemporary audience while preserving his timeless principles. The best versions of Superman are in step with current American society while also retaining the core values that lie at the character's center.

This struggle to keep Superman fresh and appealing while preserving the hero's heart has been a challenge for comic book creators since the Man of Steel's conception and appears to have only gotten more difficult as time has progressed. One interesting example of this struggle is the 2005 DC Comics mini-series *Infinite Crisis* in which the Golden Age Superman returns from a paradise dimension to a modern world that he believes is deeply misguided and inherently flawed. In doing so the world's first and greatest superhero becomes a critic of both modern comic books and contemporary American society. The original Man of Steel questions the decisions that Americans have made since 1986 and forces readers to in turn question themselves. In *Infinite Crisis*, the Golden Age Superman embraces older comic book values and detests the new type of grittier comic book heroes. This generational clash serves as an interesting lens in which to view modern comic book stories and also to understand the concept of the hero in general and Superman in particular.

The Original Is Back

In the middle of 1938, newsstands across the country contained something new and exciting; a costumed superhero. Superman's first appearance in *Action Comics #1* (June 1938) marked the beginning of a new era of American mythology, one that would create fictional superpowered champions to entertain, comfort, and inspire its citizens. The Man of Steel began his career as a New Deal social avenger but quickly transformed into what the nation's censors and readers demanded and needed. The Golden Age Superman battled evil during World War II and much of the 1950s before being replaced by an updated version during the Silver Age. During the 1960s, DC Comics creators and editors decided that the DC universe consisted of numerous parallel Earths and the original Golden Age Superman lived on Earth 2 while his more contemporary counterpart was a denizen of Earth 1.

During 1985–1986's *Crisis on Infinite Earths*, all of the parallel universes were merged into one and the Golden Age Superman was sent a paradise dimension as a well-earned reward. The Golden Age Superman was rarely seen during the next twenty years and many comic books fans assumed that he would never appear in the DC universe again. Then in 2005–2006 the Golden Age Superman left his new home/prison and returned to Earth in the pages of the *Infinite Crisis* mini-series. During his time away this Superman had been watching DC's superheroes and America's citizens and was greatly disappointed in their behavior.

One of the central themes of 2005–2006's *Infinite Crisis* is exploring dark change within DC universe and American society since 1986. The miniseries serves as a sequel to 1985–1986's *Crisis on Infinite Earth* and questions what a hero should be and asks if we can even trust ourselves and the very world around us. The storyline begins in a special countdown issue in which previous Justice League leader Maxwell Lord murders his former teammate, Ted Kord, the Blue Beetle. Both of these characters are best remembered for their appearances in the light-hearted Justice League stories of the late 1980s. When the former buffoon Max Lord brutally shoots the often silly Blue Beetle in the head, the reader understands that no one, no matter how seemingly unassuming, can be trusted.

Soon the reader learns that Lord has used his mental powers to take control of Superman, leaving the Man of Steel defenseless and untrustworthy. Superman, the ultimate American symbol and weapon, has fallen into the hands of the enemy and has literally been brainwashed to do evil. As the prequel ends Wonder Woman is forced to kill Maxwell Lord by snapping his neck and thus free Superman from his mental imprisonment setting the stage for the mini-series and leaving Superman, Batman, and Wonder Woman emotionally and morally adrift.

Heroes Divided

As *Infinite Crisis* opens the DC trinity of Superman, Batman, and Wonder Woman must each reevaluate their role as a hero. Batman has grown overly dark and cynical, Wonder Woman has become faithless and warlike, and Superman has become ineffectual and uninspiring. The three characters constantly bicker among themselves and often resemble petty schoolchildren more than superheroes. In the opening scene Batman, Wonder Woman and Superman argue about old conflicts and past actions and it becomes clear that each of them is both right and wrong. In doing this the three heroes serve as ciphers for a post–September 11th America, as fear and retribution replace truth and justice. DC Comics Executive Editor Dan DiDio notes this in his introduction to the mini-series' compilation where he states, "Remember, this story was crafted in a post 9/11 world at a time when most Americans were feeling vulnerable and in need of heroes. We saw a world [where] the human spirit was pushed to the limit, and against overwhelming odds, people persevered and heroes emerged — sadly, at the cost of their own lives."[1] While the heroic actions are displayed by the end of the story none of the trinity showcases them at the beginning.

In the first issue Batman singles out Superman and points out that the Man of Steel has become lax and submissive and Superman in turn accuses the Dark Knight of being too controlling. Batman replies, "After all of these years, you know it's not about control. It's about trying to do everything I can. And for you it's about setting an example. Everyone looks up to you. They listen to you. If you tell them to fight, they'll fight. But they need to be inspired. And let's face it, 'Superman' ... the last time you really inspire anyone was when you were dead."[2] On the next page the Golden Age Superman, his wife the Earth 2 Lois Lane, an alternate Earth's Lex Luthor (known as Alexander Luthor), and another Earth's Superboy (soon to be renamed Superboy Prime) watch from the paradise dimension in which they have been trapped since the end of *Crisis on Infinite Earths*. The four castaways of times and places that have ceased to exist watch the outside superheroes and discuss the heroes' lackluster and poor performances, with Lois serving as the new superheroes' only supporter among the group. As the Golden Age Superman punches through the glass barrier that had entrapped them he opines, "We've given them a gift they've thrown away. We sacrificed everything for them."[3]

After the Golden Age Superman and his colleagues return to Earth, the original superhero attempts to recreate his perfect Earth, so that society will be normalized and his wife Lois will not die. In an attempt to convince Batman to join his cause the Golden Age Superman explains to him, "Earth-Two was a wonderful place, Bruce. It was full of hope and love. And the heroes acted like heroes. We made mistakes, but it was nothing like what's happening here. Things have gotten out of hand. You have."[4] Golden Age Superman later adds, "Everything you've done, everything you've set in motion, is because you felt you couldn't trust the people around you. And you know what? You can't. But on my Earth it's different."[5] So in essence the first superhero has returned to Earth from heaven and declared that he is disappointed in how we live and have acted. He tells us that he does not trust any of us and we in turn should not even trust ourselves or the world around. An icon had come back to life and declared that society has not taken the wrong path but rather it was built in such a flawed and shoddy manner that it is inherently defective.

According to the Golden Age Superman, Max Lord's mental control of Superman and Wonder Woman's act of murder were not individual acts but rather symptoms of a universe that is rotten to the core. Citizens of such a place not only had to fear everyone around them but also themselves, because no one is safe from the dark forces that surround us all. This message seems to especially connect to an American society that since the 9/11 attacks had grown accustomed to terrorism, war, biological attacks, torture, and senseless violence. Seemingly, no one was safe and few people could ever be trusted. According to Superman, society's only hope is to radically return to the old ways, no matter how painful this change may be. The world had gotten darker and far more terrifying and not even the original Superman could save us.

Culture Wars

The Golden Age Superman's criticism of modern superheroes and contemporary society coincided with a post–9/11 trend toward embracing and promoting fear. Comic book stories mirrored American society by emphasizing the harsh and terrifying world around us. Much like many parts of society, formerly humane and trusting heroes became overly aggressive and jaded. In *Infinite Crisis*, the Golden Age Superman declares that the current Earth/society is so inherently flawed that it can never be acceptable. Small changes will make no difference and the only way to return society to its naturally positive state is to replace our current unacceptable living conditions with an older and better place and time.

The Golden Age Superman does not want to save our unworthy world, rather he wants to end it and recreate a world that deserves to be saved. The original Man of Steel casts off any attempt to understand or conform to modern standards and instead becomes the stern grandfather warning the world about, "these kids today" and pressing for a return to his golden age. This extremely active and opinionated Superman is contrasted to our Superman who lately has been paralyzed by inaction and self doubt. The Greatest Generation's Superman attempts to literally remake the world, while the current Superman allows the world to change and does little about it because he is afraid his intervention may cause more harm. These two Supermen represent different notions of what a hero should be and their juxtaposition force the reader to question how he/she believes Superman should act. In a post–9/11 world, does the country need a thoughtful and introspective Superman who allows people to make their own decisions or a Superman who believes in action-based answers and who believes he knows what is best?

The Golden Age Superman briefly succeeds in recreating his Earth and flies his Lois Lane their where she promptly dies, leaving the original Man of Steel in despair. The current Superman hears his predecessor's cries of anguish and the two begin to physically battle in order to decide the universe's fate. The Golden Age Superman blames his younger counterpart for Lois's death and for spreading the new Earths corruption "like a disease."[6] In a highly symbolic action the Golden Age Superman recreates the cover of *Action Comics #1* (Superman's first appearance) by smashing a car on top of the modern Superman. This scene reminds the reader of Golden Age Superman's place in comic book history and invites comic book fans to recognize the original superhero even as he is pummeling our current Superman.

Soon Wonder Woman arrives on the newly reconstituted Earth 2 and the Golden Age Superman lists the ways that she, Batman, and Superman have failed. The elder Superman then states, "And worst of all, you, Superman could've stopped this before it started. You should have! You should have led them to a better tomorrow. Instead, when the universe needed its greatest heroes, they refused to stand together. You had the opportunity to make that Earth into the perfect world it had the potential to be and you wasted it."[7] The modern Superman then counters by explaining the Earth 2 could not have been a perfect world, "because a perfect Earth doesn't need a Superman."[8] The Golden Age Superman, realizing the flaws in his beliefs, flies away to mourn his dead wife. The Golden Age Superman now understands that society has moved on and his ideas are outdated and irrelevant. While the new Superman may not have lived up to his potential there is no way to return to the past.

Superman v. Superman

As the Golden Age Superman flies away it becomes apparent that he is an artifact of a bygone age and has become irrelevant to modern readers. His outdated views and understandings no longer resonate among contemporary Americans and he has lost his ability to forge a symbolic connection with those around him. He is a prime example of what happens to Superman when he fails to change in order to meet American society's needs. The Golden Age Superman's desire to create a perfect world may have been suitable to readers during the 1940s and 1950s but modern comic book fans would no longer accept such stories.

The modern Superman soon also realizes that he too is at risk of becoming outdated and irrelevant. While the Golden Age Superman was incapable of altering his values to adjust to changing times, the contemporary Superman has been unable to find his role in the last decade. Batman's earlier contention that Superman had not inspired anyone since he was dead, references a 1992 storyline in which the Man of Steel briefly dies after saving the world from the villainous menace Doomsday. This story was immensely popular and created a comic book buying frenzy among both comic book fans and the general public. *Superman #75*, the issue in which the Man of Steel dies, was the number selling comic book of the year and a cultural and social sensation.[9] While Superman's death resonated strongly with Americans, in the years that followed the character failed to capture the public's imagination in the same way. In storylines after his death, Superman married Lois Lane and revealed his secret identity of Clark Kent to her. Superman transformed into an energy based hero and then split into two Supermen before returning to his traditional self. These gimmicks and several others failed to grab the public's attention and since 9/11 Superman appeared to have lost his way. While the Golden Age Superman was clearly wrong in his desire to return comic books to their 1950s' state, the modern Superman also needed to adjust to current American society.

Of Man and Superman

The importance of a Superman's role in American society is referenced in one of the next scenes in *Infinite Crisis*. The modern Superman and Wonder Woman find the Golden Age Superman kneeling over the recently deceased Earth 2 Lois Lane and the two Supermen make peace with each other. Wonder Woman explains to the elder Superman, "You realize that if you replace our Earth, you'll be throwing away all the good with the bad." The Golden Age Superman asks the two contemporary heroes, "How can you still have faith in your Earth?" To which the younger Superman replies, "Because they still have faith in us."[10] Here the heroes are metatextually admitting that they receive their power from comic book readers and other fans.

Although the comic book world and the real world may have become more cynical and grim since the end of *Crisis on Infinite Earths* in the mid–1980s, the heroes cannot undo these changes because this is not what their readers desire and what American society needs. Through the modern heroes the creators are acknowledging that although comic book characters can inspire and create hope, they are fictional servants who must conform to the public's current needs and desires. If they fail to do so for too long then they risk becoming irrelevant and soon will be forgotten. Superheroes exist to provide a symbol to believe in and the heroes in turn must believe in the society that created them.

Three Generations of Supermen

As the two Supermen make amends it becomes clear that Alexander Luthor and the young Superboy Prime have been manipulating the Golden Age Man of Steel in order to recreate a "perfect" Earth. Alexander Luthor is portrayed as a technological genius who wants to control the universe. Alternatively, Superboy Prime shown to be is a whiny teenager who is fixated on recreating his home Earth, Earth Prime. Superboy Prime is obsessed with remaking his birth Earth because he too believes that it was a perfect world. When battling the current Superboy and Wonder Girl, Superboy Prime questions, "Why are you still fighting me? Don't you understand? Your time is over. We're going to have good heroes again. When we bring back my Earth we'll have real heroes. Heroes who are polite and brave and honest. And no one will ever know what I had to do to bring my Earth back."[11] Superboy Prime soon kills the current Superboy and this serves as the impetus for the modern Superman, Batman, and Wonder Woman to embrace change.

The heroes admit that they have failed and as Batman seemingly looks out of the page at the reader he promises, "Never again. It never happens again. We learn from it. We learn from them."[12] The Golden Age Superman then soliloquizes, "I thought I knew the answer. It was to make the Earth a better place. Because I thought they couldn't. I thought their Superboy was unworthy of the symbol I built. But I picked the wrong one to condone. And the wrong one to condemn."[13] The Golden Age Superman admits he was wrong and that the current heroes are worthy of his mantle. The modern Superman has repented and asked both his fellow heroes and, in a way, the reader for forgiveness. He now is ready to transform to meet society's needs and prove that he is worthy of his position. There also is a third Superman, Superboy Prime, who still condescendingly believes that his Earth should replace the current version. His recklessness and arrogance are a threat to the universe and the two other Supermen must unite to stop him. In doing so, the three Supermen showcase generational attitudes and display the qualities that are necessary for an exceptional Superman.

As the two older Supermen, and a host of other heroes, chase Superboy Prime through space the story focuses on what these three Supermen represent. The Golden Age Superman is the grandfatherly figure who now embraces his role as symbolic figurehead. Clearly past his prime and no longer in touch with the current society's needs, he no longer attempts to lead or dictate change; instead he serves as the symbol of a bygone era. Creator and audience nostalgia, not need, has kept him "alive" but his time has clearly past. He is example of what happens to a Superman who cannot conform to his society's needs and desires.

The modern Superman has recently apologized for his past mistakes and has promised to be the hero that his readers demand. It is unclear if he will be able to make this transition, if another Superman will take his place, or if all version of Superman will cease to exist. Although Superman's enduring cultural connection, and his status as a corporate money generator, seem to suggest some version of his character will survive for years to come, it is not a given that a Superman will always exist. For now though, he is the one true Superman and he must carry that mantle to the best of his ability. The Golden Age Superman has given the modern Superman his blessing and there no longer is any friction between the two.

The last of the trio, Superboy Prime, is an example of a Superman gone wrong. He has taken Superman's enduring traits of honesty, desire for justice, self-confidence, strong leadership and warped them into brashness, egotism, self-centeredness, megalomania, and entitlement. Superboy Prime is what happens to Superman when common sense and love do not temper his strength and aggression. This Superboy can never be a true Superman because he cannot inspire readers and serve as a cultural icon and social mouthpiece. Instead, he is destined to become a villain and will serve as cautionary tale to both readers and fictional heroes alike. As the final battle approaches there are three Supermen; one who has outlived his usefulness, one who is searching for a way to represent his society, and one who can never carry the mantle.

Climax

In *Infinite Crisis'* climatic battle the two elder Supermen, and numerous other heroes, trick Superboy Prime into fighting on a planet near where Krypton (Superman's home planet) exploded. Under this planet's red sun the three Supermen lose their powers and the two senior heroes fight to incapacitate Superboy Prime. As their powers fail under the red sun the three heroes must fight as mortals in order to become the sole true Superman. The two elder Supermen battle the young upstart until all three are bruised and bloodied. At the end of the fight Superboy Prime asserts that he should be the real Superman because he comes from a "better Krypton." While beating Superboy Prime until he is unconscious the modern Superman counters, "It's not about where you were born. Or what powers you have. Or what you wear on your chest. Shut up! It's about what you do ... it's about action."[14] With that the modern Superman declares himself a new man of action and a populist while casting aside the whiny child of privilege. The Golden Age Superman quickly succumbs to his wounds and dies while declaring that he will always be out there somewhere even if we cannot see him. The original superhero will presumably live on in our memories, in the stories of heroes that were crafted in his image, and possibly on another alternate Earth.

When Jerry Siegel and Joe Shuster's first Superman adventure was published in *Action Comics #1* in 1938, the Man of Steel was a rough and tumble social avenger who was more worried about battling common street thugs and corrupt politicians than supervillains. This Superman did not survive long though and within a few years he was forced to transform into a super-patriot in order to inspire Americans during World War II. After the hostilities ended, the Man of Steel adjusted to postwar life by becoming a sedate champion of the state and a super-company man. During each of these changes, and the ones that would follow, Superman retained his core values while adapting to society's current needs. Comic book creators and publishers understood that Superman needed to preserve his timelessness while remaining relevant to modern readers. This served both a narrative function, ensuring that Superman mattered, and addressed business concerns, comic book readers would lose interest in a Superman that failed to meet these criteria.

Infinite Crisis provides an interesting viewpoint to examine what happens when Supermen fail to meet society's needs. The Golden Age Superman returned from paradise to inform his protégée that things needed to change. The modern Superman, indeed, had not adapted well to society's post–9/11 needs and desires and was searching for a way to become more relevant to modern Americans. Unfortunately, the older Superman did not offer a viable solution but rather showcased what can happen when a Superman becomes bound to a bygone age and thus became outdated. The two Supermen and Superboy Prime display how important it for a Superman to be both an arbiter of values and representative of his society's needs. Every era's Superman must be both constant and adaptable. Superman will always fight for "truth, justice, and the American way" but what those words mean has changed and will continue to change with each passing year. Superman's greatest superpower may be his ability to remain a beacon of American ideas and values while changing to match an evolving society.

CHAPTER NOTES

1. DiDio, Dan. "Introduction." *Infinite Crisis* (2006). New York: DC Comics, 6.
2. John, Geoff (w), and Phil Jimenez (a), George Pèrez (a), Jerry Ordway (a), and Ivan Reis (a). *Infinite Crisis* (2006). New York: DC Comics, 38.
3. Ibid., 39.
4. Ibid., 90.
5. Ibid., 97.
6. Ibid., 153.
7. Ibid., 160.
8. Ibid., 160.
9. "1992 Comic Book Sales Figures." *The Comics Chronicles*. Online. Accessed on 10 June 2011.
10. Johns, 179.
11. Ibid., 203.
12. Ibid., 211.
13. Ibid., 211.
14. Ibid., 238.

BIBLIOGRAPHY

DiDio, Dan. "Introduction." *Infinite Crisis* (2006). New York: DC Comics.
Johns, Geoff (w), and Phil Jimenez (a), George Pèrez (a), Jerry Ordway (a), and Ivan Reis (a). *Infinite Crisis* (2006). New York: DC Comics.
"1992 Comic Book Sales Figures." *The Comics Chronicles*. Online. Accessed 10 June 2011, at *http://www.comichron.com/monthlycomicssales/1992.html*.

In a World Without Superman, What Is the American Way?

John Darowski

In *Final Crisis*, Darkseid, DC Comics' god of evil, succeeds in enslaving Earth due in part to the absence of Superman. During the climatic assault on Darkseid's stronghold, this is noted when Green Lantern (John Stewart) comments to Supergirl: "It's right about now, I wish I knew what happened to your big cousin...."[1] The question "Where's Superman?" has been a theme for several years beginning in 2006. The weekly series *52* (2006-07) was billed as a year without Superman, Batman, and Wonder Woman; the weekly series *Trinity* (2008-09) showed a world without those same heroes as part of DC continuity; and the New Krypton storyline (2008–10) in his own titles saw the Man of Steel leave Earth for a resurrected home world. When Superman, the defender of truth, justice, and the American Way, vacates his post, the very nature of those standards comes into question. Such a debate is a direct reflection of real-world situations where multiple crises have led to a re-evaluation of the American Dream in the twenty-first century. In *52*, *Trinity* and New Krypton, a world without Superman creates a fictional landscape in which challenges to the preconceived notions of the American Way can be enacted for the consideration of the consumers of popular culture within a safe sphere.

"The American Way" is one of the more nebulous concepts for which Superman fights. Its meaning has been debated since the earliest years of the nation in texts such as *The Federalist Papers* and has been continually re-interpreted by each succeeding generation. In *Trinity #6* (9 July 2008), writer Kurt Busiek offers multiple interpretations of the concept. "But we all know Superman as an immigrant, who came to this world, was raised in its values, adopted it as his own. If that's not the American Way, what is?" But for Wonder Woman: "...she's not American, but the 'American Way' is about what makes up the American Dream, not what's unique about it. Things like strength, readiness, power, tempered by ideals. The hand of peace backed by a willingness to fight." And Batman is "a self-made man. Not financially [...] he's filthy rich, rolling in it ... but a man who set himself an ideal, and drove himself to study, to train, to remake himself. Until he became what he dreamed. That's another part of the American Way...."[2] Despite their differences, each reading has the same objective: the American Way is a path to achieve the American Dream.

The American Dream is another hard-to-define concept that seems to adapt every few years. At its core, it is the possibility that an individual can achieve success or a better life in the United States unlike what he or she could elsewhere. Superman is an exemplar of this ideal, even as his dual identity reveals differing definitions of success. As Clark Kent, he is a self-made man who by dint of hard work and study changed his status from small-town farmboy to metropolitan news reporter. As Superman, he is an immigrant who has used the natural abilities of his native heritage to become the world's greatest superhero; a role in which he defends the right of every American to achieve similar greatness.

It is apparent that a paradigm shift has occurred within society in the past decade that has required a new definition of the American Way. The events of 9/11 appeared to offer a new external threat against which the country could align itself and form a national identity, much as it had against the Soviet Union during the Cold War.[3] But this enemy lacked the cohesive identity or clear ideology for such a consensus. The collapse of the housing market and the resultant economic recession and accompanying rise in unemployment, coupled with increased oil prices, has fostered a distrust of large corporations and disillusionment with the government's ability to provide solutions. This has led to a growing ideological divide as demonstrated by increasingly divisive politics, exemplified by the Tea Party movement within the Republican Party.[4] With a lack of faith in leadership and business, the traditional means of achieving success have come into question.

This debate over societal values is both reflected in and enacted by popular culture. Texts, such as comic books, serve as a vehicle to evaluate and reinforce the written and unwritten rules of a society, preserving those which remain beneficial, adopting new ones as they prove valid and discarding the old as they become obsolete.[5] As Matthew J. Costello writes in *Secret Identity Crisis*:

> The heroic narrative describes a story of value and virtue, defines good and evil and offer a guide to proper action by which redemption can be achieved. In doing so it defines for a culture that which is admired and that which is feared. Because the hero exemplifies the values of a society, his role is to defend those values, to maintain a given way of life against potential threats, or to redeem it from a threat realized.[6]

In this way superheroes become defenders of the status quo. They are signifiers of stability, rarely enacting change but enforcing it when the community reaches a consensus. However, given the present state of comic book continuity, adapting new values can prove difficult, especially for a hero with seventy years of entrenched characterization. Superman has a moral certitude that can only exist in fiction. If he ever doubts, it is never for long enough to have a meaningful impact on his character; doubt only exists as a narrative contrivance. Therefore, it is only possible to have a meaningful discussion on modifying cultural rules by removing Superman from the fictional stage.

This has happened before. During the mid–90s, the United States entered a period of uncertainty following the dissolution of the Soviet Union and the end of the Cold War. Lacking an external enemy against which to define itself and compounded with rapidly progressing technology and the approaching end of a millennium, the future outlook became increasingly unknown. DC Comics reflected these fears by having Superman die in a battle with a monster aptly named Doomsday. In his place rose four replacement heroes who embodied new national identities to be tested: the Kryptonian, a super-authoritarian enforcer; the Cyborg, an integration of man and machine; Steel, the self-made man; and Superboy, a Gen-X teenager. In the end, not much changed about the U.S.'s status and Superman returned with renewed confidence in the American Way. But Steel and Superboy also remained, their values having proved worthwhile for the coming century.

But when a crisis of confidence in the American Way returned less than a decade later, the creators at DC faced a new challenge in removing Superman from the narrative; they couldn't kill him again. In the climax of *Infinite Crisis*, Superman flew a deranged Superboy-Prime through a red sun.[7] As Kryptonians receive their superpowers from a yellow sun, the rays of a red sun rob them of those abilities. While this sacrifice allowed the combined might of the DC superheroes to fell an enemy to all reality, it left Superman without his powers for a year. During that time, other heroes defended Metropolis in the pages of *52*, written by Geoff Johns, Grant Morrison, Greg Rucka and Mark Waid with art layouts by Keith Giffen.

One individual in *52* with a new vision for the twenty-first century is Lex Luthor:

> This is a country founded on a dream. A dream of equality and equanimity. A dream of hope and peace, of tolerance and perseverance. A dream where every-one — even a boy from Smallville — can become, oh, I don't know, President of the United States? We call it the American Dream. But what is that, really? A chicken in every pot? A car in every garage? That was the old dream, my friends, my guests.... I have a new dream. A dream where every man can be a super man.[8]

This is Luthor's pitch for his Everyman Project: that opportunity for every citizen to receive super powers. But within the speech lies a fundamental shift in the method to achieve the American Dream. The old models of success, "a chicken in every pot" or "a car in every garage," were the result of the government functioning as protector and provider for its citizens. Luthor's model would replace that benefactor with corporations.

Despite the best intentions, and Luthor's rarely are, this new paradigm contains a radically different motivation. Governments should have a responsibility to its citizens whereas a business seeks to make a profit. The mascots for the Everyman Project, the team Infinity Inc., may act within the traditional roles of heroes but are really flying advertisements for LexCorp. It is then with some irony that Luthor states: "Superman is gone, but there is good news. We no longer need him or any of his kind. The age of the super-citizen is dawning."[9] What he really wants are super-consumers with super powers as the commodity.

The term super-citizen implies a sense of civic duty. Superman is a hero not because of his powers; after all, most supervillains have powers, too. It is due to a higher moral code which leads him to use those powers for the benefit of society. It is doubtful that Luthor's ideal consumer would have any such compunction. As Steel asks: "Heroism is an act of altruism! How altruistic can you be when you're funded by LexCorp?"[10] Indeed, those individuals who apply for the Everyman Project are more likely seeking a different model of success: fame.

The role model for the hero-as-celebrity is Booster Gold, the first to defend Metropolis in 52. Booster does the right thing for the wrong reasons. Rather than adhering to a refined system of values, he acts for the benefit of society in order to earn endorsements and corporate sponsors, becoming a synthesis of man and product. As he boldly declares: "It's all about me!"[11]

The counter point to Booster's narcissism is the mysterious new hero Supernova. Garbed in red, white, and blue with a yellow star symbol that appears to be an amalgamation of a Christian cross and halo, Supernova moves from one crisis to the next without pause for recognition or praise. The fact that Supernova is in reality Booster Gold, who faked his death and sacrificed all those endorsements as a part of a plan to rescue his robot companion Skeets from a corrupting influence, shows that traditional morals hold more value than modern cycles of fame. As he saves his friend, Booster also redeems himself in the eyes of the reader.

If the cult of celebrity fails as a new paradigm, what of the businesses that promote it? As real corporations have failed consumers repeatedly in recent years, resulting in individuals losing everything, so too does Luthor take away what he has given. Upon learning that he is not a suitable candidate for the Everyman Project, Luthor deactivates the powers of every one of his "super-citizens," causing them to fall from the sky in the "Rain of the Supermen."[12] Such capriciousness illustrates that Luthor's vision is an untenable way to achieve the American Dream. Rather it is the hero Steel, the self-made hero, who best embodies the method to success. As writer Greg Rucka explains, Steel shows "that rewards have to be earned, that hard work is required to attain them and that strong personal responsibility are prerequisites for putting on a costume...."[13] Steel's triumph over Luthor becomes a renewal of conventional values that paves the way for the return of Superman.

Not that Superman stayed long. A year later in the weekly series *Trinity*, writer Kurt Busiek and artist Mark Bagley created another approach to a world without Superman. In this case, he is not a willing exile. Due to a set of cosmic circumstances, Superman, Batman and Wonder Woman are removed as the cornerstones of the DC Universe. A new continuity is born where those heroes never existed, the term superhero was never coined, and the Justice Society did not disband after the McCarthy hearings in the 50s.[14] The result is a world where almost all metahumans work for the paramilitary Justice Society International. What had begun as a group of like-minded individuals forming a service organization following World War II had morphed into government enforcers.

How did such a situation arise? The answer is a loss of inner direction. As stated above, superheroes adhere to a more refined set of principles to guide their actions in protecting or redeeming society. Also, they divide their time between a public space in their costumed actions and a private space in their secret identity, resulting in the inherent drama of trying to lead two lives. By revealing their secret identities during the McCarthy hearings, the Justice Society removed themselves from the personal sphere and exist solely in a public identity. But acting in a manner better than the rest of the community can lead to thinking one is better, allowing virtue to transform into hubris.[15] Without the perspective provided by a private life, morality becomes skewed and these heroes do the wrong thing for the right reasons. "We have subverted governments. Taken control where it mattered. Brainwashed people, turned them to our side. We felt we had to. [...] We did what had to be done."[16]

This loss of inner direction is then passed on to succeeding generations of metahumans. Forcing any person with powers to become a superagent under a central authority denies those individuals the opportunity to develop their own moral code.[17] And without that choice, they cannot achieve the American Dream.

The failures of the Justice Society are inverted in the saga of Superman, Batman and Wonder Woman. Thrust out of the DC Universe, they become deities of a new world, their greatest adventures recast as mythology. It is a retreat into religion, a wholly private space.[18] But this retreat has the same result of one being cut off from humanity with a skewed perspective. "Our mistake was being human. By being more than that — being the gods we have become — we will save the world."[19] Even though this god-form of Superman would have the power to solve any crisis, he would not have the ability to enjoy that success. At the end of the series, the trinity sacrifice their new-found powers to save the Earth and come through the experience with a renewed understanding that it is through a balance between public and private life that the American Way is found.

A new challenge arose during the New Krypton storyline, written primarily by James Robinson and Greg Rucka with various artists. Following the death of Jonathan Kent, Superman's surrogate father, and the arrival of 100,000 Kryptonians from the bottled city of Kandor,[20] Superman is left in a place where he is grieving with his American family and rejoicing with the Kryptonian people. And while some people of Earth believe this now means there will be 100,000 Supermen watching over them, others see the aliens as a force that could conquer the world quite easily, an allegory on the current climate concerning immigration. Fear wins out and all Kryptonians except Superman are banned from Earth.[21] The leaders of Kandor create a new planet in opposite orbit to Earth: New Krypton.[22]

This leaves Superman with a choice as to which world to call home. Ultimately, he decides to live on New Krypton where he can serve as a bridge between it and Earth. In doing so, Kal-El removes himself from the possibility of success through his natural abilities. All citizens of his new home have the same superpowers. As one citizen points out: "We make you less special."[23] But Kal-El remains unique in a different regard: his American values. As his aunt Alura notes: "Kal-El isn't like us. He's human to his core."[24] By staying true to the principles taught by his foster parents, Kal becomes an example of a different approach to resolving the crises of his native culture.

Both Superman's saga and the experiences of those characters that remain on Earth mark the importance of families. Kal-El is reunited with his aunt and uncle.[25] Lois Lane meets her estranged sister and believed-dead father.[26] The Kryptonian heroes Nightwing and Flamebird form a relationship.[27] But in each case what should have been a retreat into family is co-opted by the military.[28] Kal-El becomes a soldier in the military guild under his former enemy General Zod.[29] General Sam Lane has been in hiding preparing for what he sees as an inevitable alien attack, even if he has to manufacture a terrorist attack to blame on the Kryptonians.[30] And Nightwing and Flamebird have been tasked with hunting down Zod's sleeper cells on Earth.[31] While one may question the wisdom of portraying the military as villains at a time when the United States is at war, the salient point is that the actions of these military leaders have turned what should be a public service of a standing military into secret actions based on private fears.

Not that those fears aren't without reason. The Kryptonians have just been released from a bottled city where they were terrorized by Brainiac for years. The decision for their military to prepare so that nothing like that happens again is prudent. For the U.S., having seen the power of Superman, envisioning scenarios where that power is turned against citizens is also sound. But taking those actions in secret undercuts the freedom to choose a peaceful solution and denies the community a path to success as individuals and as a whole. It is fear that is the enemy and this story takes the results of it to a radical end in the genocide of New Krypton,[32] leaving Superman to ask just what the American Way is in the twenty-first century?

At the end of *Final Crisis*, Superman returns to literally defeat Darkseid with a wish and a song.[33] Would that the crises facing America could be resolved so simply. *52*, *Trinity* and New Krypton each explore different avenues for the American Way in a new century. However, these stories illustrate that the approaches of corporations, absolute authority, or acting in fear fail to provide an adequate pathway to the American Dream. The troubled paths resulting form these choices are ultimately smoothed by the return of Superman. This consistent conclusion validates many traditional values that have stood the test of time. But while adhering to the old, they demonstrate a constant questing for the new. Superman embodies this as a synthesis of small-town values and progressive ideals. This American way is about innovation, tempered by tradition. Harnessing the power of both can allow each individual to discover their own American Way.

CHAPTER NOTES

1. Morrison, Grant (w), and J.G. Jones (a). "Into Oblivion." *Final Crisis #5* in *Final Crisis* (2009). New York: DC Comics, 256.
2. Busiek, Kurt (w), and Mark Bagely (a). "Truth, Justice and the American Way..." *Trinity #6* (July 2008). New York: DC Comics.
3. Costello, Matthew J. *Secret Identity Crisis: Comic Books & the Unmasking of Cold War America.* (New York: Continuum, 2009), 225.
4. Costello, 85.
5. Jones, Gerard. *Men of Tomorrow: Geeks, Gangsters and the Birth of the Comic Book.* (New York: Basic Books, 2004), 281.
6. Costello, 15.
7. Johns, Geoff (w), and Phil Jimenez (a). "Infinite Crisis #7" *Infinite Crisis* (2006). New York: DC Comics, 234.
8. Johns, Geoff (w), Grant Morrison (w), Greg Rucka (w), Mark Waid (w), and Keith Giffen (a). "Dream of America." *52 #9* in *52 Vol. 1* (2007). New York: DC Comics, 189.
9. Johns, Geoff (w), Grant Morrison (w), Greg Rucka (w), Mark Waid (w), and Keith Giffen (a). "Stars in Their Courses." *52 #5* in *52 Vol. 1* (2007). New York: DC Comics, 103.
10. Johns, Geoff (w), Grant Morrison (w), Greg Rucka (w), Mark Waid (w), and Keith Giffen (a). "Halfway House." *52 #26* in *52 Vol. 2* (2007). New York: DC Comics, 283.

11. Johns, Geoff (w), Grant Morrison (w), Greg Rucka (w), Mark Waid (w), and Keith Giffen (a). "Dances with Monsters." *52 #4* in *52 Vol. 1* (2007). New York: DC Comics, 81.

12. Johns, Geoff (w), Grant Morrison (w), Greg Rucka (w), Mark Waid (w), and Keith Giffen (a). "Rain of the Supermen." *52 #35* in *52 Vol. 3* (2007). New York: DC Comics, 188–9.

13. Rucka, Greg. "Week Eight Notes." *52 Vol. 1* (2007). New York: DC Comics, 187.

14. Busiek, Kurt (w), and Mark Bagely (a). "I Remember the Day..." *Trinity #20* (15 Oct. 2008). New York: DC Comics. In DC Continuity, the members of the Justice Society of America chose to retire rather than reveal their identities during the McCarthy hearings.

15. Costello, 221.

16. Busiek, Kurt (w), and Mark Bagely (a). "Time to Suit Up." *Trinity #27* (3 Dec. 2008). New York: DC Comics.

17. Costello, 236.

18. Costello, 133.

19. Busiek, Kurt (w), Fabian Nicieza (w), Tom Derenick (a) and Wayne Faucher (a). "Much to Discuss." *Trinity #44* (April 2009). New York: DC Comics.

20. The city of Kandor was bottled and shrunk by Brainiac before the destruction of Krypton. It was returned to full size in *Action Comics #870*.

21. Robinson, James (w), and Pablo Raimondi (a). "Suspicion!" *Superman #685* in *Superman: Mon-El Vol. 1* (2010). New York: DC Comics, 54.

22. Johns, Geoff (w), Pete Woods (a) and Renato Guedes (a). "Birth of a Nation." *Action Comics #873* in *Superman: New Krypton Vol. 1* (2009). New York: DC Comics, 138.

23. Ibid., 127.

24. Ibid., 147.

25. Johns, Geoff (w), James Robinson (w), Sterling Gates (w), Pete Woods (a), Gary Frank (a) and Renato Guedes (a). "New Krypton." *Superman: New Krypton Special #1* in *Superman: New Krypton Vol. 1* (2009). New York: DC Comics, 106.

26. Gates, Sterling (w), James Robinson (w), and Eduardo Pansica (a). "The Battle for Mars." *Superman: War of the Supermen #2* in *Superman: War of the Supermen* (2011). New York: DC Comics, 65.

27. Rucka, Greg (w), and Diego Olmos (a). "The Sleeper Part Four." *Action Comics #878* in *Superman: Nightwing and Flamebird* (2010). New York: DC Comics, 88.

28. Costello, 141.

29. Robinson, James (w), Greg Rucka (w), and Pete Woods (a). "World of New Krypton Part One." *Superman: World of New Krypton #1* in *Superman: New Krypton Vol. 3* (2009). New York: DC Comics, 28.

30. Robinson, James (w), Renato Guedes (a) with Eduardo Pansica (a). "Codename: Patriot Part Four." *Superman #691* in *Superman: Codename: Patriot* (2010). New York: DC Comics, 78.

31. Rucka, Greg (w), and Eddy Barrows (a). "The Sleepers Part One." *Action Comics #875* in *Superman: Nightwing and Flamebird Vol. 1* (2010). New York: DC Comics, 20–1.

32. Gates, Sterling (w), James Robinson (w), and Jamal Igle. "The Battle for New Krypton." *Superman: War of the Supermen #1* in *Superman: War of the Supermen* (2011). New York: DC Comics, 38–9.

33. Morrison, 322.

BIBLIOGRAPHY

Busiek, Kurt (w), and Mark Bagely (a). "I Remember the Day..." *Trinity #20* (15 Oct. 2008). New York: DC Comics.

_____. "Time to Suit Up." *Trinity #27* (3 Dec. 2008). New York: DC Comics.

_____. "Truth, Justice and the American Way..." *Trinity #6* (July 2008). New York: DC Comics.

Busiek, Kurt (w), Fabian Nicieza (w), Tom Derenick (a) and Wayne Faucher (a). "Much to Discuss." *Trinity #44* (April 2009). New York: DC Comics.

Costello, Matthew J. *Secret Identity Crisis: Comic Books and the Unmasking of Cold War America.* New York: Continuum, 2009.

Gates, Sterling (w), James Robinson (w), and Jamal Igle. "The Battle for New Krypton." *Superman: War of the Supermen #1* in *Superman: War of the Supermen* (2011). New York: DC Comics.

Gates, Sterling (w), James Robinson (w), and Eduardo Pansica (a). "The Battle for Mars." *Superman: War of the Supermen #2* in *Superman: War of the Supermen* (2011). New York: DC Comics.

Johns, Geoff (w), and Phil Jimenez (a). "Infinite Crisis #7" *Infinite Crisis* (2006). New York: DC Comics.

Johns, Geoff (w), Grant Morrison (w), Greg Rucka (w), Mark Waid (w), and Keith Giffen (a). *52 Vol. 1* (2007). New York: DC Comics.

_____. *52 Vol. 2* (2007). New York: DC Comics.

_____. *52 Vol. 3* (2007). New York: DC Comics.

Johns, Geoff (w), James Robinson (w), Sterling Gates (w), Pete Woods (a), Gary Frank (a) and Renato Guedes (a). "New Krypton." *Superman: New Krypton Special #1* in *Superman: New Krypton Vol. 1* (2009). New York: DC Comics.

Johns, Geoff (w), Pete Woods (a) and Renato Guedes (a). "Birth of a Nation." *Action Comics #873* in *Superman: New Krypton Vol. 1* (2009). New York: DC Comics.

Jones, Gerard. *Men of Tomorrow: Geeks, Gangsters and the Birth of the Comic Book.* New York: Basic Books, 2004.

Morrison, Grant (w), and J.G. Jones (a). "Into Oblivion." *Final Crisis #5* in *Final Crisis* (2009). New York: DC Comics.

Robinson, James (w), Renato Guedes (a) with Eduardo Pansica (a). "Codename: Patriot Part Four." *Superman #691* in *Superman: Codename: Patriot* (2010). New York: DC Comics.

Robinson, James (w), and Pablo Raimondi (a). "Suspicion!" *Superman #685* in *Superman: Mon-El Vol. 1* (2010). New York: DC Comics.

Robinson, James (w), Greg Rucka (w), and Pete Woods (a). "World of New Krypton Part One." *Superman: World of New Krypton #1* in *Superman: New Krypton Vol. 3* (2009). New York: DC Comics.

Rucka, Greg (w), and Eddy Barrows (a). "The Sleepers Part One." *Action Comics #875* in *Superman: Nightwing and Flamebird Vol. 1* (2010). New York: DC Comics.

Rucka, Greg (w), and Diego Olmos (a). "The Sleeper Part Four." *Action Comics #878* in *Superman: Nightwing and Flamebird* (2010). New York: DC Comics.

Traveling Hopefully in Search of American National Identity

The *"Grounded" Superman as a 21st Century Picaro*

RANDY DUNCAN

A journalist (who looks suspiciously like Peter Parker) stands outside a Philadelphia diner, speaking on the phone to his editor. "He's not doing anything. He's having lunch in a diner." The "he" is Superman, who is sitting, in full costume, on a stool at the counter and eating a Philly cheese steak sandwich. The journalist continues, "This is nuts. You can't write a story about a guy walking down the street."[1]

Perhaps that last bit of dialogue is writer J. Michael Straczynski's commentary on his own bravura at attempting to do just that—devote a full year to telling a story about Superman walking across America. Taking over the writing duties on the *Superman* title, Straczynski decided he wanted Superman to re-engage with America and contrived a motivation for Superman to walk, not fly or run at super-speed, but walk across the country from shore to shore. The motivations for Straczynski's story and Superman's actions are grounded in and reacting to the epic events that had occurred in recent Superman continuity.

In a storyline that ran throughout the Superman family of titles for a span of more than a year the long-shrunken city of Kandor[2] is restored to full size and 100,000 super-powered Kryptonians, unwilling to assimilate with Earth culture, create their own planet on the other side of the solar system. Although a few of his closest confidants know better, Superman seems to abandon Earth in order to live among his own people on New Krypton. The New Krypton saga is too long and convoluted to describe here, but it is a tale full of conflict—attacks by various villains, Kryptonian leaders bent on vengeance and genocide, behind the scenes machinations of Lex Luthor, and a war between New Krypton and Earth — and culminating in tragedy with the destruction of the planet New Krypton and the deaths of all but a few thousand of the Kryptonians.

Even for a superhero, whose lives tend to be full of trauma, Superman suffers a great deal of very personal loss in a short period of time. The destruction of New Krypton is not only a real and immediate loss, but it is evocative of the destruction of the original Krypton, a loss Superman never properly grieved because he learned about it so long after the fact. The catastrophic events of the Earth–New Krypton War lead to his adopted son Chris being stranded in the Phantom Zone, the suicide of his father-in-law, General Lang, and, most devastating of all for Superman, the death of his adoptive father, Jonathan Kent.

In the wake of these events, *Superman #700* (Aug. 2010) was a giant-sized anniversary issue heralding the return of Superman to Earth. The issue contained a number of short stories, including a joyous reunion with Lois and a humorous "tale from Superman's early years" in which he helps Robin capture smugglers and complete his geometry homework. The final story is more somber. Leaving a Congressional hearing where he had been answering questions about the conflict with New Krypton, Superman is surrounded by a throng of reporters and onlookers. Suddenly, a woman pushes through the crowd, slaps Superman, and gives him a picture of her and her husband. She is angry at Superman because he was away on New Krypton when he husband died of a brain tumor, which she feels Superman could have detected with his X-ray vision and burned away with his heat vision. When a reporter admonishes her that even Superman cannot be everywhere she responds "You're right. He can't be everywhere at once." She turns to Superman. "But you were *nowhere* ... you were out *there* ... not *here*, where you were needed."[3]

Superman might have recognized that in her grief the woman was being unrealistic, and he might even have been offended by the blatant ethnocentricism that dismisses anything beyond Earth as "nowhere" and the lack of empathy for the deaths of thousands of Kryptonians. Instead, the incident triggers a powerful self-doubt. Not only does Superman wonder if he had become so involved in the world of New Krypton he lost touch with Earth, but he begins to question his sense of purpose. Later, he asks Flash what he sees when running across the country at super speed, and Flash responds "I see a blur. Unless I make an effort to see the details."[4] A nice metaphor for how a superpower can alienate one from the mundane world.[5]

Floating high above earth, looking at the picture of the woman and her husband, Superman recalls a parable his adoptive father, Jonathan Kent, told him about crop rotation: "...you have to take yourself out of where you are and put yourself back where you should be.... You have to rotate back to fertile ground ... to the soil that nourished you ... back to the Earth."[6] Superman lands in a Metropolis park, picks up a handful of dirt, and starts ... walking. Thus ends the prologue to "Grounded," a storyline that was intended to run for one year in twelve issues of the *Superman* comic book.

The "Grounded" concept (if not, as we shall see, the execution) was a radical departure from the usual superhero narrative. However, there is a long tradition of stories about a lone protagonist undertaking a lengthy journey. Four thousand years ago the Sumerian epic Gilgamesh established the template for the hero's journey, an often repeated pattern of narrative conventions Joseph Campbell dubbed the monomyth,[7] but in "Grounded" Superman is not on a hero quest. He has no clear goal. He is not seeking something akin to the Golden Fleece or the Holy Grail. What Superman seeks (although it never quite works out for him) is mundane experience rather than heroic adventure.

"Grounded" is more akin to a picaresque journey in which a lone man or woman sets out on a journey with no particular destination and only a vague purpose of discovery. Sometimes more prosaically termed a road narrative, the picaresque journey is a fairly precisely defined literary genre, the origin of which can be traced back to 16th Century Spain. Rowland Sherrill, in *Road-Book America: Contemporary Culture and the New Picaresque* (2000), identifies a variant of the road narrative more "responsive to contemporary American culture."[8] While these contemporary American road narratives are a "significant transformation of the old literary form of the picaresque narrative,"[9] the protagonist, or picaro, generally shares some traits with his literary predecessors. The protagonist is a naive drifter operating on the margins of society.[10] Perhaps Superman has led too eventful a life to be naive, but he is sincere and unpretentious. And while he is certainly far removed from the usual rascal of picaresque adventures, he is also different from and thus somewhat removed from the average person. When Dick Grayson, in his Batman guise, shows up to dissuade Superman from this journey he argues: "the world of suburban streets, and neighborhood diners, and front porches ... that isn't our world, Superman. Not anymore."[11] The choice to put on a costume and assume a superhero identity is a choice to exist on the margins of society. In attempting to reconnect with "the world of the average guy" Superman seems to be questioning that choice.

The road narrative protagonist also has an "open and essentially innocent temperament."[12] True, Superman cannot be open about his dual identity, but otherwise, whether he is Clark or Superman, he is honest, compassionate, and willing to see the good in everyone this side of Darkseid. Yet, almost from the beginning of the "Grounded" storyline there are instances in which he is a bit of a jerk. Early on in his journey he is pursued by a gaggle of curious reporters, and when one of them asks "so why aren't you flying?" Superman replies "I'm not flying because I'm walking. Are you sure you're a reporter?"[13] A few months farther into the journey, when Superman is telling Lois she cannot file a story that might get a factory shut down, he grips her by the arm and with a stern, what might even be considered a threatening look, says "I don't think you heard me. I said you can't run it."[14] In this particular instance it is clear an outside force is tampering with Superman's emotions. Nearby, the storyline's mysterious villain, inhabiting the body of a Danville, Ohio school teacher, has her fingers at her temples and seems to be concentrating (projecting thoughts?), and right after Superman proclaims "There may be a right and a wrong in this universe, Lois, but it isn't always easy to tell the difference" she mutters "That's right Superman. That's it exactly."[15] Superman's out of character behavior seems to stem not so much from any internal demons as it does from the external villain that is a necessary component of every superhero tale.

So, unusual attire and the fact he is the most powerful being on the planet aside, Superman does have some of the characteristics of the picaro. But what sort of picaresque journey is he undertaking? Ronald Primeau, in *Romance of the Road: The Literature of the American Highway* (1996), identifies four subtypes of the American road narrative: Parody, dissent narrative, search for national identity, and search for self identity.[16]

Parodies might be mocking the picaresque, such as John Updike's *Rabbit, Run* (1960), or might simply be self-conscious revisions of the road narrative, such as Joe David Brown's *Addie Pray* (1971) or Larry McMurtry's *Cadillac Jack* (1982). Jack Kerouac's dissent narrative *On the Road* (1957) is a good example of a journey imbued with a willful defiance of convention and conformity. Superman's walk across America is clearly not a parody or a counterculture protest.

Though a work of superhero fiction, "Grounded" has some elements in common with those autobiographical road narratives in which the protagonist undertakes what Primeau characterizes as "a quest for the soul of the nation."[17] For instance, feeling that he no longer knew his own country, John Steinbeck took to the road in a search for national identity that he chronicled in *Travels with Charley: In Search of America* (1962). At the conclusion of *A Walk Across America* (1979), a work that seems like it might have been a direct inspiration for the "Grounded" storyline, Peter Jenkins says of his travels: "I had started our searching for myself and my country and found both."[18] The result of Jenkins' journey sounds very similar to Straczynski's plans for Superman — "Let him set out on a journey across America, on foot, so that we can see ourselves in his eyes and he can see himself in ours."[19]

According to Sherrill, the travels of the American picaro seeking to understand his nation run the social gamut from the privileged to the impoverished and take inventory of the variety and otherness of America.[20] Superman declares that one purpose of his walk is "to reconnect with the average guy,"[21] and in the first full issue of the "Grounded" storyline he only interacts with normal human beings. He encounters some drug dealers and police in the course of solving problems, but he also has conversations with a number of average folks in a diner or on the street. By the second issue he is fighting an alien in a huge metal warsuit. In the third issue Batman makes an appearance and some of the average folks Superman encounters have been possessed and empowered by a Kryptonian artifact.

Superman walking across America didn't seem like such a hot idea to most fans, and sales steadily declined from nearly 55,000 for issue #701 to less than 39,000 by issue #711.[22] Perhaps in an effort to stimulate sales, superhero guest-stars began appearing regularly. Superman encounters Batman (Dick Grayson) in #703, Wonder Woman in #708, Flash in #709, Batman (Bruce Wayne) in #710, Livewire in #711, and Superboy and Supergirl in #713. He even travels to another dimension — the Fortress of Solidarity in "The Still Zone" — and encounters the multitude of heroes that comprise the Superman Squad. Rather than experiencing the social gamut of America, Superman spends most of his time in his usual milieu of costumes, powers and violence. Superman is so consumed with business-as-usual superhero exploits that he has little time to encounter or comprehend the variety and otherness of America.

Yet, beneath the surface action, Superman's search for a sense of purpose serves as an exploration of American identity. As the "Grounded" storyline begins the American Century has been over for nearly a decade and the nation is reassessing its role as a superpower. There is uncertainty about the legitimate and effective use of that power, and even doubts about American exceptionalism. Superman expresses a similar uncertainty: "Everything used to be so clear. Truth. Justice. The American Way. But now? Now, I'm not sure about *anything*."[23]

Most American picaros take to the road not only to understand their nation, but also to understand themselves. The picaro enters into his journey with "a nagging and troubling sense of 'self-loss'" and "an anxiety that they have lost 'America' or have somehow become 'lost' in it."[24] In the classic search-for-self autobiography *Blue Highways: A Journey into America* (1982) William Least Heat Moon's journey is prompted by feeling isolated, alienated from his land, and not able to "make things go right" in his life (having recently lost his wife and his job).[25] With the benefit of hindsight, a member of the Superman Squad from the future tells Superman "I tend to believe that you began your pilgrimage across America because you realized, on some subconscious level, that you had lost your way. You were trying to reconnect with the formative experiences that first taught you your values."[26]

In his attempt to clarify those values, to decide what he stands for, Superman must first understand who he is. Perhaps Superman is not that different from Heat Moon, who sets out on his journey not exactly knowing what he wants to discover, but as an ex-husband, an ex-teacher, a white man named William Trogdon and an Osage known as Least Heat Moon he is not at ease with his sense of self. Superman has his own multi-layered identity to reconcile.

So that he might survive the impending destruction of Krypton, Jor-el and Lara put their infant son Kal-el in a rocket and send him to Earth, where is he is raised as Clark Kent and eventually assumes the identity of Superman. Fans and, more recently, scholars have debated which aspect — Kal-el, Clark Kent, or Superman — is the true self. The argument has been made by Jules Feiffer, Mark Waid, and perhaps most famously in Bill's monologue in *Kill Bill, Part 2* that Superman is the true self and Clark Kent is the disguise. That might have been true for how the character was presented in the early stories, but the primitive version of Superman is not the definitive version. As the character and his mythos became more fully developed it is simply no longer true that Superman is "disguised as Clark Kent." When he is at home with Lois she calls him Clark or "Smallville," not Kal or "Krypton."

Thomas Andrae explores the Clark Kent/Superman paradox and concludes "that Kent is not merely a put on, and Superman the true identity, but both identities are aspects of a single personality, each autonomous in its own realm."[27] Like so many immigrants to America, Superman encompasses elements of both his "old world" heritage and his new life as an American. Gary Engle sees Superman as "an optimistic myth of assimilation" in which "Superman's powers [his "ethnic characteristics"] make the hero capable of saving humanity; Kent's total immersion in the American heartland makes him want to do it."[28]

As a fictional character who has existed for over 70 years and been depicted by hundreds of writers and artists, Superman has a rather fluid biography. In some versions he is a super baby learning to use his powers responsibly through near disastrous trial and error. In other versions he operates as a teenage Superboy with a full array of powers and his iconic costume. In still others he does not adopt the Superman identity or even discover his alien origins until adulthood. In all versions he is Clark Kent before he creates the identity of Superman. In all versions the moral examples and guidance of Jonathan and Martha Kent mold his character.

The idea that the Kents are the source of his values was there virtually from the beginning. In the expanded version of his origin in *Superman #1* (summer 1939) a caption explains "The love and guidance of his kindly foster-parents was to become an important factor in the shaping of the boy's future." And in the same panel Martha tells him he must use his power to "assist humanity."[29]

The hero we know as Superman is the product of Earth, of America, of the rural Midwest, and of Jonathan and Martha Kent. This idea is explicitly stated in Superman narratives over the decades.

John Byrne's mid–80s reinvention of the Superman mythos, *Superman: Man of Steel*, ends with a full-page panel of Superman in a heroic stance with his cape billowing in the wind. His thought balloons show that the Superman of this tale has resolved his identity crisis: "I may have been conceived out there in the endless depths of space ... but I was born when the rocket opened on *Earth*, in *America*." And a few balloons later, "Krypton bred me, but it was Earth that gave me all I am. All that matters. It was Krypton that made me Superman ... but it is Earth that makes me human!!"[30]

In the final episode of the television show *Smallville*, just before he finally puts on the costume and becomes Superman, Clark receives a final message from his Kryptonian father, Jor-el: "I ask you to remember one thing — your abilities may be of my blood, but it is your time in Smallville with Jonathan and Martha Kent and all the people there that made you a hero, Kal-el."[31]

In the lead story in *Action Comics #900* (June 2011) Luthor, having acquired godlike power, attempts to break Superman physically and emotionally but fails. In frustration Luthor screams "Why won't you break?" Superman responds, as they look at an image of the Kents, "Because of them. They made me. So that later I could make myself. They made Clark Kent. Clark Kent is Superman."[32]

Not only are his values the product of the American heartland, but his superpowers are the result of his being here. If Krypton had survived and he had remained there he would have no powers. It is beneath Earth's yellow sun that he has his exceptional abilities. As Joseph Darowski points out "it is the fact that he is in America, and not Krypton, that allows him to excel beyond what he would have been capable of in his "home country." ... The American Dream has been mythologized directly into Superman."[33]

That is why when *Action Comics #900* hit the stands (and iPads), about two-thirds of the way into the Grounded story, it created a conflagration of controversy around Superman's association with "the American way." In "The Incident," the fifth story in the over-sized issue, Superman tells the United States National Security Advisor he intends to go before the United Nations and renounce his U.S. citizenship. "'Truth, justice, and the American way' ... it's not enough anymore" he explains. "The world's too small. Too connected."[34] Those words were reported, usually in as sensational a context as possible, in every form of media. Conservative commentators saw Superman's statement as a rejection of American exceptionalism.[35] In a statement to the *New York Post* DC co-publishers Dan Didio and Jim Lee were quick to respond to the criticism. The *Post* characterized their response as an assurance that Superman "is and always will be a red-blooded American at heart," and quotes them as saying:

> Superman is a visitor from a distant planet who has long embraced American values. As a character and an icon, he embodies the best of the American Way. In a short story in *Action Comics* 900, Superman announces his intention to put a global focus on his never ending battle, but he remains, as always, committed to his adopted home and his roots as a Kansas farm boy from Smallville.[36]

American mythos being woven into the Superman mythos is consistent with Danny Fingeroth's observation that "the superhero — more than even the ordinary fictional hero — has to represent the values of the society that produced him."[37] Peter Coogan refines this idea, claiming that "superheroes embody a vision of the use of power unique to America. Superheroes enforce their own visions of right and wrong on others, and they possess overwhelming power."[38]

Straczynski, explaining his approach to the character in the "Grounded" storyline, states "For me, Superman was, is and shall forever be America's hero ... he is inexorably tied to our culture and way of life."[39] Perhaps even more than the patriotic heroes who proliferated during World War II, Superman is a representative of America. Thomas Andrae speculates that "An essential element of this [Superman's] popularity has been his canonization as an archetypal representative of the nation's highest ideals, the defender of 'truth, justice, and the American way.'"[40]

A 1942 episode of the *Adventures of Superman* radio series was the first appearance of the "truth, justice, and the American way" phrase, but it became cemented in the Baby Boomer psyche as part of the weekly introduction of the *Adventures of Superman* television series that ran from 1952 to 1958. In the theater where I was watching *Superman: The Movie* (1978) it elicited applause and cheers when Christopher Reeve spoke the line "I'm here to fight for truth, justice, and the American way."[41]

Despite the emotional resonance that particular phrase seems to have for Superman fans, it has occasionally been considered problematic, perhaps being perceived as too ethnocentric or limiting the marketability of Superman, and has been left off or replaced. In *The New Adventures of Superman* cartoons of the late 1960s Superman fought for "truth, justice and freedom." In the premiere of *Lois & Clark: The New Adventures of Superman* (1993–1997), after some prompting from Lois, Superman says he is here to fight for "truth and justice." In *Superman Returns* the American way part of the phrase got replaced with "all that stuff." Some recent DC comics have referred to Superman's mission as "truth, justice, and hope." But "the American way" makes a strong comeback in "Grounded."

The phrase "the American way" occurs so often in "Grounded" as to be a central concern of the narrative. Beginning with *Superman #707* (March 2011), in which Chris Roberson takes over as scripter working from Straczynski's outline, the concept becomes integral to Superman's search for self identity and, by extension, his exploration of national identity. Because of the change in scripting duties, it is unclear if Straczynski had planned for the American way theme to emerge, or if the sudden emphasis is Roberson's contribution.

In issue *#707* Superman asks Lois "What good am I doing really? What do I stand for?" Lois responds "How about truth, justice, and the American way? Always seemed like a pretty good lineup to me." But Superman wonders if those aren't just "words that no one seems to put much faith in anymore."[42] Later in that issue, walking across a Kansas pasture musing aloud, he says "Everything used to be so clear. Truth, justice, and the American way. But now? Now, I'm not sure about anything."[43] The next issue, a member of the Superman Squad tells him "Because of your example, all of us defend the sacred principles of truth, justice, and what your era called the American Way." "The American Way?!" he asks in astonishment. "Certainly," she replies. "Even after the nation state itself is long forgotten, the precepts on which it was founded will still be remembered. That all beings are endowed with the inalienable rights of life, liberty, and the pursuit of happiness."[44] When Batman (Bruce Wayne) argues that Superman should embrace the idea of others following in his footsteps he says "If one Superman serves the cause of truth, justice, and the American way, how much more could a whole squad of Supermen do?"[45]

One month after the controversial *Action #900* story in which he declared the American way was not enough anymore, Superman has his most patriotic moment of the "Grounded" storyline in *Superman #711* (July 2011). He is in Las Vegas contending with a super-powered young woman named Livewire who is on a rampage because fluctuations in her energy power are warping her thinking and magnifying her resentment of Superman. After putting her in a containment suit that helps her focus her thinking Superman says he will put in a good word for her with the authorities. He explains to a dubious Jimmy Olsen, "That's what America is about really. That's the American way. Life, liberty, the pursuit of happiness ... and second chances. None of us are forced to be anything we don't want to be."[46] In the final panel Superman is looking up adoringly at an American flag atop a nearby building. In *Superman #713* (Sep. 2011), an immigrant says of Superman, "He helps everyone who needs him. That's the *American way*."[47] That phrase, along with its truth and justice companions plays a central role in this issue.

Superman's doubts about his role in the world come to a climax in issue *#713* with his decision to give up the Superman identity. He intends to use his super-speed to help people without them even knowing he is there. He decides to announce this to the world in a *Daily Planet* article he will write as Clark Kent. Clark is sitting in a Portland coffee shop working on the article, titled "Must there Be a Superman?" when he encounters a stranger with a striking resemblance to longtime Superman writer Elliot S! Maggin. When "Maggin" reads the draft of Clark's article he declares "No one who understands Superman at all could have written this."[48] He insists that Clark accompany him on a walk around town to listen to stories from people on the street about what Superman means to them. Clark is moved by the stories of people's appreciation and admiration for Superman, but he still insists that it would be easier for everyone if Superman was not a symbol and just did good in secret. In response the Maggin character articulates what may well be the theme of the "Grounded" road narrative: "Superman is an aspirational figure. He shows us how to be better people ourselves by being the best person he can be."[49]

And how does Superman show us the way? "Maggin" has detailed this in an earlier panel: "Truth, justice, and the American way. Not a bad lineup, if you ask me."[50] What makes Superman exceptional among heroes, his power and idealism, is what most Americans feel makes their nation exceptional among nations. Perhaps a modern American would feel uncomfortable proclaiming as President Wilson did in 1919 that "America is the only idealistic nation in the world,"[51] but there is definitely a sense of American idealism and exceptionalism that pervades the "Grounded" narrative. In this road narrative the search for individual identity and the search for national identity coalesce so that to ask "Must there be a Superman?" is tantamount to asking "Must there be a United States of America?" And the answer worked out through the journey in "Grounded" is a definite yes to both.

Chapter Notes

1. Straczynski, J. Michael (w), and Eddy Barrows (a). "Grounded Part One." *Superman #701* (Sep. 2010). New York: DC Comics.

2. Kandor was a city from Krypton that had been shrunk to the size of a bottle prior to the planet's destruction by the alien Brainiac. Superman had freed the city from Brainiac's possession but had previously been unable to restore it and its citizens to normal size.

3. Straczynski, J. Michael (w), and Eddy Barrows (a). "Grounded Prologue: The Slap Heard 'Round the World." *Superman #700* (Aug. 2010). New York: DC Comics.

4. Ibid.

5. The metaphor was undone in issue *#709* when Flash says he was joking, he sees everything. Chief Creative Officer Geoff Johns, who writes the Flash title, might have wanted to correct what he considered an incorrect understanding of Flash's powers.

6. Straczynski and Barrows, *Superman #700*.

7. Campbell, Joseph. *The Hero with a Thousand Faces.* (Novato, CA: New World Library, 1949), 210–211.

8. Sherrill, Rowland. *Road-Book America: Contemporary Culture and the New Picaresque.* (Urbana: University of Illinois Press, 2000), 3.

9. Ibid., 3.

10. Ibid., 3–4.

11. Straczynski, J. Michael (w), and Eddy Barrows (a). "Grounded Part Three." *Superman #703* (Nov. 2010). New York: DC Comics.

12. Sherrill, 4.

13. Straczynski, J. Michael (w), and Eddy Barrows (a). "Grounded Part One." *Superman #701* (Sep. 2010). New York: DC Comics.

14. Roberson, Chris (w), and Allan Goldman (a). "Grounded Part Five." *Superman #707* (March 2011). New York: DC Comics.

15. Ibid.

16. Primeau, Ronald. *Romance of the Road: The Literature of the American Highway.* (Bowling Green: Bowling Green State University, 1996), 15.

17. Ibid., 51.

18. Jenkins, Peter. *A Walk Across America.* (New York: William Morrow, 1979), 266.

19. Segura, Alex. "J. Michael Straczynski on Superman 700 and Beyond." *DCU Blog* 23 June, 2010 http://dcu.blog.dccomics.com/201/06/23/j-michael-straczynski-on-super man-700-and-beyond/ n.d. Web. 25 May, 2011.

20. Sherrill, 4.

21. Roberson and Goldman, *Superman #707.*

22. Miller, John Jackson. "Comic Book Sales by Month." *The Comics Chronicles* http://www.comichron.com/monthlycomicssales.html n.d. Web. 11 July, 2011.

23. Roberson and Goldman, *Superman #707.*

24. Sherrill, 269.

25. Heat Moon, William Least. *Blue Highways: A Journey into America.* (Boston: Little, Brown and Company, 1982), 3.

26. Roberson, Chris (w), and Eddy Barrows (a). "Grounded Part Six." *Superman #708* (April 2011). New York: DC Comics.

27. Andrae, Thomas. "From Menace to Messiah: The History and Historicity of Superman." *American Media and Mass Culture.* Ed. Donald Lazere. (Berkeley: University of California Press, 1987), 133.

28. Engle, Gary. "What Makes Superman So Darned American?" *Superman at Fifty: The Persistence of a Legend.* Eds. Dennis Dooley and Gary Engle. (Cleveland: Octavia, 1987), 85.

29. Siegel, Jerome (w), and Joe Shuster (a). [no story title] *Superman #1* (Summer 1939). New York: DC Comics.

30. Byrne, John (w, a). "The Haunting." *The Man of Steel* (Dec. 1986). New York: DC Comics.

31. "Finale." *Smallville.* CW. KASN, Little Rock. 13 May, 2011. Television.

32. Cornell, Paul (w), and Pete Woods (a). "The Black Ring Finale: Reign of Doomsday." *Action Comics #900* (June 2011). New York: DC Comics.

33. Darowski, Joseph James. "The American Way: What Superman, Batman, Spider-Man, and the X-Men Reveal About America." MA thesis. Brigham Young University, 2006. Print.

34. Goyer, David S. (w), and Miguel Sepulveda (a). "The Incident." *Action Comics #900* (June 2011). New York: DC Comics.

35. Tobin, Jonathan S. "Superman: 'Truth, Justice and the American Way Isn't Enough Anymore.'" *CommentaryMagazine.com* 29 April, 2011. Web. 5 June, 2011.

36. Gregorian, Dareh. "Superman Renounces US Citizenship." *nypost.com* New York Post 29 April, 2011. Web. 8, July 2011.

37. Fingeroth, Danny. *Superman on the Couch: What Superheroes Really Tell Us about Ourselves and Our Society.* (New York: Continuum, 2004), 17.

38. Coogan, Peter. *Superhero: The Secret Origin of a Genre.* (Austin: MonkeyBrain Books, 2006: 231).

39. Straczynski, qtd. In Segura.

40. Andrae, 124.

41. Reeve, Christopher, perf. *Superman: The Movie.* Warner Bros. Pictures, 1978. Film.

42. Roberson and Goldman, *Superman #707.*

43. Ibid.

44. Roberson and Barrows, *Superman #708.*

45. Straczynski, J. Michael, Chris Roberson (w), and Eddy Barrows (a). "Grounded Part Eight." *Superman #710* (June 2011). New York: DC Comics.

46. Straczynski, J. Michael, Chris Roberson (w), and Eddy Barrows (a). "Grounded Part Nine." *Superman #711* (July 2011). New York: DC Comics.

47. Straczynski, J. Michael, Chris Roberson (w), and Diogenes Neves, Eddy Barrows, Jamal Igle (a). "Grounded Part Eleven." *Superman #713* (Sep. 2011). New York: DC Comics.

48. Ibid.

49. Ibid.

50. Ibid.

51. Wilson, Woodrow. *Address Supporting the League of Nations.* Sioux Falls, South Dakota, 8 September 1919, qtd. in "About Woodrow Wilson," http://www.wilson center.org. 16 July, 2011.

BIBLIOGRAPHY

Andrae, Thomas. "From Menace to Messiah: The History and Historicity of Superman." In Donald Lazere, ed., *American Media and Mass Culture.* Berkeley: University of California Press, 1987.

Byrne, John (w, a). "The Haunting." *The Man of Steel* (Dec. 1986). New York: DC Comics.

Campbell, Joseph. *The Hero with a Thousand Faces.* Novato, CA: New World Library, 1949.

Coogan, Peter. *Superhero: The Secret Origin of a Genre.* Austin: MonkeyBrain Books, 2006.

Cornell, Paul (w), and Pete Woods (a). "The Black Ring Finale: Reign of Doomsday." *Action Comics #900* (June 2011). New York: DC Comics.

Darowski, Joseph James. "The American Way: What Superman, Batman, Spider-Man, and the X-Men Reveal About America." MA thesis. Brigham Young University, 2006.

Engle, Gary. "What Makes Superman So Darned American?" In Dennis Dooley and Gary Engle, eds., *Superman at Fifty: The Persistence of a Legend.* Cleveland: Octavia, 1987.

"Finale." *Smallville.* CW. KASN, Little Rock. Aired 13 May, 2011.

Fingeroth, Danny. *Superman on the Couch: What Superheroes Really Tell Us about Ourselves and Our Society.* New York: Continuum, 2004.

Goyer, David S. (w), and Miguel Sepulveda (a). "The Incident." *Action Comics #900* (June 2011). New York: DC Comics.

Gregorian, Dareh. "Superman Renounces U.S. Citizenship." *New York Post,* 29 April, 2011. Accessed 8, July 2011 at *http://www.nypost.com/p/news/national/superman_renounces_us_citizenship_n5ZdXkQIWE7y5EoU6xTZQI.*

Heat Moon, William Least. *Blue Highways: A Journey into America.* Boston: Little, Brown and Company, 1982.

Jenkins, Peter. *A Walk across America.* New York: William Morrow, 1979.

Miller, John Jackson. "Comic Book Sales by Month." *The Comics Chronicles*. Accessed 11 July, 2011, at http://www.comichron.com/monthlycomicssales.html.

Primeau, Ronald. *Romance of the Road: The Literature of the American Highway*. Bowling Green, OH: Bowling Green State University Popular Press, 1996.

Reeve, Christopher, perf. *Superman: The Movie*. Warner Bros. Pictures. Film, 1978.

Roberson, Chris (w), and Allan Goldman (a). "Grounded Part Five." *Superman #707* (March 2011). New York: DC Comics.

_____. "Grounded Part Six." *Superman #708* (April 2011). New York: DC Comics.

Segura, Alex. "J. Michael Straczynski on Superman 700 and Beyond." *DCU Blog* 23. Accessed 25 May, 2011, at *http://dcu.blog.dccomics.com/201/06/23/j-michael-straczynski-on-superman-700-and-beyond/*.

Sherrill, Rowland. *Road-Book America: Contemporary Culture and the New Picaresque*. Urbana: University of Illinois Press, 2000.

Siegel, Jerome (w), and Joe Shuster (a). [no story title] *Superman #1* (Summer 1939). New York: DC Comics.

Straczynski, J. Michael (w), and Eddy Barrows (a). "Grounded Part One." *Superman #701* (Sep. 2010). New York: DC Comics.

_____. "Grounded Part Three." *Superman #703* (Nov. 2010). New York: DC Comics.

_____. "Grounded Prologue: The Slap Heard 'Round the World." *Superman #700* (Aug. 2010). New York: DC Comics.

Straczynski, J. Michael, Chris Roberson (w), and Eddy Barrows (a). "Grounded Part Eight." *Superman #710* (June 2011). New York: DC Comics.

Straczynski, J. Michael, Chris Roberson (w), and Diogenes Neves, Eddy Barrows, Jamal Igle (a). "Grounded Part Eleven." *Superman #713* (Sep. 2011). New York: DC Comics.

Tobin, Jonathan S. "Superman: 'Truth, Justice and the American Way Isn't Enough Any More.'" *f* 29 April, 2011. Accessed 5 June, 2011, at http://www.commentarymagazine.com /2011/04/29/truth-justice-and-the-american-way-isnt-enough/.

Wilson, Woodrow. *Address Supporting the League of Nations*. Sioux Falls, South Dakota, 8 September 1919. Qtd. in "About Woodrow Wilson." Accessed 16 July, 2011, at www.wil soncenter.org.

About the Contributors

José **Alaniz** is an associate professor in the Departments of Slavic Languages and Literatures and Comparative Literature (adjunct) at the University of Washington at Seattle. He published his first book, *Komiks: Comic Art in Russia* (University Press of Mississippi), in 2010. His research interests include death and dying, disability studies, cinema, eco-criticism and comics. He is writing two books: *Death, Disability and the Superhero: The Silver Age and Beyond* and a history of Czech comics.

Stefan **Buchenberger** is an associate professor in the Department of Cross-Cultural Studies at the Kanagawa University in Yokohama, Japan. He earned his Ph.D. in Japanese studies from the Ludwig Maximilians University in Munich, Germany. He is involved in the study of graphic narratives at the International Comparative Literature Association (ICLA) and writes regularly on graphic fiction, as well as on mystery and detective fiction.

John **Darowski** graduated from Brigham Young University with a bachelor's degree in humanities in 2004 and a master's in comparative studies in 2007. In addition to comic books, John has also presented research on anime and the Gothic at the National Popular Culture Association Conference.

Joseph J. **Darowski** is a professor of English at Brigham Young University-Idaho. He completed his Ph.D. in American studies at Michigan State University where he wrote his dissertation on the portrayals of race and gender in the X-Men comic book series. His research interests include comic books, popular culture, Chicano/a literature, and gender studies.

Thomas C. **Donaldson** is a Ph.D. candidate in U.S. cultural history at the University at Albany (SUNY), New York. His primary research focus is on the portrayal of gender in popular media, particularly comic books. He has taught history at the high school and college levels for over a decade and is writing a dissertation tentatively titled "Truth, Justice, and the Status Quo: Antifeminism, the Resurgence of Superhero Comics, and the Redemption of Masculine Hegemony as the American Way of Gender, 1955–1990."

Randy **Duncan** is a professor of communication at Henderson State University. He is the coauthor with Matthew J. Smith of *The Power of Comics: History, Form and Culture* (Continuum, 2009) and coeditor, with Smith, of *Critical Approaches to Comics: Theories and Methods* (Routledge, 2011). Duncan is the co-founder, with Peter Coogan, of the Comics Arts Conference. He also serves on the editorial board of the *International Journal of Comic Art* and the board of directors of the Institute for Comics Studies.

Jeffrey K. **Johnson** is a World War II historian for the Joint POW/MIA Accounting Command in Honolulu, Hawai'i. He is the author of *American Advertising in Poland: A Study of Cultural Interactions Since 1990* (McFarland, 2009) and has published several journal articles, including "The Countryside Triumphant: Jefferson's Ideal of Rural Superiority in Modern Superhero Mythology," in the August 2010 *Journal of Popular Culture*. He is writing a book about comic books as historical texts.

Paul R. **Kohl** is an associate professor in the Media Studies Program at Loras College in Dubuque, Iowa, where he teaches courses in television, film, and popular music. He also serves on the executive board and as Comics Area chair of the Midwest Popular Culture Society. His published work includes essays on the Beatles, situation comedies, and music as resistance.

Jason M. **LaTouche** is an assistant professor of sociology at Tarleton State University. He earned his Ph.D. in sociology from the University of North Carolina at Chapel Hill. His dissertation "Comic Books and Communities of Memory" examines how the narratives of superhero characters have evolved from the 1930s to the 2000s. He has presented research on superhero comic books at Popular Culture Association conferences and has taught a course on the sociology of superheroes.

Peter **Lee** is a graduate student at Drew University specializing in American cultural history. He has published with *Americana: The Journal of American Culture,* and has two essays on espionage comic books and Spider-Man comics in collections forthcoming from McFarland.

Lori **Maguire** is professor of British and American studies at the University of Paris VIII. She received her doctorate in modern history at St. Antony's College, Oxford. Her research interests include British and American foreign policy, media studies and contemporary political history. She is the author of a number of books and articles on these subjects.

Todd S. **Munson** is an associate professor of Asian studies at Randolph-Macon College in Ashland, Virginia. He earned a B.A. in English from the University of Massachusetts (1991), with an M.A. in East Asian studies (2000) and Ph.D. in Japanese (2004) from Indiana University. His work on comics and Asian culture has appeared in the *International Journal of Comic Art, East Asian History, Early Modern Japan: An Interdisciplinary Journal,* and *Japan Studies Review,* among others. His essay "Transformers and Monkey Kings: Gene Yang's American Born Chinese and the Quest for Identity" appears in *Comic Books and American Cultural History,* ed. Matthew Pustz (McFarland, 2012).

Daniel J. **O'Rourke** is an associate professor of communication studies at Ashland University in Ashland, Ohio. He surrendered his interest in comic books for many years until his brother insisted he read "The Man of Steel." It was good fortune in 1986 and it remains so today. His renewed interest in comics has resulted in several essays including "The Transcreation of a Mediated Myth: Spider-Man in India" with Pravin Rodrigues.

Morgan B. **O'Rourke** is an undergraduate at Ohio Wesleyan University in Delaware, Ohio. He first assisted his father Daniel O'Rourke (above) conducting research on Captain America in World War II by exploring the archives of the Library of Congress.

His contributions have grown steadily from researcher to coauthor. Father and son both quietly recognize the superior memory and knowledge of the next generation of comic book scholars.

Matthew J. **Smith**, Ph.D., is a professor of communication at Wittenberg University in Springfield, Ohio, where he teaches courses in graphic storytelling, the graphic novels of Alan Moore, and the Field Study at Comic-Con (*www.powerofcomics .com/fieldstudy*). Along with Randy Duncan, he is coauthor of *The Power of Comics: History, Form and Culture* (Continuum, 2009) and coeditor of *Critical Approaches to Comics* (Routledge, 2011).

Michael **Smith** is an associate professor of writing, rhetoric and technical communication at James Madison University, where he developed and taught a course on the rhetoric of comics and graphic novels. His comics-related publications include the essay "Finding the Joker," which appears in *Riddle Me This, Batman! The Dark Knight of the Academy* (McFarland, 2011), and the entry for Frank Miller's *The Dark Knight Returns* in Salem Press's *Graphic Novels* (2012). Other work includes "Worshipping at the Altar" (*Writing on the Edge,* fall 2011*)*, and "The American G.I." in *American Icons* (Greenwood, 2006).

Jack **Teiwes** received B.A. degrees in theatre and film studies from the University of Sydney and the University of New South Wales. He has published articles on theatre in the journal *Australasian Drama Studies* and the anthology book *Nick Enright: An Actor's Playwright* (Rodopi), and has been a regular theatre critic for *Australian Stage Online* since 2007. He is writing a Ph.D. dissertation on "The Superman Multimedia Franchise" at the School of Culture and Communication, University of Melbourne. He has delivered papers at the Comics Arts Conference, and the inaugural conference of the Popular Culture Association of Australia and New Zealand.

Louie Dean **Valencia-García** is a Ph.D. candidate studying early modern and modern European history at Fordham University in New York City. He studies cultural history, the production of space, and everyday dissent in youth and queer cultures in contemporary history. This essay is a part of a broader dissertation on Spanish youth culture and everyday dissent in the later half of the twentieth century. He has been an avid reader of Superman comic books since his own childhood and has presented internationally on topics related to youth culture.

Christopher B. **Zeichmann** is a Th.D. student of the New Testament at Emmanuel College, University of Toronto. His research concerns the construction of ethnicity in narratives from both biblical antiquity and contemporary America. As to his comic book credentials, he created the *Crazy Spider-Man Kingdom* website in 1999 (http://www.angelfire.com/myband/skacorps/), which catalogues the numerous costumes that Peter Parker has worn over the years.

Index